EU ANTITRUST LAW AND SPORT GOVERNANCE

This is the first book to examine the significance of European Union antitrust law for the future of sport in Europe.

Drawing on multi-disciplinary perspectives from law, economics, sport management and politics, and including case studies about the European Superleague (ESL) and the International Skating Union, the book explores key themes in contemporary sport, including governance, ownership and control; the European sport model; the regulatory autonomy of sports organisations; and the relationship between public policy, the law and sport.

This is important reading for any advanced student, researcher, policy-maker or practitioner with an interest in sport management, sport law, European law or European politics.

Jacob Kornbeck is a policy officer in the European Commission and a former member of its Sport Unit (2001–2014), where he was involved in the elaboration of the White Paper (COM(2007) 391) and the Communication on Sport (COM(2011) 12). An external Lecturer at the German Sport University in Cologne, Germany (sports management), and the University of Lille, France (sports law), he has published in the fields of sports law and policy, as well as social policy and social work.

Routledge Research in Sport Business and Management

Good Governance in Sport
Critical Reflections
Edited by Arnout Geeraert and Frank van Eekeren

Stakeholder Analysis and Sport Organisations
Edited by Anna-Maria Strittmatter, Josef Fahlén and Barrie Houlihan

Sport and Brexit
Regulatory Challenges and Legacies
Edited by Jacob Kornbeck

Sport Management Education
Global Perspectives and Implications for Practice
Edited by Mike Rayner and Tom Webb

Digital Business Models in Sport
Edited by Mateusz Tomanek, Wojciech Cieśliński and Michał Polasik

Sport Management, Innovation and the COVID-19 Crisis
Edited by Gözde Ersöz and Meltem Ince Yenilmez

Sport in the Iberian Peninsula
Management, Economics and Policy
Edited by Jerónimo García-Fernández, Moisés Grimaldi-Puyana and Gonzalo A. Bravo

EU Antitrust Law and Sport Governance
The Next Frontier?
Edited by Jacob Kornbeck

For more information about this series, please visit https://www.routledge.com/Routledge-Research-in-Sport-Business-and-Management/book-series/RRSBM

EU ANTITRUST LAW AND SPORT GOVERNANCE

The Next Frontier?

Edited by
Jacob Kornbeck

Routledge
Taylor & Francis Group
LONDON AND NEW YORK

Designed cover image: jacoblund / Getty images

First published 2023
by Routledge
4 Park Square, Milton Park, Abingdon, Oxon OX14 4RN

and by Routledge
605 Third Avenue, New York, NY 10158

Routledge is an imprint of the Taylor & Francis Group, an informa business

British Library Cataloguing-in-Publication Data
A catalogue record for this book is available from the British Library

Library of Congress Cataloging-in-Publication Data
Names: Kornbeck, Jacob, 1968- editor.
Title: EU antitrust law and sport governance : the next frontier? / edited by Jacob Kornbeck.
Other titles: European Union antitrust law and sport governance
Description: Abingdon, Oxon ; New York City : Routledge, 2023. | Series: Routledge research in sport business and management | Includes bibliographical references and index. | Summary: "This is the first book to examine the significance of European Union antitrust law for the future of sport in Europe. Drawing on multi-disciplinary perspectives from law, economics, sport management and politics, and including case studies about the European Super League (ESL) and the International Skating Union, the book explores key themes in contemporary sport, including governance, ownership and control; the European sport model; the regulatory autonomy of sports organisations; and the relationship between public policy, the law and sport. This is important reading for any advanced student, researcher, policy-maker or practitioner with an interest in sport management, sport law, European law or European politics"— Provided by publisher.
Identifiers: LCCN 2022036661 | ISBN 9781032306339 (hardback) | ISBN 9781032306346 (paperback) | ISBN 9781003305989 (ebook)
Subjects: LCSH: Sports—Law and legislation—European Union countries. | Antitrust law—European Union countries. | Sports—Economic aspects—European Union countries.
Classification: LCC KJE6063 .E93 2023 | DDC 344.24/099—dc23/eng/20220924
LC record available at https://lccn.loc.gov/2022036661

ISBN: 978-1-032-30633-9 (hbk)
ISBN: 978-1-032-30634-6 (pbk)
ISBN: 978-1-003-30598-9 (ebk)

DOI: 10.4324/9781003305989

Typeset in Bembo
by codeMantra

Disclaimer

The editor of this volume, Jacob Kornbeck, is a Policy Officer in the European Commission, but opinions expressed by him are strictly personal and do not render official positions of the European Commission or of the European Union. The same applies to the choice of contributors and the editorial work performed. Opinions expressed in chapters other than those signed by the editor are those of the relevant contributors.

References have been harmonised as regards literature but not with regard to sources of law (legislation and case law), where the preferences of individual authors have been respected.

The book applies a blended reference style, respecting legal traditions with those of the social sciences as far as this seemed feasible. Footnotes have been used rather than APA/Harvard style, while scholarship is listed in a Bibliography at the end of each chapter. Legal sources, media sources and all other sources which cannot be considered scholarship in a narrow sense appear in the footnotes but not in the Bibliography of a given chapter.

CONTENTS

CONTRIBUTORS

Rusa Agafonova is a Swiss, Russian and French-educated Sports Lawyer specialising in EU competition law, international arbitration and good governance. She is currently conducting doctoral research at the University of Zurich, Switzerland. Her PhD thesis focuses on the exclusivity clauses in the regulations of sports federations and on the role of EU competition law in tackling anticompetitive policies of the sports governing bodies.

Margareta Baddeley is an Honorary Professor Emerita of law at the University of Geneva, Switzerland. Following a legal career in international banking in Geneva, she has been teaching at the Universities of Fribourg and Geneva and has served as Vice-Rector of the latter. She has coordinated a range of degree programmes in sports law and is an internationally acknowledged author in the field.

Oliver Budzinski is Professor of economic theory and Director of the Institute of Economics at Ilmenau University of Technology, Germany. His main research areas are competition economics, media economics and sports economics.

Jean-Loup Chappelet is Emeritus Professor of public management at the Swiss Graduate School of Public Administration (IDHEAP) of the Faculty of law, criminal sciences and public administration of the University of Lausanne, Switzerland. He used to serve as Director of the MEMOS programme, a master programme run by 11 universities for Olympic Solidarity (1999–2011), Secretary General of the International Coubertin Committee (2003–2017) and Member of the World Anti-Doping Agency's (WADA) Education Committee (2013–2016) and social science research group and continues serving as a Member of the ASOIF's (Association of Summer Olympic International Federations) Governance Taskforce. His research is now focused on the governance of international sport organisations and events.

Dennis Cukurov is a German-qualified Lawyer at Hogan Lovells International LLP based in Munich, Germany. He focuses on European and German competition law, with particular emphasis on the sports sector. In 2021, at the Heinrich Heine University in Düsseldorf, he defended a doctoral thesis on the Superleague concept in European football.

Arne Feddersen is Professor of industrial organisation at the University of Southern Denmark, Campus Esbjerg. His main research areas include sports economics, media economics as well as regional economics.

Walter S. Palmer is Director in Alumni Relations at Dartmouth College, United States, a former Professional Basketball Player (NBA, Europe, Latin America) and former Leader of European and global athlete trade union organisations. After retirement from the court in 2003, Walter spearheaded the founding of the German basketball players association, Spieler Initiative, SP.IN (2005); the European Elite Athletes Association, EU Athletes (2007); and UNI Sport PRO, now the World Players Association (2012). During that period (2010–2014), he co-chaired the European Sectoral Social Dialogue Committee in the sport sector during its pilot phase. He served as the Deputy Executive Director for International Development and Marketing at the NBA Players Association before starting his own consulting business where he continued to advise player unions from around the world on issues related to organising, governance, career development programming and anti-doping policy. He is also a Board Member at the Centre for Sport and Human Rights and a Member of the Boston advisory board for the Concussion Legacy Foundation.

Mickaël Terrien is Assistant Professor in sport regulation at the Swiss Graduate School of Public Administration (IDHEAP) of the Faculty of law, criminal sciences and public administration of the University of Lausanne. He completed his PhD which was awarded the 2017 prize of the best French PhD in sport economics (French Ministry of Sports). His research interests include sport economics, finance and management.

Ben Van Rompuy is Assistant Professor of EU Competition Law at the Europa Institute of Leiden University, the Netherlands. He has particular expertise in the application of European competition law (antitrust, State aid) in the media and sports sectors. Ben regularly acts as an Advisor and Expert Witness for media companies, sports clubs and associations, public authorities and athletes – he represented the complainants in the European Commission's landmark antitrust case concerning the eligibility rules of the International Skating Union. Ben was previously Senior Researcher at the T.M.C. Asser Instituut in The Hague, where he headed the ASSER International Sports Law Centre.

GRUßWORT

Der Sport mit all seinen Facetten ist ein Faszinosum. Das citius, altius, fortius der olympischen Idee ist mehr denn je lebendig, es wird von Athleten und Athletinnen in der ganzen Welt auf unterschiedlichste Art und Weise gelebt. Der Sport als die „schönste Nebensache der Welt", betrieben von Amateuren, ist längst Vergangenheit. Der Amateursport ist indes die Basis für den Profisport, der die Massen zu den Wettkampfstätten und vor die TV-Screens zieht. So hat denn logischerweise auch die Kommerzialisierung des Sports vor mehr als 50 Jahren Einzug gehalten und ist in ihrer heutigen Ausprägung keineswegs am Ende.

Auf dem Weg dorthin hat es die unterschiedlichsten widerstreitenden Interessen zwischen Sportlern einerseits und den Strukturen des Sports andererseits gegeben. Ohne eine organisatorische Basis ist der Wettkampfsport nicht durchführbar. Aber welches ist die beste Basis dafür? Wer hat das Sagen? Wer darf wovon profitieren? Welche Rechte hat der Athlet überhaupt, ohne den das gesamte Spektakel gar nicht möglich wäre!?

1982 hat der Deutsche Leichtathletikverband die damals erfolgreichste deutsche Marathonläuferin, Charlotte Teske, lebenslang gesperrt, weil sie angeblich gegen die Bestimmungen eines Schuh-Ausrüstervertrags verstoßen habe. Diese anmaßende Sanktion gegen eine Athletin war damals, auch für unbefangene Beobachter, selbst in Ansätzen kaum vorstellbar. Einmal mehr wurde dadurch jedoch offenbar, dass sportrechtliche Bestimmungen einerseits und zivilrechtliche und grundrechtliche Ansprüche eines jeden Individuums andererseits, oft nur schwer vereinbar sind. Die Athletin war in dieser causa vor den Zivilgerichten erfolgreich. Für die Athletin selbst war das schon ein enormer Aufwand – physisch, zeitlich und finanziell – obwohl sie lediglich ihr Recht, als Langstreckenläuferin wieder an Wettkämpfen teilnehmen zu dürfen, einforderte.

Ein Selbstverständnis, das sie sich erkämpfen musste.

Es ist zwar nachvollziehbar, dass Sportorganisationen vom IOC, der FIFA bis hinunter zu den Sportorganisationen auf lokaler und regionaler Ebene ein Interesse daran haben, den Sport so zu organisieren, wie es scheinbar für die Sache des Sports das Beste ist. Nichtsdestotrotz sind dabei stets auch die Individualrechte eines jeden Einzelnen, der Sport treibt, zu berücksichtigen und so ergibt sich ein permanenter Widerstreit zwischen diesen beiden unterschiedlichen Positionen. Dies gilt heute mehr denn je, da supranationale, kartellrechtliche und sonstige Regelungen für alle, also auch für Athleten und Athletinnen einerseits, sowie für Sportorganisationen andererseits, gleichermaßen Gültigkeit besitzen.

Als junger Athlet und Mitglied der deutschen Leichtathletik-Nationalmannschaft habe ich schon Anfang der siebziger Jahre höchstpersönlich die Unzulänglichkeit der Funktionsträger von Sportverbänden erlebt. Später, als niedergelassener Rechtsanwalt, habe ich in Wahrnehmung der Rechte von Sportlern gegenüber Sportverbänden und Sportorganisationen immer wieder festgestellt, dass die Sportgerichtsbarkeit nur höchst unzulänglich zu entscheiden in der Lage war. Demokratische Grundrechte von Sportlern und der Respekt davor blieben allzu oft auf der Strecke. Schließlich habe ich dann als TV-Reporter selbst anhand von Wettkampfentscheidungen immer wieder erlebt, dass auch sportgerichtliche Wettkampfentscheidungen, gemessen an unserer Rechtsordnung, höchst fragwürdig sein können. Daran hat sich scheinbar bis heute nichts geändert.

Die Kommerzialisierung des Sports ist ein nicht mehr aufzuhaltendes Faktum. Sie betrifft Athleten und Athletinnen, sowie die Sportorganisationen gleichermaßen. Hier tun sich völlig neue zusätzliche rechtliche Aspekte auf, wodurch der Wettkampfsport alter Prägung einmal mehr in Frage gestellt wird. Wenn dann noch – wie aktuell – pandemische und politische Interessen (z. B. Olympische Winterspiele in Peking 2022) hinzukommen, zeigt es die ganze Misere des Sports.

Eines allerdings muss auch klar sein: Nicht alles, was legal ist, ist auch opportun. Ein weites Feld, das sich da auftut, und die Lösung lässt auf sich warten...

Bernd Heller
Stabhochspringer (1970–1972)
(Deutscher Vizemeister 1971)
Rechtsanwalt (1974–1986)
TV-Reporter, Moderator und Produzent seit 1971
(SWF, HR, ZDF, N24)
http://www.bernd-heller.com/

FOREWORD

Sport, in all its facets, fascinates us and compels us to pay attention. The Olympic ideal is not just alive but is actually lived by athletes around the world in a variety of different ways. The time when sport, the most beautiful pastime in the world, was pursued only by amateurs is long past. Today, amateur sport is the foundation upon which professional sport is built. It attracts the masses to competition while also pulling them irresistibly to the glow of their television screens. It was through amateur sport that commercialisation gained a toehold more than 50 years ago and its expansion is nowhere near complete.

Along the way, a set of very different and competing interests developed with athletes on one side and sport organisations on the other. Indeed, competitive sport is not possible without an organisational foundation. But which organisational form is the best? Who should make the decisions? Who should profit? What rights do athletes have, considering that without them the entire spectacle would not be possible?

In 1982, the German Athletics Federation gave a life ban to the most successful German marathon runner at that time, Charlotte Teske, because she allegedly violated the terms of the federation's shoe sponsorship contract. Even to outsiders, this sanction seemed unimaginably disproportionate. Once again, it was made clear in this case that it is often impossible to reconcile sports rules with civil and constitutional rights. I represented the athlete in her case - and was successful. Even though the violations of Ms. Teske's rights were so obvious, it took an incredible effort on her part – physically, emotionally, and financially – just to win back her right to participate in sport competitions.

It is evident that sport organisations, from the IOC and FIFA to those at the regional and local levels, have an interest in organising sport in a way that is best for sport as a whole. However, each athlete has their own rights as an individual that must be respected, which results in a fundamental conflict between these two positions. That is true today, more than ever, because supranational competition laws and rules apply equally to both athletes and sport organisations.

As a young athlete and member of the German Athletics Federation in the early 1970s, I also experienced in a deeply personal way the inadequacy of the approach taken by those running sport organisations. Later, as an independent lawyer representing athletes, I came to realise that sport's disciplinary system was entirely inadequate in taking athletes' rights into account. Athletes' fundamental democratic rights were too often lost along the way. As a TV reporter, I often witnessed decisions made during competitions that were highly questionable when measured against our democratic legal standards. Apparently, not much has changed since then.

The commercialisation of sport is a force that can no longer be denied. It affects athletes and sport organisations equally. Commercialisation brings with it an entirely new set of legal considerations for competitive sport heaping new questions on top of old issues. The dreadful state of sport governance has been further exposed by the dual crises of a global pandemic and increasing geopolitical tensions (i.e. Beijing Winter Olympic Games).

One thing, however, remains clear: not everything that is legal is also appropriate. The chasm between the two sides is becoming wider, and the solution remains elusive.

Bernd Heller
Pole vaulter 1970–1972
(four international championships)
(German vice champion 1971)

Attorney-at-Law 1974–1986
TV reporter, moderator and producer since 1971
(ZDF, SWF, HR, n-tv, N24)
http://www.bernd-heller.com

Translated by **_Walter Palmer_**
Former basketball player
NBA 1990–91, 1992–93, Europe 1991–92,
1993–2003, Argentina 1993
Trade unionist (2005–2015)

1

INTRODUCTION

The slow yet steady rise of EU sports antitrust law (1982–2022)

Jacob Kornbeck

1.1 Introduction

Is EU antitrust law going to be (one of) the main driver(s) of change in European sport governance? When two speed skaters filed an antitrust complaint targeting the selection rules of the International Skating Union (ISU), they triggered a major controversy. Their complaint led to an antitrust investigation by the European Commission, a Commission decision, a judgment of the General Court and an appeal to the Court of Justice. At this writing (1 July 2022), the oral hearing was scheduled for 11 July 2022 and the judgment was expected to make headlines. When a handful of football clubs launched an initiative to set up a European Superleague, they too sent shock waves through the sports establishment. Here too, the Court of Justice of the European Union (CJEU) was likely to hand down a landmark ruling, starting with oral hearings to be held on 11–12 July 2022. Finally, in a case brought by a Belgian football player and his former club, challenging the Home-Grown Player (HGP) rule of the Union of European Football Associations (UEFA) restricting the number of foreign-trained players to be fielded at any given time, the Court again had to resolve a case on the basis of EU antitrust law, one of the main fields of EU competition law and policy. As this book was going to press, three paradigmatic test cases were pending before the CJEU: *International Skating Union, European Superleague Company* (ESL) and *Royal Antwerp FC.*

- In *International Skating Union*[1] the Court, upon appeal from the General Court,[2] had to decide whether an antitrust decision by the European

1 International Skating Union v Commission. Case C-124/21 P (pending).

2 GC, 16.12.2020. International Skating Union v European Commission. Case T-93/18. ECLI:EU:T:2020:610.

DOI: 10.4324/9781003305989-1

Commission[3] had assessed the selection rules of the International Skating Union (ISU) correctly. The case struck a nerve because it touched upon the funding model of European sports, based on a 'pyramid' encasing elite with grassroots, professional with amateur and competitive with recreational sports, while also raising concerns regarding the extent to which funds are really distributed all the way down to the grassroots. The case revealed a potential for conflicts of interest whenever sports governing bodies (SGBs) regulate sports markets while also participating in marketing rights derived from the same sporting activities. In 2021, ISU received some indirect support from the European Parliament (EP) in a generic resolution 'on EU sports policy,'[4] although the role of EP resolutions as a source of law seems debatable.

- In *European Superleague Company*,[5] the Court had to answer prejudicial questions submitted by the Commercial Court N° 17 of Madrid in a case opposing the European Superleague Company (ESL) to UEFA and the Fédération Internationale de Football Association (FIFA). The questions related to the interpretation, application and enforcement of EU antitrust rules were substantial, while the proposed so-called 'breakaway league'[6] was seen in many quarters as a threat to the financial stability of the established European sport 'pyramid.' The case raised the same concerns as the *ISU* case as regards the risk of conflicts of interest in a governance system attributing a regulatory and a commercial role to the same SGB, while steps taken by UEFA and its affiliates – national football associations (FAs) – to discourage clubs and their

3 Decision C (2017) 8240 final. Commission Decision of 8.12.2017 relating to proceedings under Article 101 of the Treaty on the Functioning of the European Union (the Treaty) and Article 53 of the EEA Agreement Case AT.40208 – International Skating Union's Eligibility rules (Only the English text is authentic). http://ec.europa.eu/competition/antitrust/cases/dec_docs/40208/40208_1384_5.pdf; See also Summary of Commission Decision of 8 December 2017 relating to a proceeding under Article 101 of the Treaty on the Functioning of the European Union and Article 53 of the EEA Agreement (Case AT.40208 – International Skating Union's Eligibility Rules) (notified under document C(2017) 8240). OJ C 148, 27.4.2018, pp. 9–12.

4 European Parliament resolution of 23 November 2021 on EU sports policy: assessment and possible ways forward (2021/2058(INI)). P9_TA(2021)0463. A9-0318/2021. https://www.europarl.europa.eu/doceo/document/TA-9-2021-0463_EN.html, at 11–17, in particular at 11: 'Acknowledges the importance of a European sports model based on values, voluntary activities and solidarity,' at 13: 'a European sports [...] integrating the principles of solidarity, sustainability, inclusiveness for all, open competition, sporting merit and fairness' and 15: 'sports clubs as the foundation of a European sports model offering everyone the opportunity to engage in sport locally.'

5 European Superleague Company, S. L. v Union of European Football Associations (UEFA) and Fédération Internationale de Football Association (FIFA). Date lodged: 27 May 2021. Referring court: Juzgado de lo Mercantil n.° 17 de Madrid (Commercial Court No 17, Madrid, Spain). Case C-333/21 (pending). See working document: https://curia.europa.eu/juris/showPdf.jsf?text=&docid=244284&pageIndex=0&doclang=EN&mode=lst&dir=&occ=first&part=1&cid=5967904.

6 For a sport law theory of breakaway league, see Pijetlovic (2015).

commercial partners from participating in the proposed league only exacerbated such concerns. UEFA and FIFA received some support from the EP as part of the 2021 resolution referred to above,[7] as well as in the related report of its Committee on Culture and Education (CULT) (in charge of Sport).[8]

- In *Royal Antwerp FC*,[9] finally, the French-speaking Court of First Instance of Brussels was putting a prejudicial question to the Court in a matter regarding an Israeli-born, Belgian-naturalised football player and his former employing club, as opposed the Belgian FA. The heart of the matter was the compatibility of national rules, enacted by the FA to comply with UEFA's so-called Home-Grown Player (HGP) rule,[10] with EU antitrust law. Adopted by UEFA in 2005, these rules had received explicit backing from the EP in a resolution adopted in 2006.[11]

These three cases meant that all eyes were turned towards Luxembourg, the capital of the Grand-Duchy and seat of the General Court and the Court, in the

7 EP resolution (2021/2058(INI)) (fn 4), at 13: 'Calls for a European sports model that recognises the need for a strong commitment to integrating the principles of solidarity, sustainability, inclusiveness for all, open competition, sporting merit and fairness, and accordingly strongly opposes breakaway competitions that undermine such principles and endanger the stability of the overall sports ecosystem; stresses that these principles should be encouraged by all sports stakeholders and national authorities.' *Ibid.*, at 14: 'Recognises the role of federations in governing their sport and encourages closer coordination and cooperation with authorities and all relevant stakeholders.'

8 A9-0318/2021. 8.11.2021. Report on EU sports policy: assessment and possible ways forward (2021/2058(INI)). Committee on Culture and Education. Rapporteur: Tomasz Frankowski, https://www.europarl.europa.eu/doceo/document/A-9-2021-0318_EN.html, p. 16: 'In particular, the debate has been stymied by semantics about the name, rather than focusing on the substance of the relevant features of the model, what they mean and how best to promote them. Whilst this confusion and inaction persists, the forces that threaten the European dimension in sport and seek to undermine its features only stand to benefit. The European Superleague was a prime example of this, which, for now, has fortunately failed due to the strong European opposition to it.'

9 SA Royal Antwerp Football Club v Union royale belge des sociétés de football association ASBL. Date lodged: 11 November 2021. Referring court: Tribunal de première instance francophone de Bruxelles (Belgium). Case C-680/21 (pending). Working document: https://curia.europa.eu/juris/showPdf.jsf?text=&docid=251818&pageIndex=0&doclang=EN&mode=lst&dir=&occ=first&part=1&cid=5969529.

10 The HGP rule was adopted by the UEFA Executive Committee (2 February 2005) and confirmed by the 52 UEFA affiliates – national football associations (FAs) – at the UEFA Congress in Tallinn (21 April 2005). It is not enshrined in any UEFA regulation but has been incorporated into various FA regulations, including the Belgian one who was targeted by Royal Antwerp FC.

11 European Parliament resolution of 29 March 2007 on the future of professional football in Europe (2006/2130(INI)). P6_TA(2007)0100. A6-0036/2007. https://www.europarl.europa.eu/doceo/document/TA-6-2007-0100_EN.html, at 34: 'Expresses its clear support for the UEFA measures to encourage the education of young players by requiring a minimum number of home-grown players in a professional club's squad and by placing a limit on the size of the squads; believes that such incentive measures are proportionate and calls on professional clubs to strictly implement this rule.'

summer of 2022. The objective of the present book is, in a timely manner, to respond to this situation by presenting critical perspectives from the disciplines of law, economics and sports management on some of the more salient aspects of the three cases, and of the underlying problems and challenges.

What is the deeper, long-term significance of such initiatives and what do they reveal about structural change happening in European sports? Prepared and published within a short timeframe, in an effort to respond in a timely fashion to ongoing events in a fast-moving environment, this book aims to provide answers to some currently pressing questions. Academically robust yet relevant to practice, it is about far more than just the *ISU, ESL* and *Royal Antwerp* cases. Authors include established authorities alongside rising stars, with people from practice as well as from academia. Lawyers, economists and experts on sports management, as well as an athlete representative, have all contributed to this book project. The Preface has been written by an athlete-turned-lawyer-turned-TV-producer who had the privilege to represent an athlete, back in 1982, in what could have become the first case of applying Community (now Union) antitrust law to sport.

To frame the discussion, the present Introduction will provide a brief, analytically selective chronology of EC/EU[12] case law and decisional practice during the 40-year period until now (1982–2022) in an effort to show whether a mature doctrine of EU sports antitrust law was in place in 2022.

1.2 The incremental formation of EC/EU sports antitrust law (1982–2022)

1.2.1 Pre-enforcement (c. 1982–1994)

When West German athlete Charlotte Teske won the 1982 Boston Marathon, she did not wear shoes from Adidas, the official sponsor of the German Athletics Association (DLV). According to a newspaper article[13] published by Hartmut

12 The text below refers both to Community and Union law, and to the European Community (EC) and the European Union (EU) as appropriate. In covering the entire period concerned, this differentiated terminology is of necessity because the Union was only introduced with the entry into force of the Treaty of Maastricht (1.11.1993), and only acquired legal personality with the entry into force of the Lisbon Treaty (1.12.2009) (Article 47 TEU). For quite some time, therefore, the EU was a *de facto* political entity without being a legal entity, its enforceable secondary law being Community law (while there was Union law within the so-called second and third pillars of the Maastricht Treaty), with agreements (such as the numerous grant agreements and service contracts in the field of sport in which the present editor was involved in those days) being signed in the name of the Community, not the Union. That the media of many Member States (especially the more Northern ones) started referring to the EU in a more generic sense, already in the 1990s, does not change the fact that such usage was, in many cases, imprecise or even misleading.

13 Johannes, H. (1999) Wie eine Marathonläuferin den DLV schlägt. *Neue Zürcher Zeitung (NZZ)*, 15 September (on file with author).

Johannes (1931–2021),[14] all she had received from Adidas was two pairs of shoes and a sports bag. When her assiduous training on the streets of Boston had used up her official shoes, she had stocked up in a local store, which in those days only had domestic sports shoes, leading to the purchase of a pair of Nike Élite. As she crossed the finish line, she was photographed and the pictures, including the incriminating shoes, went round the world (sports news were already more globalised than the sports goods retail market), which prompted Adidas to approach DLV asking for a compensation in accordance with the sponsorship agreement. In an apparent effort to economise, and according to Johannes, DLV offered a disciplinary solution, consisting in a life ban for Teske. The Directorate-General for Competition (then DG IV, now DG COMP) of the Commission of the European Communities (now the European Commission) started investigating unofficially, though a formal procedure was never opened, which explains why no decision was published and also why the case was not mentioned in the annual report.[15] Still according to Johannes, two different federal ministries of Germany intervened in various ways and the matter was settled out of court. Teske was represented by Bernd Heller, an athlete-turned-lawyer (and later TV producer) whose Preface is printed at the beginning of this book. Thus, nothing became of the 'Teske case,'[16] which was nipped in the bud, and SGBs – understandably – did not have an opportunity to realise the applicability of Community antitrust law to their role as private regulators. And while a range of sports antitrust enforcement did begin in the 1990s (see below), still no ruling was handed down by the Court of First Instance (CFI) of the European Union (now the General Court), or the Court of Justice, based on antitrust rules until *Meca Medina* (2006), although some cases could have been.

Community antitrust law was already well established, notwithstanding, when the Court ruled in *Walrave*[17] (1974) that Community law also applied to sport; at least to the extent that sport was part of economic life. The Court's use of the phrase 'only as far as'[18] must have seemed rather restrictive at that time: a

14 In 1982, Dr Hartmut Johannes (20/05/1931–22/01/2021) was an official of DG IV (now DG COMP) of the Commission of the EC (now the European Commission). The NZZ article was published after his retirement from the Commission, at a time when he was working in private practice, still in Brussels. Unfortunately, there was no way Dr Johannes could be approached in connection with the present book – the editor would have been delighted to let him write a Preface or a Postscript – as he had passed away in 2021 (source: European Commission, DG HR).

15 Johannes (1999) (fn 13).

16 It seems impossible to use italics (*Teske*) for a case which was never opened official.

17 ECJ, 12.12.1974. B.N.O. Walrave and L.J.N. Koch v Association Union cycliste internationale, Koninklijke Nederlandsche Wielren Unie and Federación Española Ciclismo. Reference for a preliminary ruling: Arrondissementsrechtbank Utrecht – Netherlands. Case 36-74. ECR 1974 01405. ECLI:EU:C:1974:140.

18 *Ibid.*, p. 1421, at 1: 'Having regard to the objectives of the Community, the practice of sport is subject to Community law only in so far as it constitutes an economic activity within the meaning of Article 2 of the Treaty.'

reading which the qualifying phrases 'of purely sporting interest' and 'nothing to do with economic activity'[19] would seem to corroborate. Even if they were semantically connected to a remark about the formation of national teams (an admittedly punctual, even if highly mediatised, occurrence in the life of European sports), they seemed to suggest a blanket exemption (at least a partial one). The vagueness of this ruling was to create legitimate yet unrealistic expectations, leading sports governing bodies (SGBs) and policy makers alike down an unhelpful alley whence they were not to emerge for the next 32 years, believing until then that some 'purely sporting' rules must qualify for exemption from EC/EU law. It was not until *Meca Medina*[20] (2006) that they were to be definitively disabused, even if some[21] were having difficulties in accepting the unambiguously phrased decision in the very first case adjudicated by the Court of Justice of the European Union (CJEU) based on antitrust rules applied to sport. Given that competition law and policy – and its component antitrust law – had been enshrined in the Treaty since the 1950s, the fact that the first such case should be adjudicated half a century after the European Economic Community (EEC) started operating (1958), was and remains remarkable. Equally striking was the fact that it should occur 32 years after the Court had established that Treaty provisions were applicable to the private rules of SGBs, especially whenever their application risked curbing the exercise of freedoms guaranteed by the Treaty. In view of the protection of an 'objective of the Community,' it is immaterial that SGBs are organised under private law, since avoiding violations of a Treaty guarantee is primordial.[22] That was already the position in 1974, when interpreting free movement law in the context of sport.

In *Meca Medina*, the Court finally made it clear that the economic/non-economic binary did not imply any substantive distinction allowing to discard the possibility of oversight by regulators and courts. In a sense, however, this decision should perhaps not have been such a big surprise after all, given the

19 *Ibid.*, p. 1421, at 2: 'The prohibition on discrimination based on nationality contained in Articles 7, 48 and 59 of the Treaty does not affect the composition of sport teams, in. particular national teams, the formation of which is a question of purely sporting interest and as such has nothing to do with economic activity.'

20 CJEU, 18.06.2006. David Meca-Medina and Igor Majcen v Kommission. Case C-519/04 P. ECR 2006 I-06991. ECLI:EU:C:2006:492.

21 See e.g. the commetary by Infantino (at that time UEFA Legal Director): Infantino, G. (2006) Meca-Medina: A Step Backwards for the European Sports Model and the Specificity of Sport? https://editorial.uefa.com/resources/01ba-0f8425be6c58-211e02039f19-1000/meca-medina_summary_a_step_backwards_for_the_european_sports_model_and_the_specificity_of_sport_pdf.

22 See ECJ, 12.12.1974. *Walrave* (fn 17), p. 1419, at 18: 'The abolition as between Member States of obstacles to freedom of movement for persons and to freedom to provide services, which are fundamental objectives of the Community contained in Article 3 (c) of the Treaty, would be compromised if the abolition of barriers of national origin could be neutralized by obstacles resulting from the exercise of their legal autonomy by associations or organizations which do not come under public law.'

scope of EC/EU competition rules for horizontal application, with frequently unexpected (possibly even unintended) consequences. That certain entities were sports governing bodies (SGBs), or that the activities concerned qualified as sport and that the litigious rules were sporting rules enacted, applied and enforced by private entities (SGBs), could not qualify for exemptions, although such arguments were routinely relied upon by SGBs, and often employed successfully vis-à-vis national authorities. The problem with this line of reasoning was that the concept of an undertaking, under EC/EU competition law, was already directed towards an assessment of economic realities rather than bound to accept certain legal formalities. This 'functional approach'[23] had already been established in *Consten*[24] (1966) and *Höfner* (1991)[25] and was to be followed by the Commission in its FIFA 1990 World Cup decision[26] (1992). Drawing on *Walrave* (for the application of EC law to sport), and on *Höfner* (for the concept of an undertaking), the Commission emphasised that the nature of the economic activities of an undertaking must be assessed 'regardless of its legal form,'[27] thereby offering a powerful rebuke to the defence habitually used by SGBs, that their frequent legal form as non-profit organisations should entail exemptions. Drawing on *Italy v UK (British Telecommunications)*[28] (1985), the Commission retained that the non-profit status of an entity pursuing an economic activity could not be relied upon to escape assessment of that activity as economic in nature.[29] In this context, it should be recalled that competition law and policy is, alongside the Single Market, the centrepiece of European integration. As its horizontal application has the potential to reach all economic sectors, it was only going to be a question

23 Ezrachi (2016), p. 1.

24 ECJ, 13.07.1966. Établissements Consten S.à.R.L. and Grundig-Verkaufs-GmbH v Commission of the European Economic Community. Joined cases 56 and 58–64. ECR. 1966 00429. ECLI:EU:C:1966:41, p. 327: 'independently of the legal form taken.' *Ibid.*, p. 342: 'Besides, for the purpose of applying Article 85 (1), there is no need to take account of the concrete effects of an agreement once it appears that it has as its object the prevention, restriction or distortion of competition.'

25 ECJ, 23.04.1991. Klaus Höfner and Fritz Elser v Macrotron GmbH. Reference for a preliminary ruling: Oberlandesgericht München, Germany. Case C-41/90. ECR 1991 I-01979. ECLI:EU:C:1991:161, at 21: 'It must be observed, in the context of competition law, first that the concept of an undertaking encompasses every entity engaged in an economic activity, regardless of the legal status of the entity and the way in which it is financed and, secondly, that employment procurement is an economic activity.'

26 92/521/EEC: Commission Decision of 27 October 1992 relating to a proceeding under Article 85 of the EEC Treaty (IV/33.384 and IV/33.378 – Distribution of package tours during the 1990 World Cup) (Only the French and Italian texts are authentic). OJ L 326, 12.11.1992, pp. 31–42.

27 *Ibid.*, p. 35, at 43: 'In accordance with the case law of the Court of Justice, any entity carrying on activities of an economic nature, regardless of its legal form, constitutes an undertaking within the meaning of Article 85 of the EEC Treaty.'

28 ECJ, 20.03.1985. Italian Republic v Commission of the European Communities. Case 41/83. ECR 1985 00873. ECLI:EU:C:1985:120.

29 *Ibid.*, p. 35, at 43: 'An activity of an economic nature means any activity, whether or not profit-making, that involves economic trade.'

of time until the sport sector would feel the full brunt of the law; that it took so long, remains remarkable regardless and may say more about the reluctance, within the sector, to turn to public authorities for conflict resolution, than about the nature of the Community/Union legal order.

Had the history of EC sports law started – very tentatively – in 1974 with the *Walrave* ruling (see above), then the fast-aborted 'Teske case' marked, in 1982, the theoretical starting point of EC sports antitrust law. For while free movement rules were to remain the mainstay of the sports law of the Community for a long time, the theoretical possibility of challenges grounded in antitrust rules could not be discarded categorically. Whereas the Court's 1995 *Bosman* ruling was to become the pivotal moment in the development of EC/EU sports law and policy, the Court resolved the case solely on the basis of free movement rules, although AG Lenz[30] had acknowledged the applicability, in principle, of antitrust rules to the case; at least, he could see 'no reason' why the rules at issue (the Belgian FA's rules governing international player transfers) 'should not be subject both to Article 48 [then: free movement of workers] and to EC competition law'.[31] And while SGBs where, then, still convinced that some sporting activities and structures must *per se* qualify for exemptions – the Court seemed to have promised this to them in *Walrave* (1974) with its 'purely sporting'[32] phrase – they should have been disabused by AG Lenz who recalled that the non-profit status of the sending and receiving clubs, or of any clubs for that sake, was immaterial in determining if their rules entered into the scope of EC competition law.[33] In so doing, he was merely recalling what was then the established law regarding the notion of an undertaking, with a focus on economic reality rather than legal form,[34] a notion which was likely to apply horizontally to sport, like to any other sector.

1.2.2 Emerging enforcement (c. 1994–2008)

The decade starting with *Bosman* (1995–2006) was one of doctrinal transition, as the applicability of Community law to wider areas of sporting activities started being acknowledged *de facto*, if not always *de jure*.

30 GA Lenz, 20.09.1995. URBSFA ./. Jean-Marc Bosman u.a, Royal club liégeois SA ./. Jean-Marc Bosman u.a. und UEFA ./. Jean-Marc Bosman. Rs. C-415/93. ECLI:EU:C:1995:293, Rn. 126, 255, 263, 266, 273, 286.

31 *Ibid.*, at 253.

32 ECJ, 12.12.1974, *Walrave* (fn 18), p. 1421, at 2.

33 GA Lenz, 20.09.1995. *Bosman* (fn 31), at 255. 'The activities of US Dunkerque and RC Liège are not different in character from those of bigger clubs. What is different is only the economic success obtained by the clubs in question from their activity. That circumstance is not relevant, however, to the question of whether there is an undertaking. The Italian Government's objection that football clubs are non-profit-making organizations is thus also wide of the mark. Even if that assertion were correct – which I consider very doubtful – it would be of no importance, since the concept of undertaking which underlies EC competition law does not presuppose a profit-making intention.'

34 See ECJ, 13.07.1966. *Consten* (fn 24); ECJ, 23.04.1991; ECJ, 23.04.1991 *Höfner* (fn 26).

Yet the idea of 'purely sporting rules' was still alive and kicking, ever since *Walrave*,[35] leading to legitimate yet unattainable expectations. Because the previous decade had been marked by the frenetic rush to complete the Single Market programme within a mere seven years (1985–1992), an (almost) 360° exercise had taken place scanning all potentially relevant sectors for relevance to Community law. After all, the Internal Market programme had been launched in 1985, by Jacques Delors and Lord Cockfield, with the publication of a White Paper[36] listing hundreds of areas of regulation proposed for harmonisation. In line with this logic, these were the years when the press and mass media (especially but not solely the British tabloid press) started reporting on the curvature of cucumbers and bananas as apparent proof of bureaucratic zeal (even if each piece of European legislation meant a simplification compared with 12 extant set of rules, in each case). It was also the time when the European Commission commissioned a study to Coopers & Lybrand,[37] identifying a number of sports regulatory issues of some salience in relation to Single Market. The 1990s and early 2000s therefore did see some administrative procedures of the Commission involving the production of sports equipment (*Tretorn* (tennis balls) (1994),[38] federations and event organisers and owners of media rights (*FIA* (motor sport) 2001),[39] *Champions League* (media rights derived from football matches) 2003[40]). It was also the time when European sports law emerged as a visible subdiscipline of law and sports law. In Germany, a sports law section was established under the German Lawyers' Association (*Arbeitsgemeinschaft Sportrecht im DAV*) in 1999,[41]

35 ECJ, 12.12.1974. *Walrave* (fn 17).

36 Commission of the European Communities. COMC85) 310 final. Brussels, 14 June 1985. Completing the Internal Market: White Paper from the Commission to the European Council (Milan, 28–29 June 1985). https://op.europa.eu/en/publication-detail/-/publication/4ff490f3-dbb6–4331-a2ea-a3ca59f974a8/language-en.

37 Coopers & Lybrand (1991) Gaming in the Single Market: a Study of the Current Legal and Market Situation. Brussels: Coopers & Lybrand (previously on file with author). Coopers & Lybrand (1994) The Impact of EC Activities on Sport. Brussels: Coopers & Lybrand (previously on file with author).

38 94/987/EC: Commission Decision of 21 December 1994 relating to a proceeding pursuant to Article 85 of the EC Treaty (IV/32.948–IV/34.590: Tretorn and others) (Only the English, French, German, Italian and Dutch texts are authentic) (Text with EEA relevance). OJ L 378 , 31/12/1994 P. 0045–0053.

39 Notice published pursuant to Article 19(3) of Council Regulation No 17 concerning CasesCOMP/35.163 – Notification of FIA Regulations, COMP/36.638 – Notification by FIA/FOA of agreements relating to the FIA Formula One World Championship, COMP/36.776 – GTR/FIA & other. OJ C 169, 13.6.2001, pp. 5–11.

40 2003/778/EC: Commission Decision of 23 July 2003 relating to a proceeding pursuant to Article 81 of the EC Treaty and Article 53 of the EEA Agreement (COMP/C.2-37.398 – Joint selling of the commercial rights of the UEFA Champions League) (Text with EEA relevance.) (notified under document number C(2003) 2627).
OJ L 291, 8.11.2003, pp. 25–55.

41 See Steiner (2022), as well as an unsigned and undated text on the website of the association, hosted by one of its members: http://www.ra-kraehe.de/5.html.

while an unaffiliated 'Constance Circle' (*Konstanzer Arbeitskreises für Sportrecht*) (today *Deutsche Vereinigung für Sportrecht*) (DVSR) emerged in 1982.[42]

Between the *Bosman* (1995) and *Meca Medina* (2006) rulings, sports governing bodies (SGBs) deployed various attempts and strategies to achieve insulation of their regulatory (and, by implication, also their commercial) functions from the reach of EC/EU law. While the immediate, short-term response to *Bosman* had been something like disbelief, consternation and even outrage,[43] SGBs gradually learnt that 'joining them' was better than 'beating them,' as the saying goes. Rather than confronting the unpopular outcome, they started instead engaging meaningfully with EU Institutions – the sort of lobby work which is everyday business for actors interested in achieving some policy outcomes and avoiding others – and developed this strand of activity over the following years: 'engaging with the EU in order to minimise its impact.'[44] The EU Institutions listened and engaged in a process which led from the Amsterdam Declaration[45] of the European Council (Heads of State and Government), over the Commission's 'Helsinki report'[46] on a so-called European model of sport towards the Nice Declaration,[47] again adopted by the European Council conjointly with that of a new Treaty. These documents have been quoted in many judgments, although their exact legal implications can be hard to gauge. As a *minimum minimorum*, they may represent a certain declaratory attachment to the pyramidal European model, conflating top-level with grassroots, professional with amateur and

42 Krähe, C. (2012) 30 Jahre Konstanzer Arbeitskreis für Sportrecht, http://www.ra-kraehe.de/12.html.

43 Anderson (2010), p. 333: 'Without overly exaggerating or trivialising the matter, it might be said that the immediate reaction of UEFA and the football authorities worldwide to the Bosman litigation displayed the classic four stages of grief – denial; then anger; followed by depression; and finally acceptance.'

44 García & Weatherill (2012).

45 Treaty of Amsterdam amending the Treaty on European Union, the Treaties establishing the European Communities and certain related acts, signed at Amsterdam, 2 October 1997. OJ C 340, 10.11.1997, pp. 1–144, p. 136: 29. Declaration on sport: 'The Conference emphasises the social significance of sport, in particular its role in forging identity and bringing people together. The Conference therefore calls on the bodies of the European Union to listen to sports associations when important questions affecting sport are at issue. In this connection, special consideration should be given to the particular characteristics of amateur sport.'

46 Brussels, 10.12.1999. COM(1999) 644 final. Report from the Commission to the European Council with a view to safeguarding current sports structures and maintaining the social function of sport within the Community framework – The Helsinki Report on Sport –, p. 8, sec. 4.2.1: In terms of the economic activity that it generates, the sporting sector is subject to the rules of the EC Treaty, like the other sectors of the economy. The application of the Treaty's competition rules to the sporting sector must take account of the specific characteristics of sport, especially the interdependence between sporting activity and the economic activity that it generates, the principle of equal opportunities and the uncertainty of the results.'

47 European Council Nice, 7–10 December 2000. Conclusions of the Presidency (Annexes), https://www.europarl.europa.eu/summits/nice2_en.htm, Annex IV. Declaration on the specific characteristics of sport and its social function in Europe, of account should be taken in implementing common policies.

competitive with recreational sports. While a duty for EU Institutions to check the sport-friendliness of envisaged decisions can be deduced, the question of the voice(s) of sport remains unaccounted for, where the notion of 'sport-friendly' decisions may be grounded in a flawed understanding of sport as a monolith devoid of internal conflicts. Such a doctrine, and the outright rejection of the notion that opposed 'camps' can be found in sports (SGBs versus athletes), found an implausibly enthusiastic protagonist in the Federal Court of Justice (*Bundesgerichtshof*) (BGH) of Germany in the *Pechstein* case.[48] Yet the same did not happen so far as regards Treaty on the Functioning of the European Union (TFEU) and its interpretation through the General Court and the Court.

That the constitutional legislator at European level (the Member States) did not respond in kind to the advances made by sports governing bodies (SGBs), with the support of some Governments, is interesting, as their efforts reached quite a stage of advancement in 2002 when the so-called Freiburg Draft of the European Constitutional Treaty[49] was published in the name Erwin Teufel, Minister-President of the German Land of Baden-Württemberg. The text included an Article 24 on 'Respect for the Sovereignty of the Member States.'[50] The ambition behind this move was clear enough – a blanket exemption for sport from the scope of application of Union law – although one wonders just how many sport-specific rules would have been covered by such an exemption in practice. Sport would have been recognised as an untouchable emanation of national identity and would have been insulated from the law – and probably also from judicial review – had the text been maintained; yet 'there was no appetite among the majority of delegates to introduce such a brake.'[51] Thus the final draft Constitution did not include this unusual language and, while the Constitution was soon to be abandoned after unsuccessful referenda in France and the Netherlands, the text included in today's Article 165 TFEU is the one included in the last Constitution draft,[52] albeit amended by the 'taking into account' phrase.

48 BGH, Az. KZR 6/15, Pechstein ./. International Skating Union (ISU), 7. Juni 2016, Tenor, at d). See also Ehle & Guaia (2017).

49 European Convention. The Secretariat. Brussels, 20 January 2003. CONV 495/03. CONTRIB 198. Contribution submitted by Mr Erwin Teufel, member of the Convention: "Freiburg Draft of a European Constitutional Treaty", https://ec.europa.eu/dorie/fileDownload.do?docId=184349&cardId=184349.

50 *Ibid:* '(1) When exercising the competencies assigned to it by this Treaty, the Union shall respect the sovereignty of the Member States and their regional entities especially in the following areas which are characteristic for their national identity and their fundamental constitutional legal order: [...] (a) the organisation of the state and administrative structures including the principle of communal self-governance; (b) the public welfare services and the social security systems; (c) the media order; (d) culture and sports policy and education services; (e) the role of the churches and religious communities; (f) the fundamentals of regional planning and development; (g) the fundamental requirements of public safety, public order and health. (2) Under no circumstances, measures by the Union may encroach upon the core area of these sovereign rights.'

51 Weatherill (2017), p. 145.

52 Draft Treaty establishing a Constitution for Europe. Adopted by consensus by the European Convention on 13 June and 10 July 2003. Submitted to the President of the European Council

This text merely requires EU institutions to take the 'specific nature of sport,' including 'its structures based on voluntary activity and its social and educational function,' 'into account.'[53] What exactly 'taking into account' implies remains debatable, as the Court's judgments in a number of cases involving State aid to Spanish professional football clubs illustrate.[54] In *Hércules CF and Spain v Commission*, for instance, the club (supported by Spain) had based a plea for disregarding the R&R Guidelines[55] on the 'special characteristics,' peculiarities of the book-keeping of football clubs,[56] as well as the 'context of a sector' which was 'subject to specific protection under Article 165 TFEU.'[57] Yet the General Court took no notice of these pleas in its findings, just like repeated pleas by the clubs and the Kingdom of Spain invoking Article 165 and the 'special characteristics,' in some of the other trials in this category, would appear to have had no influence on its findings and the final outcome in this case regarding State aid, another branch of EU competition law and policy.[58] The only deduction conceptually and systematically defensible against this backdrop must be that there is no impediment to an orthodox interpretation of EU competition law, in this case the requirements of antitrust law, beyond a brief look at the 'special characteristics' of sport without any specific tests being required.

Antitrust enforcement in the field of sport was now beginning to take off, with the Commission establishing the main principles of the joint sale of media

---

in Rome – 18 July 2003. OJ C 169, 18.7.2003, pp. 1–105, Article III-182 (1): 'The Union shall contribute to the promotion of European sporting issues, given the social and educational function of Sport.'

53 Article 165 (1) TFEU: 'The Union shall contribute to the promotion of European sporting issues, while taking account of the specific nature of sport, its structures based on voluntary activity and its social and educational function.'

54 These cases fall into three categories, including tax relief Commission decision 2016/2391, SA.29769) concerning four clubs: Real Madrid, FC Barcelona, Athletic Bilbao, Atletico Osasuna; land swaps (Commission decision 2016/2393, SA.33754) with Real Madrid; and bank guarantees (Commission decision 2017/365, SA.36387) for the benefit of three Valencian clubs: Valencia CF, Hércules CF, Elche CF. For more details, see Kornbeck (2021).

55 Communication from the Commission. Guidelines on State aid for rescuing and restructuring non-financial undertakings in difficulty. OJ C 249, 31.7.2014, pp. 1–28.

56 GC, 20.03.2019. Hércules Club de Fútbol, SAD and Kingdom of Spain v Commission. Case T-766/16. ECLI:EU:T:2019:173, at 37. 'The applicant submits that it was not a firm in difficulty at the date on which the disputed guarantee was issued. First of all, the criteria set out in point 10(a) of the R&R guidelines do not apply to the football market. Only the method used by the Union of European Football Associations (UEFA) and the Liga Nacional de Fútbol Profesional which compare the accounts of one club with the average of the other clubs participating in tournaments in the same Member State are relevant, in view of the specific features of the football market. The applicant was in a better situation than the average club in the first division and second division A of the Spanish football championship and, moreover, in a situation similar to the average for European football overall.'

57 *Ibid.*, at 56.

58 For a detailed discussion of all of these cases, see Kornbeck (2021).

rights in its *UEFA Champions League* (2002),[59] *FA Premier League* (2008)[60] and *Bundesliga* (2005)[61] decisions. While an entirely orthodox application of antitrust rules would have required that clubs should market their media rights individually, the centralised marketing mechanisms were accepted subject to certain governance criteria being met, including transparent tender procedures, limitation of duration of the relevant arrangements and division of rights into different packages (no single buyer). A similar doctrine was developed by the CFI in its *Eurovision I*[62] and *Eurovision II*[63] judgments, with sports dimensions. In other words, unusual arrangements were accepted as long as robust procedures were in place offering safeguards against arbitrary and abusive decision-making. The same period also witnessed some missed enforcement opportunities, including when the *Balog* case was referred to the Court by the Court of First Instance of Charleroi (Belgium) (1998) but removed from the register in 2001.[64] *Balog* was a dispute involving a Hungarian football player and a Belgian club (Hungary only joined the EU in 2004) regarding a clause enshrined in the rules and circulars of the national and international football federations (URBSFA, UEFA, FIFA), requiring the payment of a transfer fee when moving between clubs within EU or EEA Member States. The national court wanted to know if such a requirement violated antitrust rules as per (then) Articles 85 TEC and 53 EEA Agreement: worthy prejudicial questions. In the *Mouscron* case,[65] the Belgian club Excelsior Mouscron had, under the UEFA 'home and away' rule, been denied the right to play a match at the stadium of FC Metz (France). 'In an unpublished Decision, the Commission rejected the complaint on *de minimis grounds*; in other words, there was insufficient EU interest to intervene.'[66] Knowing the general

59 Notice published pursuant to Article 19(3) of Council Regulation No 17 concerning case COMP/C.2/37.398 – Joint selling of the media rights of the UEFA Champions League on an exclusive basis (Text with EEA relevance). OJ C 196, 17.8.2002, pp. 3–5.

60 Summary of Commission Decision of 22 March 2006 relating to a proceeding pursuant to Article 81 of the EC Treaty (Case COMP/38.173 – Joint selling of the media rights to the FA Premier League) (notified under document number C(2006) 868). OJ C 7, 12.1.2008, pp. 18–18.

61 2005/396/EC: Commission Decision of 19 January 2005 relating to a proceeding pursuant to Article 81 of the EC Treaty and Article 53(1) of the EEA Agreement (Case COMP/C.2/37.214 – Joint selling of the media rights to the German Bundesliga) (notified under document number C(2005) 78) (Text with EEA relevance). OJ L 134, 27.5.2005, pp. 46–46.

62 CFI, 11.07.1996. Metropole télévision SA and Reti Televisive Italiane SpA and Gestevisión Telecinco SA and Antena 3 de Televisión v Commission of the European Communities. Joined cases T-528/93, T-542/93, T-543/93 and T-546/93.
ECR 1996 II-00649. ECLI:EU:T:1996:99.

63 CFI, 08.10.2002. Métropole Télévision SA (M6), Antena 3 de Televisión, SA, Gestevisión Telecinco, SA and SIC – Sociedade Independente de Comunicação, SA v Commission of the European Communities. Joined cases T-185/00, T-216/00, T-299/00, T-300/00. ECR 2002 II-03805. ECLI:EU:T:2002:242.

64 Tibor Balog v. ASBL Royal Charleroi Sporting Club (RCSC). Case C-264/98. Application: OJ C 278 from 05.09.1998, p.28. Removal from the register: OJ C 173 from 16.06.2001, p.32.

65 Unpublished Commission Decision of 9 Dec. 1999, Case 36851, C.U. de Lille/UEFA (Mouscron); see Cattaneo & Parrish (2020), p. 90, fn. 363.

66 Cattaneo & Parrish (2020), p. 90, at 214.

reluctance of athletes and sports officials to take disputes to court, reserving arbitration as the preferred means of dispute resolution, an expectation sometimes even presented openly to governments by sports governing bodies (SGBs),[67] it does not seem far-fetched to assume that many other cases could have been adjudicated, had they been brought before the CJEU. *Ubi non accusator, ibi non iudex.*[68]

1.2.3 Confident enforcement (c. 2008–2022)

In the past 21 years (2001–2022), two particularly high-profile antitrust cases stand out among all the cases decided by the Commission: the 2001 FIA decision[69] and the 2017 ISU decision.[70]

At the beginning of this period, EU antitrust enforcement was decentralised as proposed by the Commission in a White Paper published in 1999.[71] Enshrined in Regulation 1/2003[72] with entry into force on 1 May 2004, the framework was reformed structurally and profoundly. As opposed to Regulation 17/62,[73] which it replaced, Regulation 1/2003 provided for a competence shared between the Commission and national competition authorities (NCAs), and for national courts to interpret EU rules in their entirety. All authorities thus empowered have since then been subjected to a formal requirement of 'uniform application of Community competition law' (Article 16) with specific powers reserved for the Commission and mechanisms ensuring consistency. This decentralisation – where NCAs are the first port of call while the Commission takes the more 'European' cases – explains why up to 15 sports cases[74] were decided by NCAs between 2008 and 2015, while the ISU case (2017) was investigated and decided by the Commission.[75] These include the decisions of the Italian NCA in the *FISE* (equine sports) (2008) and *Corse Garcano* (motor sports) (2009) cases; of

67 See the World Anti-Doping Code 2021, Article 22.6: 'Each government should respect arbitration as the preferred means of resolving doping-related disputes, subject to human and fundamental rights and applicable national law.'

68 'Where there is no plaintiff, there is no judge.'

69 Notice published pursuant to Article 19(3) of Council Regulation No 17 concerning CasesCOMP/35.163 – Notification of FIA Regulations, COMP/36.638 – Notification by FIA/FOA of agreements relating to the FIA Formula One World Championship, COMP/36.776 – GTR/FIA & other. OJ C 169, 13.6.2001, pp. 5–11.

70 Decision C (2017) 8240 final (fn 3). For more details, see Kornbeck (2019).

71 White Paper on modernisation of the rules implementing Articles 81 and 82 (formerly Articles 85 and 86) of the EC Treaty. Brussels, 28.04.1999. COM(99) 101. https://europa.eu/documents/comm/white_papers/pdf/com99_101_en.pdf

72 Council Regulation (EC) No 1/2003 of 16 December 2002 on the implementation of the rules on competition laid down in Articles 81 and 82 of the Treaty (Text with EEA relevance). OJ L 1, 4.1.2003, pp. 1–25.

73 EEC Council: Regulation No 17: First Regulation implementing Articles 85 and 86 of the Treaty. OJ 13, 21.2.1962, pp. 204–211.

74 This is the number reported and assessed by Cukurov (2021), though the list is variable.

75 For details see Van Rompuy (2015); Verdonk (2017); Kornbeck (2020), the latter with a comparative table; most recently, Cukurov (2021).

the Swedish NCA in the *SBF* (motor sports) (2011) and the *SKKF* (bodybuilding) (2014) cases; of the Irish NCA in the *SJI* (equine sports) (2012) case; of the Belgian NCA in the *FEI* (equine sports) (2015); and, of course, of the Commission in the *ISU* (skating) (2017) case. The Swedish NCA's *SBF* decision and the Belgian NCA's *FEI* decision were both appealed to national courts, who confirmed and even strengthened the verdict made by NCAs. A case ruled under a slightly different constellation was that from Germany, in *Euroleague Properties S.A, et al. v FIBA Europe and FIBA,* where the ruling of the Munich Regional Court (LG München I) 2016 (Basketball) included an injunction for two sports governing bodies (SGBs) to cease and desist from applying pressure on alternative organisers and their business partners.[76] The outstanding role of national courts is further underscored by the case of the German Wrestling League (Deutsche Ringer Liga) (DLR): facing pressure from SGBs, it litigated successfully in first and second instances,[77] and was able, on that basis, to take up business operations alongside the SGB (Deutscher Ringer Bund) (DRB).[78] Most recently, the Frankfurt Higher Regional Court (OLG Frankfurt)[79] ruled about the compatibility of the regulation of the German FA (DFB) on players' agents with antitrust law.[80]

The root cause of many antitrust challenges is the 'one federation' principle[81] according to which one SGB holds a regulatory monopoly over a particular sport within a particular geographical area: global (e.g. FIFA), continental (e.g. UEFA), national (the relevant FA), etc. Elsewhere, the present editor has argued that SGBs have three types of solutions at their disposal to maintain this principle, while also remaining (more or less) in compliance with antitrust law. Solutions range from the 'splitting' or 'unbundling' of their regulatory and commercial roles; over the 'revocation of statutory rules' targeted by complaints and/or investigations; to a 'light-touch application and sanctions renunciation'[82] – each of which comes with specific advantages and disadvantages. Almost all cases subjected to decisions by NCAs in recent years ended with commitments by SGBs to amend or revoke problematic rules,[83] including the Commission's ISU decision (2017).[84] The FIA decision (2001) represents the truly 'nuclear' solution of 'splitting' or 'unbundling,' not unlike unbundling practised in markets with

76 LG München I: 1 HK 0 8126/16. 2.6.2016; discussed by Kornbeck (2020).

77 OLG Nürnberg, 26.01.2021, Az. 3 U 894/19.

78 See Bücher (2018), M. Juristischer Punktsieg in Reichweite. Ringer-Liga atmet auf. *Badische Neueste Nachrichten (BNN),* 14.12.2018, p. 19; Bücher, M. (2019) Ringer-Urteil mit Signalwirkung. Verbände dürfen DRL nicht mehr ausbremsen. *BNN,* 1.03.2019, p. 20; Bücher, M. (2021) Ringerliga atmet auf Gericht bestätigt Urteil gegen DRB und Weltverband. BNN, 30.01.2021, p. 17.

79 OLG Frankfurt/M., 30.11.2021, 11 U 172/19 (Kart) – DFB-Reglement für Spielervermittlung.

80 Ackermann (2022).

81 Vieweg (1983); Kornbeck (2020).

82 Kornbeck (2020).

83 Van Rompuy (2015); Verdonk (2017); Kornbeck (2020).

84 Decision C (2017) 8240 final (fn 3).

network effects such as transports, energy or telecommunications. In the sport sector, this solution remains seldom so far (the FIA case is the only one identified to far) and one which would seem to go counter to most of the traditions of the sector, although it definitely has its merits. The FIA case started with several notifications, by FIA to the Commission, of regulations and agreements with FIA's business partners, and ended amicably with the publication of FIA's wide-ranging structural reform in the *Official Journal of the European Union*. From the summary published by the Commission, it emerges unambiguously that the investigation had given rise to concerns over conflicts of interest arising from the fact that FIA profited commercially from arrangements for which FIA was the sole private regulator.[85] The Commission accepted FIA's reforms and closed the case because they appeared to offer the necessary safeguards against abuse of dominant position.[86]

During the same period, far from standing still, case law developed considerably as the Court started adjudicating cases on the basis of antitrust rules. *Meca Medina*[87] was – and remains – significant for at least three reasons. First, for being grounded in antitrust rules (where *Bosman* was resolved by relying on free movement rules); until 2006, SGBs could still be legitimately excused for thinking that such rules could not be invoked to challenge their regulations. Second, because the Court threw out the judgment of the CFI,[88] which had considered – generously from the perspective of SGBs, frustratingly for athletes – that 'sport is essentially a gratuitous and not an economic act, even when the athlete performs it in the course of professional sport.'[89] In this respect, the

85 *Ibid.*, p. 8, sec. 5: 'The Commission's Statement of Objections issued in June 2000 made the preliminary assessment that FIA had a 'conflict of interest' in that it was using its regulatory powers to block the organisation of races which competed with the events promoted or organised by FIA (i.e. those events from which FIA derived a commercial benefit). Moreover, for a certain period of time, FIA may have been abusing a dominant position under Article 82 of the EC Treaty by claiming the TV rights to motor sport series it authorised.'

86 *Ibid.*, p. 10, sec. 6: 'The proposed changes to the regulatory framework and to the commercial arrangements appear to the Commission to introduce sufficient structural remedies minimising the risk of possible future abuse and to set the basis for a healthy competitive environment in economic activities related to motor sport. The Commission considers that, inter alia, the following elements are of particular relevance to this assessment.'

87 CJEU, 18.06.2006. *Meca-Medina* (fn 20).

88 CFI, 30 September 2004. David Meca-Medina and Igor Majcen v Commission of the European Communities. Case T-313/02. ECR 2004 II-03291. ECLI:EU:T:2004:282.

89 *Ibid.*, at 45: 'It must also be made clear that sport is essentially a gratuitous and not an economic act, even when the athlete performs it in the course of professional sport. In other words, the prohibition of doping and anti-doping rules concern exclusively, even when the sporting action is performed by a professional, a non-economic aspect of that sporting action, which constitutes its very essence.' Note, however, that the English version of the judgment refers – rather broadly – to 'sport,' the French, however, to 'le geste sportif' and the German version to 'das Sporttreiben,' as observed by Kornbeck (2017). These semantic differences are far from anodyne.

Court[90] took the diametrically opposite position.[91] Had the Court upheld the doctrine of the CFI, EU sports law could have taken a different turn, sheltering SGBs in part from the reach of EU law. Third, by adapting the *Wouters*[92] test to sport and anti-doping, thereby providing a practical tool for performing tests in an area explicitly submitted to the requirement of case-by-case analysis; without handing down such a test, the Court would have left a considerable vacuity and lack of legal certainty. The three-step test consists of the elements context, necessity and proportionality, where each subsequent step must be inherent to the previous one. First, the context-inherence step reflects the Court's finding that no abstract, overarching rule can be identified which would discharge regulators and courts of their duty to assess each case individually and on its own merits.[93] Second, the necessity of the measures taken to reach an otherwise legitimate aim must be demonstrated separately, as must its inherence. Whereas in the case at issue, an antitrust complaint directed against an anti-doping procedure concerning two swimmers had been rejected by the Commission, the Court considered that the Commission could very well be entitled to consider the objectives of the litigious anti-doping rules legitimate, although this would by necessity be subject to confirmation through a case-specific assessment.[94] When performing such tests, attention should be paid to the gravity of the sanctions imposed by SGBs.[95] Third

90 CJEU, 18.07.2006. David Meca-Medina and Igor Majcen v Commission of the European Communities. Case C-519/04 P. ECR 2006 I-06991. ECLI:EU:C:2006:492.

91 *Ibid.*, 33: 'In holding that rules could thus be excluded straightaway from the scope of those articles solely on the ground that they were regarded as purely sporting with regard to the application of Articles 39 EC and 49 EC, without any need to determine first whether the rules fulfilled the specific requirements of Articles 81 EC and 82 EC, as set out in paragraph 30 of the present judgment, the Court of First Instance made an error of law.'

92 ECJ, 19.02.2002. J. C. J. Wouters, J. W. Savelbergh and Price Waterhouse Belastingadviseurs BV v Algemene Raad van de Nederlandse Orde van Advocaten, intervener: Raad van de Balies van de Europese Gemeenschap. Reference for a preliminary ruling: Raad van State, Netherlands. Case C-309/99. ECR 2002 I-01577. ECLI:EU:C:2002:98.

93 CJEU 18.06.2006, *Meca Medina* (fn 21), at 42: 'Next, the compatibility of rules with the Community rules on competition cannot be assessed in the abstract (see, to this effect, Case C-250/92 DLG [1994] ECR I-5641, paragraph 31). Not every agreement between undertakings or every decision of an association of undertakings which restricts the freedom of action of the parties or of one of them necessarily falls within the prohibition laid down in Article 81(1) EC. For the purposes of application of that provision to a particular case, account must first of all be taken of the overall context in which the decision of the association of undertakings was taken or produces its effects and, more specifically, of its objectives. It has then to be considered whether the consequential effects restrictive of competition are inherent in the pursuit of those objectives (Wouters and Others, paragraph 97) and are proportionate to them.'

94 *Ibid.*, at 43: 'As regards the overall context in which the rules at issue were adopted, the Commission could rightly take the view that the general objective of the rules was, as none of the parties disputes, to combat doping in order for competitive sport to be conducted fairly and that it included the need to safeguard equal chances for athletes, athletes' health, the integrity and objectivity of competitive sport and ethical values in sport.'

95 *Ibid.*, at 44: 'In addition, given that penalties are necessary to ensure enforcement of the doping ban, their effect on athletes' freedom of action must be considered to be, in principle, inherent itself in the anti-doping rules.'

and finally, even if the necessity of the measures taken were to be confirmed, this would not *per se* imply their proportionality; it would have to be demonstrated separately and persuasively.[96]

The risk of conflicts of interest arising from the (almost ubiquitously) bundled regulatory and commercial functions of SGBs came into renewed focus in the MOTOE case, where the Court's ruling[97] was preceded by a particularly thoughtful opinion by AG Kokott.[98] The case in question concerned a national legal framework whereby the Greek state had delegated powers to ELPA, the national SGB regulating motorsports, allowing it to vet applications from alternative event organisers prior to the authorisation of motor races on public roads by the Greek authorities. The Greek rules appeared devoid of procedures or mechanisms which could have prevented ELPA from taking biased decisions, harming the gainful activities of alternative organisers while protecting ELPA's own income. AG Kokott specifically found that 'legislation such as that in force in Greece invites abuse,' insisting that the existence of actual abusive behaviour was not required in the light of a structural predicament making it possible or even likely.[99] The first reason behind this finding was the fact that ELPA regulated activities from which it also profited as an entrepreneur,[100] giving ELPA an objective interest in administering its powers in a self-interested way. The second reason was the absence of rules and procedures which could have made abuse impossible or at least unlikely.[101] This reasoning is still very much at the heart of

96 *Ibid.*, at 45: 'Therefore, even if the anti-doping rules at issue are to be regarded as a decision of an association of undertakings limiting the appellants' freedom of action, they do not, for all that, necessarily constitute a restriction of competition incompatible with the common market, within the meaning of Article 81 EC, since they are justified by a legitimate objective. Such a limitation is inherent in the organisation and proper conduct of competitive sport and its very purpose is to ensure healthy rivalry between athletes.'

97 CJEU, 01.07.2008. Motosykletistiki Omospondia Ellados NPID (MOTOE) v Elliniko Dimosio. Reference for a preliminary ruling: Dioikitiko Efeteio Athinon, Greece. Case C-49/07. ECR 2008 I-04863. ECLI:EU:C:2008:376.

98 AG Kokott, 06.03.2008. Motosykletistiki Omospondia Ellados NPID (MOTOE) v Elliniko Dimosio. Reference for a preliminary ruling: Dioikitiko Efeteio Athinon, Greece. Case C-49/07. ECLI:EU:C:2008:142.

99 *Ibid.*, at 97: 'Irrespective of whether any abuse actually exists, it is sufficient, for the purposes of establishing an infringement of Article 86(1) EC in conjunction with Article 82 EC, that a State measure merely creates a risk of abuse. In the present case, the risk that ELPA will abuse its dominant position in exercising its right of co-decision under Article 49 of the Greek Road Traffic Code is particularly high, for two reasons.'

100 *Ibid.*, at 98: 'Firstly, rules on consent such as those in question here lead to a conflict of interest: ELPA, which itself organises and markets motorcycling events, receives from the Greek State a right of co-decision in the authorisation of motorcycling events of other, independent service providers. ELPA thus not only has the legal means that allow it effectively to prevent other service providers from entering the Greek market, but also an economic interest in limiting access to the market by its competitors to its own advantage.'

101 *Ibid.*, at 99: 'Secondly, ELPA is not subject, under those rules on consent, to any restrictions, obligations or controls in relation to the grant or refusal of its consent to the authorisation of motorcycling events. This makes it particularly easy for ELPA to refuse to give consent to the

the cases which were pending before the Court in 2022, as well as of the cases decided administratively between 2008 and 2015.[102]

Among the cases decided administratively, as referred to, three were appealed to courts of law. In the first case, regarding motorsports, a decision taken by the Swedish NCA was appealed to the Swedish Market Court which upheld and even strengthened the verdict of the NCA.[103] In the second case, concerning equine sports, a decision taken by the Belgian NCA regarding the rules of the worldwide SGB which happened to have its seat in Belgium was confirmed by an ordinary Belgian court of appeal.[104] In the third case, the Commission's *ISU* decision (2017) was appealed to the General Court, and later thence to the Court of Justice. The General Court, among other things, focused on the same constellation as AG Kokott had once done, emphasising the 'obligations imposed on a sports federation which has a power of authorisation.' Here, too, the reasoning was inspired by the acknowledgement that ISU regulated the same sport in which it was involved itself as an entrepreneur, resulting in an objective need for safeguards against abuse.[105] The General Court noted that athletes and alternative event organisers had no alternative to the route foreseen by ISU[106] which, in turn, meant that ISU – in the absence of rules and procedures which could have prevented abuse – could wield its power arbitrarily.[107]

---

authorisation of the motorcycling events of other, independent service providers. As the present case clearly shows, the mere fact that ELPA omitted to act was sufficient to thwart the plans of another service provider – in this instance, MOTOE – in the year 2000.'

102 See Kornbeck (2020).

103 Marknadsdomstolen, Beslut 2012:16. 2012-12-20 Dnr A 5/11, see Kornbeck (2020), p. 207.

104 Arrêt défnitif de la Cour d'appel de Bruxelles. Dossier n°: VM-15–016. Décision n°: 15-VM-23. See Kornbeck (2020), p. 217.

105 GC, 12.12.2020, *International Skating Union* (fn 3), at 70: 'In that regard, it must be noted that, according to that case-law, when a rule entrusts a legal person, which itself, organises and commercially operates competitions, with the task of designating the persons authorised to organise those competitions and to determine the conditions under which they are organised, it grants that entity an obvious advantage over its competitors. Such a right may therefore lead the undertaking making use of it to prevent access by other operators to the market concerned. The exercise of that regulatory function should therefore be made subject to restrictions, obligations and review, so that the legal person entrusted with giving that consent may not distort competition by favouring events which it organises or those in whose organisation it participates (see, to that effect, judgment of 1 July 2008, MOTOE, C-49/07, EU:C:2008:376, paragraphs 51 and 52).C, 16.20.21) (Case T-93/18).'

106 *Ibid.*, at 74: 'It must be noted that the eligibility rules laid down in the exercise of the applicant's regulatory function provide for ineligibility penalties in the event that skaters take part in an unauthorised competition. Since skaters cannot miss the opportunity to take part in more important events organised by the applicant, it follows that third party organisers that intend to organise a speed skating event must obtain prior authorisation from the applicant if they wish skaters to take part.'

107 *Ibid.*, at 75: 'Therefore, having regard to the fact that the applicant organises events and also has the power to authorise events organised by third parties, it must be held that that situation is capable of giving rise to a conflict of interests. In those circumstances, it follows from the case-law cited in paragraphs 70 and 71 above that the applicant must ensure, when examining

On balance, this rather cursory overview of developments having unfolded during the 40-year period (1982–2022) will have revealed that an orthodox application of EC/EU antitrust rules to sport has gradually been established as the default approach to antitrust cases involving sports governing bodies (SGBs). According to Cukurov, an analysis of a total of 15 cases decided by NCAs (and the Commission) revealed 'no particular difficulties' in applying standard concepts and tests.[108] Lack of problem awareness did not shelter SGBs from the reach of the law in the 21st century, just like attempts made between 1995 and 2006 to achieve insulation did not pay out either, at that earlier point in time, while Article 165 TFEU and its 'taking into account' phrase seem to have been to no avail. Facilitated by the decentralisation of antitrust enforcement brought about by Regulation 1/2003, the increasing national enforcement between 2008 and 2015 shows a new confidence in NCAs, a trend apparently confirmed by the Commission's decisions in 2001 (*FIA*) and 2017 (*ISU*). The three test cases pending before the CJEU (*ISU, ESL, Royal Antwerp*) can be expected to provide further legal certainty,[109] while it seems a reasonable hypothesis that the orthodox interpretation is likely to be confirmed, by and large. Even if a modicum of sympathy leads to some leniency, the currently unbridled regulatory and disciplinary structures of the SGBs concerned (which are probably matched by those of many others) call for action by NCAs and courts. It would seem natural for the Court to acknowledge this, in continuation of its case law of many years, including the thoughtful analysis of AG Kokott in *MOTOE*.

1.3 Chapter plan

Following this Introduction, authors will respond to the questions identified above through the substantive chapters of this edited book, including conceptual essays as well as case studies.

In direct continuation of the Introduction, Chapter 2 by *Ben Van Rompuy* traces back the recent uptick in antitrust enforcement action vis-à-vis sports governance to developments in the case law of the EU courts, which gradually determined the scope of application of Articles 101 and 102 TFEU and shaped the principles for the assessment of sporting rules and practices under these provisions. This introduction of the relevant analytical framework reveals the unique function of EU sports antitrust law as a meaningful accountability mechanism. But to what extent has it been a motor of change? Van Rompuy observes that the seminal *Meca Medina* ruling did not open the floodgates to large numbers of antitrust challenges against SGBs, as some had anticipated. A number of legal

applications for authorisation, that those third parties are not unduly deprived of market access to the point that competition on that market is distorted.'

108 Cukurov (2021), p. 140: 'Die Analyse hat ergeben, dass die Institutionen mit den allgemeinen Kartellrechtsinstrumenten und Prüfungsrastern offenbar zurechtkamen, da sich keine Schwierigkeiten offenbarten, das Kartellrecht auf sportverbandliche Maßnahmen anzuwenden.'

109 See Chapter 9 for more details.

and practical hurdles (limiting access to public and private antitrust enforcement) have continued to undercut EU antitrust law's potential to play a more significant role in promoting procedural and substantive principles of good sports governance. The chapter offers some concluding thoughts on substantive and procedural developments we can expect to see going forward, however, suggesting that change may well be afoot.

Rusa Agafonova follows with Chapter 3 on the *ISU* case, raising the question 'on a mission to defend the weaker party?' Drawing on ongoing doctoral research,[110] this first of two discipline-specific case studies focuses on athletes as the main actors, but also on their structurally weak position in litigation of this kind. In recent years, EU competition law has proven itself an efficient instrument for challenging restrictive policies and decisions of SGBs. Sports undertakings, such as breakaway leagues and promoters, not integrated into the official structure of sport but striving to get a share of the markets for the organisation and exploitation of sports events, have been particularly keen to use this tool. Nevertheless, it is individual athletes who are the most vulnerable subjects in the sports industry and who, according to Agafonova, should take advantage of competition law in the first place. In their relations with SGBs, athletes are placed *de facto* in the position of the weakest party. In order to participate in official competitions, they have no alternative rather than to adhere to SGBs' rules and policies. Athletes – especially in the less economically developed sports disciplines – are also normally weaker economically. Finally, SGBs possess a well-established network in the industry and are better equipped in case of disputes. The statistics of CAS awards demonstrate the overwhelming success of sports institutions when these confront athletes in the framework of an arbitration procedure. The chapter looks at the reasons why and how individual athletes should benefit from EU competition law and, most importantly, why this will be vital for the functioning of sport in general.

From skating we shall then turn to football, in the second discipline-specific case study. Chapter 4 by *Dennis Cukurov,* dedicated to the *European Superleague* case, will draw on insights gained from his recently defended doctoral thesis on the compatibility of a possible future European Superleague (ESL) in football with EU antitrust competition law.[111] Beyond questioning the compatibility of the response chosen by established SGBs to avert initiatives like that of the ESL, the author also looks into the question whether the ESL would not itself be a cartel problematic under EU competition law, leading to proposals for a more compatible league structure. This second case study will focus on the role of investors and financial markets as drivers of change and will blend legal and conceptual with economic and empirical insights and arguments.

Chapter 5, by Margareta Baddeley, is the reflection of a seasoned expert on the Swiss regulatory model under which top level sports governing bodies (ISGBs) operate when organised as Swiss associations. As an exploration of the legal,

110 See the paper by Agafonova (2019).
111 Cukurov (2021).

political and social reality of international sports governance on Swiss soils, the chapter shows why (EU) competition law is seldom applied to the regulations, operations and decisional practice of the ISGBs. This is due to several factors, as this contribution explains. The first factor is the large autonomy of associations under Swiss law, given the application of law (*Rechtsanwendung*) on associations in general and in particular on sports associations, of which the ISGBs incorporated as non-profit organisations under Swiss association law benefit largely. State law, including EU law, is therefore rarely enforceable and enforced by courts against the rules and decisions of the ISGBs. Furthermore, violations of EU antitrust are rarely argued in litigation between the actors of the world of sports, and finally, Swiss (international) arbitration law does not provide for the necessary application of mandatory EU antitrust law.

From this empirical-legal analysis, readers can now turn towards a conceptual and theoretical paper from the perspective of sport economics. In Chapter 6, *Oliver Budzinski and Arne Feddersen* ask whether organising premier-level European football should be a monopoly, and who should be in charge. In their attempt to locate the scope for a necessary monopoly, the two economists discuss the merits and shortcomings of the established European pyramidal model of sports governance. In economics, monopolies are associated with severe consumer (fan) welfare loss and massive dynamic inefficiencies. Therefore, effective competition in every market is the generally preferred organisation of commercial activities and, subsequently, the main goal of competition law and policy. Yet they also find that there may be situations where a single supplier of a good may exceptionally be superior to competition. Organising premier-level sports is often viewed to be such an exception, they argue, as in the EU with the pyramid structure of sports associations governing professional (and commercial) sports. Budzinski and Feddersen revisit this assertion from a modern economics perspective, looking for economic arguments in favour of the pyramid structure, counter-arguments as well the potential for balancing the two. For the identified monopoly areas, they ask who should run them in order to maximise social and consumer (fan) welfare, suggesting that regular competitions for the market such as tender procedures for regulatory packages could be implemented, so that different suppliers can offer their service. Based on transparent criteria, this would allow the best to get their trial for a defined number of seasons.

Taking the economic analysis to the operational level is Chapter 7 in which *Mickael Terrien and Jean-Loup Chappelet* look at the economic and legal stakes of breakaway leagues in the field of football. The authors seek to identify the opportunities that the creation of a Superleague would offer to key stakeholders in the professional football ecosystem, considering economic alongside legal conditions, first by questioning the interests of the clubs: is the Superleague intended to maximise their revenues? Should it help establish regulatory mechanisms that end the arms race in the talent market? Or is this project just a negotiating lever used by the big clubs against UEFA? This raises the question of the interest for the competition organiser. Several strategic resources and conditions necessary for the success of independent leagues can be identified in the literature. Beyond the legal barriers to entry, how does a sport competition manage to impose itself over its competitors? Finally, this chapter examines the consequences of the Superleague for (tele)spectators. Given the erosion of the competitive balance in continental and domestic football competitions, could the independent league have a beneficial effect on the interest of competitions?

Under the evocative title 'An Olympic Choice,' Chapter 8 by *Walter Palmer* investigates antitrust law, sport and the European social model. In this final chapter, a former NBA player who is also an experienced European and worldwide trade union representative discusses the role, experience and perspectives of athletes and fans. Palmer finds that the collision between European competition law and the governance models preferred by sport administrators has affected the experience of athletes and spectators in a variety of ways. Athletes, especially, bring rights with them into the arena that can be negatively impacted by pyramidal governance structures that embed already imbalanced power dynamics. While sport administrators advocate for a de facto exemption from competition law using a variety of code phrases, such as 'specificity,' 'autonomy' and the 'European model of sport,' experience shows that collective bargaining and social dialogue offer an already established path to derogations from laws and regulations that may impinge upon the business of sport. Athletes, spectators and sport organisations, it is argued, all stand to gain if the risks posed by competition law to some of the accepted practices in sport are addressed collectively. Palmer also explores the impacts that current sport governance practices have on athletes and spectators through the lens of European competition law.

1.4 Terminology: antitrust as a portion of competition policy

Having mentioned this last chapter from the USA, a note on terminology may be required at this stage, since some colleagues may think that 'antitrust' is a quintessentially US term while 'competition law' would be more appropriate in an EU context. Indeed, the editor has several times heard and read such remarks while for the title of present book, after consultation with some of the contributors, he resolved to use the term 'antitrust' due to its specific and unambiguous meaning. As anyone can see from the website of the Commission's Directorate General of Competition (DG COMP),[112] Antitrust is one of the main areas of competition law and policy, in theory and in practice, alongside Cartels, Mergers and State Aid. While Antitrust, Cartels and Mergers are closely intertwined and hard to disentangle, State Aid is an entirely different ballgame; the former all have Articles 101–102 TFEU as their legal base, the latter Articles 107–109 TFEU. The confusion may stem from the absence of a specific subventions regime in US federal law, reflecting a surprisingly relaxed attitude to grants provided by public authorities at regional or local level to enterprises willing to settle on their

112 https://ec.europa.eu/competition-policy/index_en.

territory. Such arrangements would often be illegal under EU law and likely to trigger sanctions like those decided by the Commission in the Apple Ireland case (where Ireland was ordered to claim a big amount of tax not claimed[113]), which may account for an apparently generalised incomprehension towards this – apparently very European concept – in the USA. Franco-American prize-winning economist Thomas Philippon,[114] for instance, affirms that most of his US colleagues have not heard of the concept and do not seem grasp why subventions to selected businesses should pose a problem. And yet, although EC/EU state aid enforcement (just like antitrust enforcement) took time to develop and assume its present vigour, the basic principles have accompanied European integration since the very beginnings, where the Spaak Report (1956)[115] preceding the adoption of the EEC Treaty (1957) took an unambiguous position against subventions capable of distorting competition. Interestingly, the functional perspective adopted by EC/EU competition law and policy, applicable to antitrust as well as to state aid cases, where the form and legal nature of anticompetitive arrangements is immaterial when anticompetitive objectives and/or effects can be established, was emphasised already at that point in time with the phrase 'no matter how' the aid is provided.[116] Yet 'antitrust' is not synonymous with 'competition law' or 'competition policy,' as it has its own legal base, principles and instruments. For these reasons, the present book carries the term 'antitrust' in its title and aims to foster debate on the relevance of EU antitrust law to the development of sports law and governance.

Disclaimer

The author is a civil servant in the European Commission, yet opinions expressed are strictly personal and do not render any official positions of the European Commission, nor of the European Union.

Bibliography

Ackermann, T. (2022) Grenzen der Sportverbandsautonomie nach der Wouters-Doktrin. *Wirtschaft und Wettbwerb (WuW)*, 3, 122–127.

113 C(2016) 5605 final. Commission decision of 30.8.2016 on State aid SA.38373 (2014/C) (ex 2014/NN) (ex 2014/CP) implemented by Ireland to Apple; see also CJEU, Commission v Ireland and Others. Case C-465/20 P (pending).

114 Philippon (2019), p. 135.

115 Comité intergouvernemental créé par la conférence de Messine. Rapport des chefs de délégation aux ministres des Affaires étrangères. Bruxelles, 21 avril 1956. http://aei.pitt.edu/996/1/Spaak_report_french.pdf, p. 57: 'La règle générale est que sont incompatibles avec le marché commun les aides, sous quelque forme qu'elles soient accordées, qui faussent la concurrence et la répartition des activités en favorisant certaines entreprises ou certaines productions.'

116 *Ibid.*

Agafonova, R. (2019) International Skating Union versus European Commission: Is the European sports model under threat? *International Sports Law Journal*, 19:1–2, 87–101.

Anderson, J. (2010) *Modern Sports Law: A Textbook*. Oxford: Hart.

Cattaneo, A. & Parrish, R. (2020) *Sports Law and the European Union*. Aalphen a/d Rijn: Wolters Kluwer.

Cukurov, D. (2021) *Kartellrechtliche Zulässigkeit von Superligen im Fußball. Der europäische Ligasport vor dem Umbruch*. Baden-Baden: Nomos & Munich: C.H. Beck.

Ehle & Guaia, I. (2017) Bundesgerichtshof, Az. KZR 6/15, Pechstein v. International Skating Union (ISU), 7 June 2016. In: Duval, A. & Rigozzi, A. (eds) *Yearbook of International Sports Arbitration 2016*. The Hague: T.M.C. Asser Press, 415–427.

Ezrachi, A. (2016) *EU Competition Law: An Analytical Guide to the Leading Cases*. Oxford: Hart.

García, B. & Weatherill, S. (2012) Engaging with the EU in Order to Minimize Its Impact: Sport and the Negotiation of the Treaty of Lisbon. *Journal of European Public Policy*, 19:2, 238–256.

Kornbeck, J. (2017) Le geste sportif: ein alternatives Unterscheidungsmerkmal zu den besonderen Merkmalen des Sports nach Artikel 165 AEUV? *Europäische Zeitschrift für Wirtschaftsrecht (EuZW)*, 28:15, 603–606.

Kornbeck, J. (2019) Specificity, Monopoly and Solidarity in the European Commission's ISU (International Skating Union) Decision: Anything New Under the Sun? *Journal of European Competition Law & Practice (JECLAP)*, 10:2, 71–79.

Kornbeck, J. (2020) What Can SGBs Do to Comply with Antitrust Rules While Maintaining the 'One Federation' Principle? *International Sports Law Journal*, 20:3–4, 203–226.

Kornbeck, J. (2021) Spanish Professional Football Clubs: How Salient Is the Exact Nature of the Aid Provided? *European State Aid Law Quarterly (EStAL)*, 20:1, 120–138.

Kornbeck, J. (ed) (2022) *Sport and Brexit: Regulatory Challenges and Legacies*. Abingdon: Routledge.

Philippon, T. (2019) *The Great Reversal. How America Gave Up on Free Markets*. Cambridge, MA, Belknap Press.

Pijetlovic, K. (2015) *EU Sports Law and Breakaway Leagues in Football*. Den Haag: T.M.C. Asser Press & Heidelberg: Springer.

Steiner, U. (2022) 50 Jahre Sportrechtswissenschaft in Deutschland. *Zeitschrift für Sport & Recht (SpuRt)*, 29:2, 79–80.

Van Rompuy, B. (2015) The Role of EU Competition Law in Tackling Abuse of Regulatory Power by Sports Associations. *Maastricht Journal of European and Comparative Law*, 22:2, 179–208.

Verdonk, T. (2017) Rivalry among Sports Associations: The Compatibility of Sports Associations' Exclusivity Clauses with EU Competition Law. *European Competition Law Review*, 38:2, 80–88.

Vieweg, K. (1983) Zur Einführung: Sport und Recht. *Juristische Schulung (JuS)*, 23, 825–830.

Weatherill, S. (2017) *Principles and Practice in EU Sports Law*. Oxford: Oxford University Press.

2

A MOTOR OF CHANGE? EU ANTITRUST LAW AND SPORTS GOVERNANCE FROM *MECA-MEDINA* TO THE *EUROPEAN SUPERLEAGUE*[1]

Ben Van Rompuy

2.1 Introduction

The earliest interactions between European Union (EU) law and sports governance, most famously in the *Bosman* case, concerned the internal market rules. A select number of athletes challenged rules and practices of their sports governing bodies (SGBs) before national courts, alleging that they were discriminatory and interfered with their free movement rights. Through preliminary references, the Court of Justice brought sport within the scope of the Treaty, but for a long time, it exclusively handled sports-related cases on the basis of the free movement provisions on workers and services. Concerns that the measures in question also may distort competition within the internal market remained somewhat of an afterthought.

Since the turn of the century, however, EU antitrust law began to play a more prominent role. The growing economic significance of various sports-related activities, in itself driven largely by technological and regulatory developments in the European audiovisual sector, was the main catalyst for enforcement action, initiated by the European Commission. Its application of Articles 101 and 102 TFEU to business activities such as the licensing of sports media rights or the sale of tickets was generally uncontroversial. By contrast, its scrutiny of regulatory choices made by SGBs – now also brought firmly within the realm of antitrust law because of their economic implications – was met with fierce opposition. SGBs considered matters of 'internal' sports governance to be a part of their

1 This chapter is based in part on Van Rompuy (2022a). Disclaimer: the author represented the complainants in the proceedings before the European Commission that resulted in its decision of 8 December 2017 in Case AT.40208 – International Skating Union's Eligibility, which is discussed in this chapter.

DOI: 10.4324/9781003305989-2

autonomous preserve and were afraid that antitrust enforcement would not pay due regard to the distinctive features of sport and its structures.[2] Following an at times highly political, uphill battle, the Commission concluded several antitrust investigations into the rules and practices of the Fédération Internationale de Football Association (FIFA), the Union of European Football Associations (UEFA) and the International Automobile Federation (FIA) in 2001 and 2002.[3] It then refrained, for almost a decade and a half, from intervening in the regulatory aspects of sport. The Commission received several sports-related antitrust complaints, but these were all rejected on priority grounds.[4] National competition authorities (NCAs), which became the main public enforcers since the decentralisation of EU antitrust enforcement in 2004, also adopted few decisions in this area.[5] Their enforcement action in the sports sector focused predominantly on the joint selling of media rights by national football associations.[6]

Against this background, the recent uptick of antitrust enforcement action *vis-à-vis* sports governance is certainly remarkable. The European Commission's decision in 2015 to open an investigation into the International Skating Union's (ISU) eligibility rules may have been a one-off. And the headline-grabbing private action brought by the European Superleague Company against UEFA and FIFA is exceptional in its own right. Yet the growing string of national cases – some also high-profile, such as the decision of the German competition authority concerning the application of Rule 40 of the Olympic Charter,[7] others less so – may signal a trend.[8] EU antitrust law had already emerged as a potentially

2 See e.g. Infantino (2006); Zylberstein (2007).

3 European Commission Press release of 5 June 2002, 'Commission closes investigations into FIFA regulations on international football transfers,' IP/02/824; Press release of 18 April 2002, 'Commission closes investigations into FIFA rules on players' agents,' IP/02/585; Press release of 30 October 2001, 'Commission closes its investigation into Formula One and other four-wheel motor sports,' IP/01/1523.

4 After being informed of the Commission's preliminary conclusion that there are insufficient grounds for acting, the complainant will usually (implicitly) withdraw its complaint. In a number of cases, this did not happen, prompting the need for the Commission to formally reject the complaint by decision. See e.g. Case AT.40105 (UEFA Financial Fair Play Rules); Case AT.40296 (Interdiction du TPO par la FIFA; Case AT.39732 – BRV/FIA, certain Formula One engine manufacturers, FIM, Dorna, Honda); Case AT.39464 (Supporters Juventus Turin v FIGC-CONI-UEFA-FIFA); Case AT.40022 (Match fixing in sanctions in tennis); Case AT.39471 (Certain joueur de tennis professionnel/Agence mondiale antidopage+ATP+CIAS); Case AT.39899 (Licensing of intellectual property rights for football collectibles); and Case AT.40490 (Spanish Football Trainers).

5 Most of the national cases dealt with the rules and practices of national SGBs governing the sanctioning of sports events and the participation of their members in non-sanctioned events. See Van Rompuy (2015).

6 Van Rompuy (2014).

7 Bundeskartellamt, Decision pursuant to Section 32b GWB Public version, B-226/17 (25 February 2019).

8 See e.g. Lithuanian Competition Authority, 'By agreeing not to pay players' salaries, the Lithuanian Basketball League and its clubs infringed competition law,' press release of 18 November 2021; German Competition Authority, 'Bundeskartellamt provides preliminary assessment of

powerful tool to curb the transnational private power of SGBs. But public authorities, athletes, clubs and other stakeholders are increasingly tapping into that potential.

The aim of this chapter is to trace back these recent developments to the case law of the Court of Justice and the General Court, together referred to as the EU courts, which clarified the scope of application of Articles 101 and 102 TFEU and established a specific analytical framework for the assessment of sporting rules and practices under these provisions. This will set the stage for the subsequent chapters. Section 2.2 charts how the Court of Justice eventually refused to give antitrust immunity to a category of 'purely sporting' rules. Section 2.3 outlines the key principles set out in the case law – and in particular the judgments in *Meca-Medina, MOTOE* and *ISU* – which now guide and structure the antitrust analysis of sporting rules and practices. Section 2.4 offers some concluding thoughts on the unique function of EU antitrust enforcement in this area and on the developments that we can expect going forward.

2.2 Scope of application of the EU antitrust rules

Already in the 1970s, the Court of Justice established, in response to preliminary questions from national courts, that sport is subject to EU law where it constitutes an economic activity. It was only in 2006, however, that the Court fully recognised the difficulty of separating the economic aspects from the sporting aspects and made clear that, as a result, sporting rules and practices cannot escape from the application of the EU antitrust rules.

2.2.1 The erosion of the purely sporting exemption: from Walrave to Meca-Medina

In *Walrave and Koch v Union Cycliste Internationale* (*Walrave*) (1974) the Court of Justice was faced with the prospect that the prohibition to discriminate on the basis of nationality, now contained in Article 18 TFEU, would condemn the selection of athletes for national representative teams. The Court, however,

DFL's 50+1 ownership rule,' press release of 31 May 2021; Polish Competition Authority, 'The President of UOKiK brings charges of limiting competition against basketball clubs,' press release of 12 April 2021; Belgian Competition Authority, 'The Competition College has decided to impose certain interim measures following the application filed by Royal Excelsior Virton against the Royal Belgian Football Association (RBFA),' press release of 23 November 2020; Portuguese Competition Authority, 'Covid-19: AdC imposes interim measure on the Portuguese Football League that suspends no-poach agreement,' press release of 25 May 2020; Italian Competition Authority, 'A378E – Sanzione di 450mila euro alla Federazione Italiana Sport Equestri (FISE),' press release of 16 October 2019; Belgian Competition Authority, 'The Investigation and Prosecution Service of the Belgian Competition Authority closed an investigation against Fédération Equestre Internationale (FEI) pursuant to commitments,' press release of 20 December 2018.

explained that the provisions of the Treaty, which then exclusively pursued economic objectives, do not affect a practice 'of purely sporting interest' that has 'nothing to do with economic activity.'[9] Rules about the composition of national teams, the Court reasoned, only exclude foreign athletes for sporting reasons. Two years later, in *Donà v Mantero* (1976), the Court repeated that the internal market rules do not apply to matters of purely sporting interest. It left it to the national court to verify whether the challenged rules of the Italian Football Federation, which only permitted players of Italian nationality to participate in certain matches, discriminated 'for reasons which are not of an economic nature, which relate to the particular nature and context of such matches, and are thus of sporting interest only.'[10]

When the next sports-related case reached the Court of Justice, almost 20 years later, it gave a restrictive interpretation of the 'purely sporting' exemption. In its *Bosman* judgment (1995), the Court reiterated that the internal market rules do not preclude rules or practices justified on non-economic grounds, but it made clear that the exemption 'cannot be relied upon to exclude the whole of a sporting activity from the scope of the Treaty.'[11] The Court's earlier position that participation in international competitions between national teams could be disassociated from economic activity was already contentious.[12] But in any event, the same could not be said about rules governing the international transfer of professional football players. The Court further distinguished nationality clauses that concern 'specific matches between teams representing their countries' from the challenged system of nationality-based discrimination in European club football competitions.[13]

The European Commission started to enforce the antitrust rules based on these principles set out by the Court, but the precise scope of the exemption remained unclear. In an attempt to give guidance, the Commission sought to draw a dividing line between practices of SGBs that fall outside the reach of EU antitrust law ('the sporting activity strictly speaking') and commercial activities generated by that sporting activity, to which the antitrust rules apply.[14] Yet the

9 Case 36/74 *Walrave and Koch v UCI* [1974] ECLI:EU:C:1974:140.

10 Case 13/76 *Gaetano Donà v Mario* Mantero [1976] ECLI:EU:C:1976:115, at 14.

11 Case C-415/93 *Union royale belge des sociétés de football association and Others v Bosman and Others* [1995] ECLI:EU:C:1995:463, at 76.

12 Weatherill (2017), pp. 75–76; Van den Bogaert & Vermeersch (2006).

13 Case C-415/93 *Union royale belge des sociétés de football association and Others v Bosman and Others* [1995] ECLI:EU:C:1995:463, at 128.

14 European Commission Preliminary Guidelines on the application of the competition rules to sport (internal memo to the Commission), SEC(1999) 249; Commission Report from the Commission to the European Council with a view to safeguarding current sports structures and maintaining the social function of sport within the Community framework – The Helsinki Report on Sport, COM(1999) 644 final; European Commission, press release of 24 February 1999, 'Commission debates application of its competition rules to sport,' IP/99/133; European Commission, press release of 9 December 1999, 'Limits to the application of Treaty competition rules to sport: Commission gives clear signal,' IP/99/965.

increasing interdependence between those two levels of activity made it ever more difficult to locate that line of separation.

In its judgment in *Meca-Medina* (2006), the first case in which it applied one of the antitrust provisions to a sporting rule, the Court of Justice rejected the applicability of the purely sporting exemption. Two professional swimmers, who had been banned for two years for failing a drug test, had complained to the Commission alleging that the anti-doping regulations of the International Olympic Committee (IOC) violated the EU antitrust rules. The General Court dismissed an appeal against the Commission's decision rejecting their complaint. It considered, citing *Walrave*, that the anti-doping rules escape the application of the antitrust rules on the sole ground that they are based on purely sporting considerations.[15] On further appeal, the Court of Justice invalidated that reasoning and held that 'the mere fact that a rule is purely sporting in nature does not have the effect of removing from the scope of the Treaty the person engaging in the activity governed by that rule or the body which has laid it down.'[16] It thus became clear that sporting rules and practices are subject to scrutiny under the EU antitrust rules. The Court explained that even when a sporting rule falls outside the scope of the free movement provisions because it has nothing to do with economic activity, this still does not mean – as the General Court erroneously assumed – that it is also excluded straightaway from the scope of the EU antitrust rules. Instead, it must be determined, on a case-by-case basis, whether a particular sporting rule or practice fulfils the specific requirements of Articles 101 and 102 TFEU.[17] Two of these requirements still delimit the personal scope of these provisions and their jurisdictional reach and will therefore be discussed first.

2.2.2 SGBs as (associations of) undertakings

Article 101 TFEU catches collusive practices between 'undertakings' and Article 102 TFEU applies to the conduct of 'undertakings' with a dominant position. This concept, broadly defined as 'any entity engaged in economic activity, regardless of the legal status of the entity or the way in which it is financed,'[18] thus determines the categories of actors to which the antitrust rules apply.[19]

There is no doubt that SGBs, leagues, clubs (or teams) and even individual athletes act as undertakings with respect to the commercial activities in which they are involved (such as the sale of tickets, media rights and merchandising, the transferring of players or the conclusion of sponsorship contracts). The fact that in addition to professional clubs a large number of amateur clubs belong to

15 Case T-313/22 *David Meca-Medina and Igor Majcen v Commission* [2004] ECLI:EU:T:2004:282.

16 Case C-519/04 P *David Meca-Medina and Igor Majcen v Commission* [2006] ECLI:EU:C:2006:492, at 27.

17 *Idem*, at 30–33.

18 Case C-41/90 *Höfner and Elser* [1961] ECLI:EU:C:1991:161, at 21.

19 Jones, Sufrin & Dunne (2019), p. 141.

a SGB does not call into question that it engages in economic activities.[20] While the economic success obtained by the clubs may certainly be different, their activities are not different in character.[21] The concept of undertaking also does not presuppose a profit-making intention.[22]

The question whether SGBs also can be regarded as undertakings when they act in a purely regulatory capacity is less straightforward. For Article 101 TFEU this would not raise difficulties. That provision also refers to 'decisions by associations of undertakings' and thus will in any event cover the rules and practices by which SGBs coordinate the conduct of their members. The situation is different as regards Article 102 TFEU. When SGBs regulate (access to) markets on which they themselves are not active, Article 102 TFEU can only capture this rule-making activity through the notion of collective dominance. In *Laurent Piau* (2005), the General Court found that the European Commission erred in law by taking the view that FIFA cannot hold a dominant position on the market for football players' agents' services simply because FIFA is not an actor on that market. According to the Court, FIFA, as 'the emanation of the national associations and the clubs,' effectively operates – through its members – on any market that it regulates. In other words, FIFA's involvement stems from its regulatory measures. Based on this premise, the Court considered that FIFA and the clubs (i.e., the undertakings operating on the players' agents market), 'being so linked in the long term as to their conduct' by binding rules, present themselves on that market as a collective entity.[23] Following a similar reasoning, the German NCA recently considered the individual conduct of the German Olympic Committee and the IOC a manifestation of a dominant position collectively held by all members of the Olympic Movement.[24]

20 The mere fact that certain members are not undertakings is not sufficient to remove an association from the scope of the EU antitrust rules. See e.g. Case T-23/09 *CNOP and CCG v Commission* [2010] ECLI:EU:T:2010:452, at 74; Case T-217/03 *FNCBV and Others v Commission* [2010] ECLI:EU:T:2010:452, at 55.

21 Opinion of Advocate General Lenz in Case C-415/93 *Union Royale Belge des Sociétés de Football Association and others v. Bosman and others* [1995] ECLI:EU:C:1995:293, at 255–256. See also e.g. Joined Cases C-51/96 and C-191/97 *Christelle Deliège v Ligue Francophone de Judo et Disciplines Associées ASBL and others* [2000] ECLI:EU:C:2000:199, at 46; Case T-193/02 *Laurent Piau v Commission* [2005] ECLI:EU:T:2005:22, at 70.

22 What matters is whether the offering of goods of services on the market is potentially in competition with other entities. Even when these other entities equally operate without seeking to make profit, it can be concluded that the entities' economic survival ultimately depends on being able to impose their services to the detriment of the services offered by the competitor. Case C-49/07 *Motosykletistiki Omospondia Ellados NPID (MOTOE) v Elliniko Dimosio* [2008] EU:C:2008:142, at 28.

23 Case T-193/02 *Laurent Piau v Commission* [2005] ECLI:EU:T:2005:22, at 112–116.

24 Bundeskartellamt, Decision pursuant to Section 32b GWB Public version, B-226/17 (25 February 2019), at 89–90.

2.2.3 Effect on trade between EU Member States

Articles 101 and 102 TFEU only apply to agreements, decisions or conduct that appreciably affect trade between Member States. This jurisdictional requirement defines the boundary of the areas respectively covered by these provisions and the national antitrust rules.[25] It is not required that the agreement, decision or conduct will actually have or has had cross-border effects within the internal market. It is sufficient that they are 'capable' of having such an effect.[26]

Sporting rules and practices of international SGBs, which coordinate the conduct of their members worldwide, are generally liable to affect trade between Member States.[27] The same is true for most activities in relation to the transfer of players or the commercial exploitation of (participation in) international and even national sports events. Since national sporting rules and practices often apply to the whole territory of a Member State, they may also have an impact on cross-border economic activity, in particular when they have potential foreclosure effects.[28]

2.3 The substantive antitrust assessment of sporting rules

Given the wide scope of application of Articles 101 and 102 TFEU, the main inquiry will generally focus on the question whether a sporting rule or practice is, on balance, anti-competitive. Most rules and practices of SGBs restrict the freedom of action of their individual members. And in a professional sports context, these restrictions will often be capable of having anti-competitive effects. Yet this does not necessarily imply that they constitute a 'restriction of competition' under Article 101 TFEU or an 'abuse' under Article 102 TFEU.

2.3.1 Restriction of competition

In order to violate Article 101 TFEU, a sporting rule or practice must have an anti-competitive object or actual or potential restrictive effects on competition, which are not outweighed by public benefits. When a restriction of competition within the meaning of Article 101(1) TFEU has been proven, Article 101(3) TFEU can, in all circumstances,[29] be invoked as a defence. It provides for an exception from the prohibition of otherwise anti-competitive collusive behaviour. Four cumulative conditions must be satisfied. The agreement, decision or

25 Joined Cases 56 and 58/64 *Consten and Grundig v Commission* [1966] EU:C:1966:41, at 341.

26 EU Commission, Guidelines on the effect on trade concept contained in Articles 81 and 82 of the Treaty (Notice) [2004] C 101/81, at 24–32.

27 See e.g. Decision of the Commission of 8 December 2017 in Case AT.40208 – International Skating Union's eligibility rules, at 310–313.

28 European Commission, Guidelines on the effect on trade concept contained in Articles 81 and 82 of the Treaty (Notice) [2004] C 101/81, at 77–99.

29 See e.g. Case C-439/09 *Pierre Fabre Dermo-Cosmétique* [2011] ECLI:EU:C:2011:649, at 57.

concerted practice must: (1) improve the production or distribution of goods or promote technical or economic progress; (2) allow consumers a fair share of the resulting benefits; (3) not impose restrictions that are not indispensable to the achievement of the benefits; and (4) not eliminate competition in a substantial part of the internal market.

Given the bifurcated structure of Article 101 TFEU, the General Court and the European Commission have rejected the suggestion that a US-style 'rule of reason' analysis should be conducted at the Article 101(1) stage. It is Article 101(3) that provides the appropriate forum for weighing the pro-competitive benefits and anti-competitive effects of collusive behaviour.[30] Nonetheless, in a line of case law dealing with professional bodies, the Court of Justice did apply a rule of reason type of analysis to determine the applicability of Article 101(1), allowing public interest benefits raised by the defendant to offset competition concerns. In the primary case *Wouters* (2002), the Court had to assess whether a regulation adopted by the Netherlands Bar, prohibiting partnerships between lawyers and accountants, violated Article 101 TFEU. The Court considered that the rule – a decision by an association of undertakings – was liable to distort competition. It stressed, however, that Article 101(1) does not necessarily catch every restriction of the freedom of action of the parties or one of them. To determine whether the decision constitutes a restriction of competition within the meaning of Article 101, the overall context in which the decision was taken or produces its effect must be taken into account. More particularly, 'account must be taken of its objectives' and it 'has then to be considered whether the consequential effects restrictive of competition are inherent in the pursuit of those objectives.'[31]

When asked whether the anti-doping regulations of the IOC amount to a restriction of competition within the meaning of Article 101(1) TFEU in *Meca-Medina*, the Court of Justice chose to apply the test it had articulated in *Wouters*. The Court first recognised that the rules, which are capable of restricting competition by banning athletes from sporting events following a positive doping test,[32] had legitimate objectives; namely 'to combat doping in order for competitive sport to be conducted fairly' and 'the need to safeguard equal chances for athletes, athletes' health, the integrity and objectivity of competitive sport, and ethical values in sport.'[33] Then, the Court examined whether the restrictions caused by the rules are suitable and necessary to achieve these objectives. Considering that the penal nature of the rules did not appear to go beyond what is necessary to ensure enforcement of the doping ban – the swimmers had neither

30 The balancing of overall effects under Article 101(1) TFEU would render the substantive analysis under Article 101(3) TFEU redundant. Case T-112/99 *Métropole télévision and Others v Commission* [2001] ECLI:EU:T:2001:215, at 74.

31 Case C-309/99 J. *C. J. Wouters, J. W. Savelbergh and Price Waterhouse Belastingadviseurs BV v. Algemene Raad van de Nederlandse Orde van Advocaten* [2002] EU:C:2002:98, at 97

32 Case C-519/04 P *David Meca-Medina and Igor Majcen v Commission* [2006] ECLI:EU:C:2006:492, at 47.

33 *Idem*, at 43.

demonstrated that the permitted dosage threshold were set unjustifiably low nor argued that the penalties imposed were excessive – it found the limitations on the athlete's freedom of action to be inherent in the proper conduct of competitive sport and proportionate.[34] The Court therefore concluded that the anti-doping rules did not constitute a restriction of competition and, subsequently, fell outside the prohibition in Article 101(1) TFEU.

The Court of Justice in *Meca-Medina* thus put forward an analytical framework for sporting rules and practices that allows sports-specific justifications to offset a *prima facie* case of competitive harm at the Article 101(1) stage of the assessment. At the Article 101(3) stage, such justifications would have a far lesser impact.[35] It follows that the *Wouters* test is the linchpin of the substantive antitrust analysis. It must be determined whether the rule or practice is appropriate for the organisation and proper conduct of competitive sport (the suitability subtest) and does not go beyond what is necessary to attain the purported legitimate objective (the necessity or least-restrictive-means test). If not, the anti-competitive object or effect of the measure is not neutralised and a – most likely prohibited – restriction of competition is established.

While the party or authority alleging an infringement has the burden of proving the existence of an infringement of Article 101(1) TFEU, it is for those claiming the benefit of a defence against such a finding to demonstrate, 'by means of convincing arguments and evidence,' that the conditions for applying such defence are satisfied.[36] The exceptional use of the *Wouters* test at the 101(1) stage does not alter this allocation of the legal burden.[37]

Contrary to organisational sporting rules and practices, business activities connected to sport, such as the licensing of sponsoring or merchandise rights, are generally subject to an orthodox analysis. To the extent that sports-specific justifications would be relevant, they can only be accepted as efficiencies gains under Article 101(3) TFEU. As discussed, however, the dividing line between regulatory and commercial aspects can only be found on a case-by-case basis. For example, in three major cases involving the joint selling of exclusive football media rights, the European Commission established the conditions under which it considered

34 *Idem*, at 44–55.

35 The European Commission advocates a narrow interpretation of Article 101(3) TFEU that only allows improvements in economic efficiencies that sufficiently compensate the consumers affected by the restriction. European Commission, Guidelines on the application of Article 81(3) of the Treaty [2004] OJ C 101/105. Article 101(3) TFEU additionally requires that the agreement (or decision or concerted practice) must not lead to the elimination of competition.

36 Recital 5, Council Regulation (EC) No 1/2003 of 16 December 2002 on the implementation of the rules on competition laid down in Articles 81 and 82 of the Treaty. OJ L 1, 4.1.2003, p. 1–25

37 See e.g. Joined Cases C-204/00 P, C-205/00 P, C-211/00 P, C-213/00 P, C-217/00 P and C-219/00 P *Aalborg Portland A/S and Others v Commission* [2004] ECLI:EU:C:2004:6, at 78–79. There is also no presumption of legality of sporting rules and practice. Decision of the Commission of 8 December 2017 in Case AT.40208 – International Skating Union's eligibility rules, at fn 329.

that practice permissible under Article 101 TFEU. The parties involved – UEFA, the German League Association and the English Football Association Premier League – invoked a financial solidarity argument as the main justification for their joint selling arrangements. The aim of maintaining a financial and competitive balance between clubs participating in the same competition has been accepted by the Court of Justice as a legitimate regulatory objective,[38] justifying in theory the application of the *Wouters* test. Joint selling arrangements have been shown to facilitate horizontal financial solidarity.[39] Yet the joint selling of media rights is not an indispensable prerequisite for a fair distribution of revenues between the clubs. This can be achieved through other mechanisms that do not restrict competition on the market for the acquisition of the media rights. In its *UEFA Champions League* decision (2003) the Commission therefore stressed that the solidarity justification could only be considered under Article 101(3) TFEU.[40]

2.3.3 Abuse

Article 102 TFEU only prohibits the 'abuse' of a dominant position within the internal market or a substantial part of it. The provision lists certain types of conduct that may be abusive (such as tying and bundling and the imposition of unfair trading conditions) but this list is not exhaustive.[41] The EU courts have generally defined abuse as conduct that cannot be regarded as 'competition on the merits.'[42] This may include exploitative practices, exclusionary practices, discriminatory practices and practices that are otherwise harmful to the internal market. While a number of basic principles underlie the approach to the different categories of abuses,[43] there is no general test to distinguish between

38 Case C-415/93 *Union Royale Belge des Sociétés de Football Association and others v Bosman and others* [1995] ECLI:EU:C:1995:293, at 106.

39 T.M.C. Asser Institute (2014) *Study on Sports Organisers' Rights*, Study commissioned by the European Commission, https://www.asser.nl/media/2624/final-report_sor-2014.pdf, pp. 74–91. See also e.g. Opinion of Advocate General Lenz in Case C-415/93 *Union Royale Belge des Sociétés de Football Association and others v. Bosman and others* [1995] ECLI:EU:C:1995:293, at 226–234.

40 The Commission, however, avoided addressing the merits of the argument that a joint selling arrangement ensures a fairer distribution of revenue. Because UEFA's amended joint selling arrangement could be justified on other economic efficiency grounds (the creation of a single point of sale, the creation of a packaged league product and the branding of content by a single entity), the Commission concluded that 'it is not necessary for the purpose of this procedure to consider the solidarity argument any further.' Commission Decision of 23 July 2003 in Case COMP/C.2–37.398 – Joint selling of the commercial rights of the UEFA Champions League, paras. 131, at 164–167.

41 See e.g. Case 6/72 *Europemballage and Continental Can v Commission* [1973] EU:C:1973:22, at 26; Case C-457/10 P *AstraZeneca v Commission* [2012] EU:C:2012:770, at 134.

42 See e.g. Case 85/76 *Hoffmann-La Roche v Commission* [1979] EU:C:1979:36, at 6; Case C-280/08 P *Deutsche Telekom v Commission* [2010] EU:C:2010:603, at 175.

43 For a detailed discussion, see O'Donoghue & Padilla (2020); Nazzini (2011). See also European Commission, Guidance on the Commission's enforcement priorities in applying Article 82 of the EC Treaty to abusive exclusionary conduct by dominant undertakings [2009] C 45/7.

anti-competitive practices and competition on the merits. In order to establish the abusive nature of a certain conduct, specific conditions must be met (that do not necessarily apply when assessing other types of conduct).[44]

Even though the wording of Article 102 TFEU does not provide for an exception like Article 101(3) TFEU, the EU courts have established that a dominant undertaking may seek to justify conduct that would otherwise be an abuse. It may do so by demonstrating either that its conduct is objectively necessary or that any harm to competition is outweighed by efficiency benefits.[45] This pursuit for consistency in the analytical principles for an efficiency defence under Articles 101 and 102 TFEU supports the European Commission's view that the *Wouters* test is equally transferrable to Article 102 TFEU.[46] This has not yet been confirmed in the jurisprudence of the EU courts, however.

2.3.2 SGBs as gatekeepers: a specific obligation to ensure equality of opportunity

In situations where particular undertakings control access to certain (downstream) markets, the EU courts have held that 'a system of undistorted competition can be guaranteed only if equality of opportunity is secured as between the various economic operators.'[47] Most of this case law concerns newly liberalised or regulated markets. Yet it is also of importance for sports governance. The general obligation of equal treatment that this jurisprudence imposes on gatekeepers was central to the European Commission's decision on the ISU's eligibility rules (2017) and will also be front and centre in the pending *European Superleague* case. Its underlying principles thus deserve special attention here.

In the exercise of their regulatory power, SGBs restrict access to various markets, but antitrust concerns have predominantly revolved around exclusion from the markets for the organisation and marketing of sporting events.[48] Indeed, the regulations of most international and national SGBs include provisions on the 'sanctioning' of third-party competitions and on the participation of their members in non-sanctioned events. This can be justified. As governing body of a particular sport, a SGB has a legitimate role in, for instance, ensuring compliance

44 Case C-52/09 *Konkurrensverket v TeliaSonera Sverige AB* [2011] EU:C:2011:83, at 55.

45 Case C-209/10 *Post Danmark A/S v Konkurrencerådet* [2012] ECLI:EU:C:2012:172, paras. 40–41; Case C-413/14 Intel Corp. v Commission [2017] *ECLI:EU:C:2017:632*, para. 140.

46 European Commission, White Paper on Sport, COM(2007) 391 final, Annex I, pp. 64–69.

47 See e.g. Case 612/17 *Google and Alphabet v Commission (Google Shopping)* [2021] ECLI:EU:T:2021:763, at 180; Case C-1/12 *Ordem dos Técnicos Oficiais de Contas v Autoridade da Concorrência* [2013] ECLI:EU:C:2013:127, at 88; Case C-280/08 P *Deutsche Telekom AG v Commission* [2010] ECLI:EU:C:2010:603, at 230; Joined Cases C-327/03 and C-328/03 *ISIS Multimedia Net and Firma O2* [2005] ECLI:EU:C:2005:622; Case C-18/88 *RTT v GB-Inno-BM SA* [1999] ECLI:EU:C:1991:474, at 25.

48 For a discussion and analysis of national antitrust cases concerning this issue, see Van Rompuy (2015).

with uniform standards for their discipline and maintaining a properly structured calendar.[49] A pre-authorisation system can be considered a suitable mechanism to achieve this.[50] Yet it is clear that where the regulator also organises and commercially exploits events, a conflict of interest may arise. Sanctioning rules could be enforced to entrench market power. Rules prohibiting members from participating in events not sanctioned by the SGB may then raise insurmountable barriers to entry for competitors.

In its preliminary ruling in *MOTOE* (2008) the Court of Justice addressed the question how the dual role of SGBs ought to be measured against the demands of the Treaty.[51] The reference was made in the course of national proceedings between the Greek State and MOTOE, the Greek Motorcycling Federation. Greek legislation requires authorisation from the minister for public order for the organisation of motorcycling events on public and private roads, which can only be given following the consent of the national association that is recognised by FIA – at that time the Automobile and Touring Club (ELPA). When ELPA rejected its application to organise a series of races, MOTOE sought financial compensation for the damage it claimed to have suffered.

The Court of Justice did not object to the fact that ELPA, which itself organises and commercially exploits events, was entrusted with the power to decide which events may take place. The Court did consider, however, that ELPA not only had the means to prevent rivals from entering the Greek market, but also an economic interest in limiting market access and favouring its own events. To ensure equal conditions of competition, the exercise of ELPA's power to authorise events should therefore be made subject to restrictions, obligations and review.[52] The Court of Justice left it to the national court to assess whether the Greek legislation sufficiently ensured that applications for authorisation would be dealt with in an objective, transparent and non-discriminatory way. If it did not do so, the legislation risked leading to an abuse of a dominant position and should therefore be considered incompatible with Article 106(1) TFEU in conjunction with Article 102 TFEU.[53]

The European Commission relied on these principles to insist that the ISU's pre-authorisation system could only pass the *Wouters* test if it would provide for authorisation criteria and sanctions that are clearly defined, transparent, non-discriminatory, reviewable and capable of ensuring third parties effective

49 See Opinion of Advocate General Kokott in Case C-49/07 *MOTOE* [2008] ECLI:EU:C:2008:142, at 91–96.

50 Case T-93/18 *International Skating Union v Commission* [2020] ECLI:EU:T:2020:61, at 108.

51 Case C-49/07 *MOTOE* [2008] ECLI:EU:C:2008:142.

52 *Idem*, at 52.

53 Pursuant to Article 106(1) TFEU the Member States shall, in respect of undertakings to which they confer exclusive rights, neither enact nor maintain in force any measure contrary to the rules contained in the Treaties, in particular the antitrust rules.

access to the market.[54] In its appeal against the Commission decision, the ISU argued that the obligations arising from *MOTOE* and related case law were not applicable. The General Court disagreed.[55] If a SGB is both an operator in and regulator of a market, the Court made clear, it must ensure that 'third parties are not unduly deprived of market access to the point that competition on that market is distorted.'[56] It follows that both Articles 101 and 102 TFEU place an obligation on SGBs, in the exercise of their power to regulate market access, not to unfairly discriminate against rivals.

The precise scope and content of this equal treatment obligation will no doubt be the focus of much future litigation. In the particular context of the organisation of sports events, for instance, it remains unclear to what extent a SGB may favour its own competitions and those of its members when controlling and coordinating the official calendar of (international) sports events. Disputes about calendar conflicts have already been framed as potential EU antitrust law violations, but to the best of the author's knowledge, they have not yet been resolved on those grounds in legal proceedings.[57]

2.4 Antitrust challenges to sports governance: a motor of change?

Because of its broad scope of application, EU antitrust law has the unique potential to assert control over the transnational private regulation of sports. It is also, in principle, well equipped to subject sporting rules and practices to meaningful review. When the Court of Justice in *Meca-Medina* denied antitrust immunity for sporting rules and practices, it at the same time put forward an analytical framework that leaves sufficient flexibility to take into account the special features of professional sport and its structures. EU antitrust law grants, as Weatherill puts it, conditional autonomy to sport.[58] It reasonably demands that SGBs can make the case that their rules and practices are suitable and necessary for the organisation and proper conduct of their sport. Measures that pass this proportionality requirement should withstand antitrust scrutiny. It is only when a substantially less restrictive and workable alternative can be identified that the collateral anti-competitive effects of sporting rules and practices will be caught by Articles 101 and 102 TFEU.

The utility of antitrust law as an accountability mechanism is, however, contingent on enforcement. And while some asserted that the *Meca-Medina*

54 Decision of the Commission of 8 December 2017 in Case AT.40208 – International Skating Union's eligibility rules, at 339–342.

55 Case T-93/18 *International Skating Union v Commission* [2020] ECLI:EU:T:2020:61, at 69–75.

56 *Idem*, at 75.

57 Alexander Engelhard and Luka Milanovic, 'An overview of the dispute between FIBA & Euro League – Is there an end in sight?', LawInSport, 28 February 2018, https://www.lawinsport.com/topics/sports/item/an-overview-of-the-dispute-between-fiba-euroleague-is-there-an-end-in-sight.

58 See e.g. Weatherill (2017).

judgment would open the floodgates to large numbers of antitrust challenges against SGBs,[59] that is not really what happened.

Compliance with EU antitrust law is ensured through a dual enforcement system that combines public and private enforcement. Because competition authorities must make effective use of their limited resources, private antitrust enforcement is often presented as an alternative. The European Commission, for instance, typically rejects sports-related complaints on the (sole) ground that the complainant can alternatively bring an action before the national courts.[60] Private antitrust challenges to sports governance can, however, hardly substitute for public enforcement.

Firstly, the possibility of private litigation crucially depends on having access to legal services and sufficient financial means. In this respect, there are evidently serious imbalances between the major stakeholders in, for instance, European football and the overwhelming majority of other (semi-)professional sports clubs or athletes, who may additionally fear retaliation or reputational damage. Although private antitrust enforcement is usually aimed at compensation for harm done, in a sports-related context, the grant of injunctive relief (i.e., ordering the infringer to cease and desist the anti-competitive practices) may be as important.[61] But also here, cases are initiated and pursued according to private cost-benefit calculations. Only a select number of stakeholders in sports is therefore capable of truly exploiting the deterrence properties of EU antitrust law through private action.

Secondly, there are jurisdictional hurdles. In *ISU*, the General Court considered that arbitration rules and the exclusive jurisdiction of the Court of Arbitration for Sport would not prevent athletes from bringing an action for damages before a national court.[62] Yet this is far from certain. In 2016, the highest civil court in Germany considered the private damages action initiated by speed skater Claudia Pechstein inadmissible because the ISU's arbitration rules exclude ordinary jurisdiction.[63]

Thirdly, and most importantly, public antitrust enforcement is a far more suitable forum for scrutinising the proportionality of sporting rules and practices. Unlike civil courts, whose task is to safeguard the individual rights of the plaintiff, competition authorities act in the public interest, focusing less upon the fault of the infringing undertaking and more upon the overall harm to the market that results.[64] This polycentric dimension as well as the inquisitorial character of the procedure makes decision-making markedly different from that followed

59 See e.g. Infantino (2006).
60 See Van Rompuy (2022b).
61 Ullrich (2021).
62 Case T-93/18 *International Skating Union v Commission* [2020] ECLI:EU:T:2020:61, at 159.
63 Bundesgerichtshof, Urteil des Kartellsenats vom 7.6.2016 – KZR 6/15, at 57.
64 Dunne (2017); Wils (2017).

in courts.[65] Competition authorities have wider investigative powers and can employ various (in)formal tools and procedures, such as the commitments procedure, to effectively calibrate degrees of reasonable necessity. For example, to determine the proportionality of the advertising restrictions that the IOC imposes on Olympic athletes and their sponsors, the German NCA did not simply second-guess less restrictive alternatives but surveyed, in addition to the parties involved in the proceedings, approximately 500 German athletes and 200 (potential) sponsors.[66] Intervention by competition authorities can also result in positive remedial action: they can co-design, impose and subsequently monitor compliance with remedies that go beyond nullity (and monetary compensation) as a sanction (or restitution) for infringing conduct.

In the transnational realm, intervention by the European Commission, the only antitrust enforcer that can demand EU-wide reforms, has indeed been most transformative. For instance, the proceedings initiated by Jean-Marc Bosman before a Belgian court certainly flicked the first domino, but these proceedings came to an end with a monetary settlement. It was the Commission's antitrust investigation that provided the forum for negotiations between different stakeholders and that eventually brought FIFA's rules on international football transfers in line with EU law's requirements in 2001.[67] The detailed remedies concluding the Commission's investigations into various FIA rules and commercial arrangements, including a separation of the SGB's regulatory and commercial powers, were similarly the result of lengthy and complex negotiations.[68] Yet since then, the Commission has not considered sports governance an enforcement priority, with the inquiry into the ISU's eligibility rules, concluded in 2017, as a notable exception.

So, the *Meca-Medina* ruling may have been a game-changer, but legal and practical hurdles limiting access to private and public enforcement have continued to undercut EU antitrust law's potential to play a more significant role in promoting procedural and substantive principles of good sports governance. The limited enforcement action at EU level has achieved *specific* deterrence for at least some of the few international SGBs involved. FIFA and UEFA's legal teams have compliance most certainly in mind. And EU antitrust enforcement has probably also achieved at least some *general* deterrence (i.e., dissuaded other SGBs from violating the antitrust rules).[69] However, most transnational sporting rules and

65 Lianos (2013), pp. 78–79.

66 Bundeskartellamt, Decision pursuant to Section 32b GWB Public version, B-226/17 (25 February 2019).

67 See e.g. Duval (2016).

68 Van Miert (2000), pp. 168–192.

69 For instance, the decision of the International Swimming Federation (FINA) to no longer prevent swimmers from participating in unsanctioned events may have been influenced not only by the antitrust class action in the United States but also by the decisional practice of the European Commission and the Belgian competition authority. See BBC, Fina backs down on ban

practices have so far been vulnerable to EU antitrust scrutiny only on certain fronts – if at all.

Changes might be ahead, however. The more public enforcers and even self-interested plaintiffs tap into its potential, the greater the function of EU antitrust law as a meaningful accountability mechanism in sports governance will become manifest. Most attention today is given to the *European Superleague* and the *ISU* cases currently pending before the Court of Justice. But maybe the most interesting developments will come from the NCAs. They have been paying increasing attention to the rules and practices of national SGBs and leagues in recent years.[70] And their enforcement actions against the gatekeeper power of technology giants like Meta, Apple, Amazon and Google demonstrate how NCAs can have an outsized influence on transnational quasi-regulatory practices. International SGBs perhaps should take note.

Bibliography

Dunne, D. (2017) The Role of Private Enforcement within EU Competition Law. *Cambridge Yearbook of European Legal Studies*, 16, 143–187.

Duval, A. (2016) The FIFA Regulations on the Status and Transfer of Players: Transnational Law-Making in the Shadow of Bosman. In Duval, A. & Van Rompuy, B. (eds) *The Legacy of Bosman: Revisiting the Relationship between EU law and Sport*. The Hague: TMC Asser Press, 81–116.

Engelhard, A. & Milanovic, L. (2018) An Overview of the Dispute Between FIBA & EuroLeague – Is There An End In Sight? *LawInSport*, 28 February 2018, https://www.lawinsport.com/topics/sports/item/an-overview-of-the-dispute-between-fiba-euroleague-is-there-an-end-in-sight.

Infantino, G. (2006) Meca-Medina: A Step Backwards for the European Sports Model and the Specificity of Sport? UEFA Paper, 2 October 2006, https://www.uefa.com/MultimediaFiles/Download/uefa/KeyTopics/480401_DOWNLOAD.pdf

Jones, A., Sufrin, B. & Dunne, N. (2019) *EU Competition Law: Text, Cases and Materials*. 7th edition. Oxford: Oxford University Press.

Lianos, I. (2013) Some Reflections on the Questions of the Goals of EU Competition Law. In Lianos, I. & Geradin, Damien (eds) *Handbook on European Competition Law*. Cheltenham: Edward Elgar, 78–79.

Nazzini, R. (2011) *The Foundations of European Union Competition Law: The Objective and Principles of Article 102*. Oxford: Oxford University Press.

O'Donoghue, R. & Padilla, J. (2020) *The Law and Economics of Article 102 TFEU*. 3rd edition. Oxford: Hart Publishing.

Ullrich, H. (2021) Private enforcement of the EU Rules on Competition – Nullity Neglected. *International Review of Intellectual Property and Competition Law (IIC)*, 52, 606–635.

Van den Bogaert, S. & Vermeersch, A. (2006) Sport and the EC Treaty: A Tale of Uneasy Bedfellows? *European Law Review* 31:6, 826–827.

---

threat over International Swimming League, 15 January 2019, https://www.bbc.com/sport/swimming/46878438.

70 For references, see fn 8.

Van Miert, K. (2000) *Mijn jaren in Europa*. Tielt: Lannoo.

Van Rompuy, B. (2014) The Impact of EU Competition Policy on the Sale of Sports Media Rights: Trends and Developments at the National Level. In Donders, K., Pauwels, C. & Loisen, J. (eds) *The Palgrave Handbook of European Media Policy*. London: Palgrave Macmillan, 442–460.

Van Rompuy, B. (2015) The Role of EU Competition Law in Tackling Abuse of Regulatory Power by Sports Associations. *Maastricht Journal of European and Comparative Law*, 22:2, 179–208.

Van Rompuy, B. (2022a) Antitrust Challenges to Sports Governance: EU and US Perspectives. In Nafziger, J.A.R. & Gauthier, R. (eds) *Handbook on International Sports Law*. 2nd edition. Cheltenham: Edward Elgar, 423–455.

Van Rompuy, B. (2022b) The European Commission's Handling of Non-Priority Antitrust Complaints: An Empirical Assessment. *World Competition*, 45:2, 265–294.

Weatherill, S. (2017) *Principles and Practice in EU Sports Law*. Oxford: Oxford University Press.

Wils, W. (2017) Private Enforcement of EU Antitrust Law and its Relationship with Public Enforcement: Past, Present and Future. *World Competition*, 40:1, 3–45.

Zylberstein, J. (2007) Collision entre idéaux sportifs et contigences économiques dans l'arrêt Meca – Medina. *Cahiers de droit européen*, 43, 213–237.

3

THE *INTERNATIONAL SKATING UNION* CASE

On a mission to defend the weaker party?

Rusa Agafonova

3.1 Introduction

The antitrust litigation in Europe is currently marked by two major cases, *ISU v Commission*[1] and *Superleague v UEFA*.[2] From the first sight, they are similar: there is a breakaway league (active or prospective), a sports governing body (hereinafter: 'SGB') protecting its organisational system, a sport which nurtures professional aspirations of millions of athletes, be it an Olympic champion or a little kid, provides employment opportunities for many people, mounts a captivating show for fans and embodies the entire philosophy for European society.[3]

That said, there is a considerable difference between the ISU and the Superleague cases. Namely, who plays the role of David opposing the sport-governing Goliath. In the former case, these are two athletes representing a more than modest sport of speed skating, in the latter, a company led by three prominent European football clubs, which, only during the 2020/21 season (affected by COVID-19) generated cumulatively more than €1.6 billion.[4]

The fact that these are 'just' a couple of skaters facing harsh sanctions 'just' for participating in a sports event not included in the official calendar might

1 Case T-93/18 International Skating Union v Commission [2020] ECLI:EU:T:2020:610.

2 Case C-333/21 European Superleague Company, S. L. vs. UEFA and FIFA, lodged on 27 May 2021.

3 Resolution of the Council and of the representatives of the Governments of the Member States meeting within the Council on the key features of a European Sport Model. 30 November 2021, General Secretariat of the Council, No. prev. doc.: 13711/21.

4 Football Money League, Deloitte Sports Business Group, March 2022, available at https://www2.deloitte.com/content/dam/Deloitte/uk/Documents/sports-business-group/deloitte-uk-dfml22.pdf. Accessed on 3 April, 2022. During the season 2020/21, Real Madrid earned €640.7 million (second overall place among the European football clubs), FC Barcelona €582.1 million (fourth place), Juventus €433.5 million (ninth place).

DOI: 10.4324/9781003305989-3

have contributed to the Commission's decision to open the investigation back in 2014:[5] Commissioner Vestager referred to this case as 'extreme'.[6] That said, the problem of imbalance of bargaining power embedded in the relations between athletes and SGBs (and in the sports industry more generally) deserves a more complex and systematic approach. While some useful tools have been introduced to mitigate local disparities (e.g., when signing an employment agreement with a club or when being a party to arbitral proceedings), a more global imbalance rooted in the structural characteristics of sport, remains untouched.

Furthermore, since most SGBs, holding a very powerful market share, stick to a traditionally protectionist approach towards their policy-making competences and are generally reluctant to share market with other undertakings, the traditionally contract law problem of the protection of a weaker party overlaps considerably with the antitrust issues.

The goal of the present contribution is to analyse why athletes remain the most unprotected stakeholders in the sports industry and why antitrust interference can (and should) tackle the bargaining abuses.

3.2 Bargaining imbalance and weaker parties

The notion of weaker party is rooted in the principle of freedom of contract, an essential underlying principle of private law, according to which anyone should be able to decide when, with whom and on which conditions to enter a contract. Bargaining power of parties is dynamic and, thus, hardly definable.[7] Its degree is usually affected by a combination of factors, such as information asymmetries, mental or intellectual disadvantage, limited means of protection, economic and social dependence.[8] In the relations between undertakings, the important criteria are also the probability of finding an alternative trade partner, supply and demand forces of the product or service, difference in scale of business between the parties, position of the abusing firm in the industry.[9] The US courts usually apply the availability-of-alternatives criterion and the 'negotiability' test (by testing whether one party has afforded the other a meaningful opportunity to negotiate terms of a contract).[10]

5 While some bigger cases safeguard their pending status for years.

6 EU to sports chiefs: Get your skates on, 8 December 2017, available at https://www.politico.eu/article/margrethe-vestager-orders-skating-union-to-change-rules/ (Accessed on 3 April, 2022): 'Vestager said: "This decision doesn't mean the Commission is trying to be the referee in every dispute about sport," she said. "By taking an extreme case like this, I do hope we can send a message."'

7 Helveston & Jacobs (2014), p. 22; Niedermaier (2015), p. 146.

8 Rühl (2014), pp. 342–346.

9 See ICN, Task Force for Abuse of Superior Bargaining Position, ICN Special Program for Kyoto Annual Conference Report on Abuse of Superior Bargaining Position, (7th ICN Conference, Kyoto, Japan, April 2008), available at https://centrocedec.files.wordpress.com/2015/07/abuse-of-superior-bargaining-position-2008.pdf. p. 19. Accessed on 3 April, 2022.

10 Helveston & Jacobs (2014), pp. 9–14.

The danger of unequal bargaining power lies in the inequality of substantive and procedural rights and in the risk of abuse of rights by the stronger party. For this reason, many legal orders adopt special legislation protecting the categories generally placed in the position of a weaker party, such as employees, consumers, tenants and patients.[11] This list keeps on growing in view of new business realities,[12] as the imbalances eventually become omnipresent.[13]

3.3 Athletes as the weaker party

In sport, the role of the weaker party is attributed to athletes and smaller clubs vis-à-vis SGBs.[14] The imbalance of bargaining power is caused by numerous factors and, first of all, by the structural aspects of sport. The European sports model in its classic form is highly hierarchical.[15] Athletes are placed at the very bottom of the pyramid, i.e., are subject simultaneously to the rules and policies of several sports governing bodies on the different levels (regional, national and international), depending on the level of professionalisation and sporting success.[16] The most powerful organisations, international SGBs, take their institutional and political legitimacy from their recognition by the IOC as the sole administrators of the respective sports discipline.[17] The monopolist position granted by the IOC endows the SGBs with a significant weight at the bargaining table. Primarily, this monopoly allows them to impose regulations on their direct members (affiliated associations) as well as on indirect members (athletes and clubs, as direct members of the affiliated associations).[18] In the framework of their regulatory competence, SGBs adopt different policies to maintain a stable calendar of competitions, guarantee the compliance with health and security standards, etc. In order to compete in the official events, athletes must adhere to these rules. In practice, they do so by signing either a licence (for an extended period of time) or a registration form (for a particular event), but in both cases, it is a pre-drafted contract comprising standard terms, meaning that the formation of the agreement is deprived of any individual negotiations between the parties.[19]

Such agreements include different sets of rules, often by reference to other documents (e.g., the statutes, disciplinary code, etc.). The biggest debate has been

11 Hondius (2004), p. 245; Rühl (2014), pp. 340–342.
12 Hondius (2004), p. 245.
13 Rösler (2010), p. 730; Niedermaier (2015), p. 146.
14 Baddeley, 2020, p. 7; Niedermaier, p. 145.
15 European Commission, European Model of Sport: Consultation Document of DG X (1998), para. 1.1.
16 Szymanski & Ross (2007), p. 618.
17 Rules 3 and 25 of the Olympic Cherter, in force as from 8 August 2021. Available at https://library.olympics.com/Default/doc/SYRACUSE/1088617/olympic-charter-in-force-as-from-8-august-2021-international-olympic-committee
18 Agafonova (2019), p. 89.
19 Rutgers & Sauter (2021), p. 344.

sparkled, undoubtedly, by the arbitration rules (in many cases commonly known as 'the CAS clause'). In effect, the absolute majority of SGBs refer the appeals against the final disciplinary decisions rendered by their internal organs to the exclusive competence of CAS.

The Swiss-based associations as well as the Lausanne-headquartered CAS largely benefit from the Swiss legal order (primarily, the Civil Code and the Swiss Act on International Private Law that governs international arbitration), which traditionally favours the freedom of party autonomy, grants considerable space for self-regulation and very narrow possibilities for legal review of SGBs' decisions and the CAS's awards.[20]

Since the arbitration rules are integrally incorporated in the regulations of an SGB and not detachable from the rest of the agreement between an organisation and an athlete,[21] the latter faces a take-it-or-leave-it choice considering whether to entrust his only means of legal protection to the arbitral institution, which, despite the numerous advantages and ongoing improvements, still provokes doubts about its independence.[22] The ECtHR recognised the SGBs' bargaining superiority, notably, in appointing arbitrators.[23]

Furthermore, as Szymanski and Ross point out, the hierarchical organisation of sport imminently affects the economic possibilities of athletes.[24] There is, undoubtedly, a strong market interdependence between sportsmen and SGBs. On the one hand, athletes are the essential input for the proper organisation of sports competitions: without securing their services, neither an SGB, nor a third-party promoter will mount an event.[25] Moreover, athletes are a very scarce resource: unlike employees in non-sports industries who possess relatively homogeneous skills, it is extremely difficult to substitute a skillset of an elite athlete.[26] On the other hand, as most SGBs have a significant share of the market for the organisation of sports events, they also hold a significant buying power, thus leaving athletes with a limited employment market.[27] Normally, elite sportsmen specialise only in a single discipline from the young age, and are not able to switch to a different sport.[28] For this reason, most athletes become tied to a particular market, and are forced to accept unfavourable terms of the buyers of their services (SGBs).

20 Baddeley (2020), p. 7.
21 Freeburn (2021), pp. 299–300.
22 ECtHR, Mutu and Pechstein v. Switzerland, 2 October 2018, CE:ECHR:2018:-1002JUD004057510, paras. 10, 157–159.
23 Nevertheless, the Court did not find it a sufficient ground to constitute a violation of Article 6§1 of the Convention. On the other hand, in the widely acclaimed dissenting opinion, Judges Keller and Serghides reopened the door for discussion.
24 Szymanski & Ross (2007), p. 618.
25 Decision of the Commission in case AT. 40208 – International Skating Union's Eligibility rules, para. 98.
26 Feldman, 2018, p. 214.
27 Decision of the Commission in case AT. 40208 – International Skating Union's Eligibility rules, para. 198.
28 *Ibid.*, para. 92.

Among these terms, there is often a ban on participation in the events organised by third parties. The non-compliance can be potentially sanctioned with an ineligibility period, putting at risk the chances to further compete at the highest level. As a result, the fear of compromising the entire career often deters athletes from coming aboard a breakaway league.[29] In the conditions of the deficit of available sportsmen, promoters meet considerable difficulties in setting up events, and prospective competitors lose any incentive in entering this market. In the absence of competition, no new investments are made and the financial conditions offered to participants deteriorate. For example, only few official events offer good prize money: primarily, the Olympic Games, sometimes World Championships and/or World Cups. For this reason, in most sports, prize money is not a single source of income.[30] Except for a very limited number of sport stars in commercially onerous sports disciplines,[31] most athletes depend on financial support of family, subsidies or private foundations.

Finally, the weaker position of athletes is complemented by the residual circumstances inherent to sport: the lack of a stable and reliable social network due to frequent traveling,[32] young age, lack of knowledge and of experience in business and legal questions.[33] To put it in terms suggested by Marc Galanter,[34] when it comes to litigation, athletes are 'One-Shotters': they are generally reluctant to have recourse to courts, but when they do, 'the stakes are … high'.[35] In contrast, SGBs are 'Repeat Players': they have more experience in litigation in general, and in specific, repeated cases in particular. In addition, professional athletes have relatively short careers, and try to make the most of their potential during the active years on the top level. Therefore, any litigation is especially time- and money-consuming as it 'jeopardizes a disproportionate percentage of career earning potential'.[36]

All these factors represent different dimensions of the bargaining disadvantage of the individuals who play the central role in the sporting show. Breakaway leagues, organisations and clubs are less vulnerable in this sense: even in the conditions of structural asymmetry, they usually have a better and more sophisticated legal and economic support. Moreover, unlike employees and consumers, athletes do not benefit from any specific provisions designed to protect their substantive and procedural rights from bargaining abuses by stronger contracting partners.[37] Therefore, this function is entirely left to internal sports mechanisms and to general legal provisions.

29 *Ibid.*, paras. 195–196.
30 *Ibid.*, para. 40.
31 *Ibid.*, para. 38.
32 Niedermaier (2015), p. 147.
33 *Ibid.*, p. 147.
34 Galanter (1974), p. 97.
35 Niedermaier (2015), p. 151.
36 Feldman (2018), p. 214.
37 Rutgers & Sauter (2021), p. 344; Baddeley (2020), p. 15.

3.4 Internal sports mechanisms

Some useful mechanisms have been implemented in order to mitigate the weaknesses of the athletes' bargaining position. For instance, as a result of the 2013 Revision to the Code of Sports-related Arbitration (CAS Code), the mechanism of legal aid was implemented in the CAS system. This was a breakthrough as it allowed many athletes with financial difficulties to access the CAS arbitration system and to effectively exercise their legal rights. From a more global perspective, the availability of legal aid contributes to sustaining the legitimacy of the CAS arbitration.[38] Some other sport dispute resolution institutions and sports federations have followed the trend set by the CAS.[39]

Second, players' associations and unions serve to ensure the minimum guarantees of athletes' rights. The term 'players' union' first conjures up the idea of the North American professional sports leagues and collective bargaining agreements (the famous CBAs). A CBA is an agreement reached between a league's owners and the players' union, which serves as the primary governing authority for the relationship between players and their respective teams. Today virtually every employment aspect – from minimum and maximum salaries to practice times and travel expenses – is negotiated and subsequently included in a uniform players' contract.[40] On the one hand, CBAs give players more rights and more leverage by reaching the 'arms' length bargained' standard terms of employment,[41] and, on the other hand, it serve a ground for the non-statutory exemption of the league's rules from the Sherman Act.[42] In Europe, among the most powerful organisations representing athletes are FIFPro (International Federation of Professional Footballers)[43] and EU Athletes (the European multi-sport federation of athlete and player associations).[44] Although these institutions are not yet comparable to the North American players' unions, they play a non-negligible role in discussions with the SGBs. The trend for the democratisation of policy-making is probably the most viable way to strike the balance of forces among all the stakeholders. However, it is unlikely that the democratic regime would be established by itself.

The available sports-specific instruments might be efficient but bring only a limited remedy to the power asymmetries. In practice, the more global imbalance

38 Rigozzi, Hasler & Quinn (2013), para. 92.

39 E.g., FIFA introduces new legal aid system and opens applications for pro bono counsel, 2 September 2019, available at https://www.fifa.com/legal/news/fifa-introduces-new-legal-aid-system-and-opens-applications-for-pro-bono-counsel. (Art. 42 of the FIFA Disciplinary Code); IIHF introduces legal aid program, 14 November 2019, available at https://www.iihf.com/en/news/15933/iihf-introduces-legal-aid-program.

40 Feldman (2018), pp. 212–213.

41 O'Leary (2017), p. 180.

42 O'Leary (2017), pp. 102–103.

43 https://fifpro.org/en/who-we-are.

44 https://euathletes.org/.

caused by structural hierarchy, market dominance and governance unilateralism is likely to be redressed through the pressure from outside.[45]

3.5 EU antitrust mechanisms

And antitrust system can impose such pressure. In the recent decades, the number of antitrust disputes related to sport has been at the rise. The case law of the Court of Justice is very clear in that, while respecting the specific nature of sport, sporting rules are subject to the application of EU competition law.[46]

The crux of the antitrust problem of sport lies in the market dominance of SGBs overlapping with the unresolved conflict of interest between their regulatory and commercial functions. Being the sole governing body in charge of establishing and enforcing sporting rules, SGBs are placed in a perfect position[47] to leverage this regulatory monopoly to the market advantage when they act as organisers and agents exploiting commercial rights in relation to sports events.[48] To obtain such an advantage, it suffices to set up an authorisations system, making the issuance of approvals conditional on various criteria, thus performing a role of a gatekeeper. Before the ISU case, the disputes around the gatekeeping problem had been engaged mostly by third-party promoters and breakaway leagues. The case of ISU stands out because it started with a complaint lodged by athletes.

In the complaint, the two Dutch skaters challenged the eligibility rules of the skating federation,[49] arguing that these provisions violated Articles 101 and 102 TFEU by depriving athletes of the opportunity to commercially exploit their professional skills.[50] In 2017, the Commission rendered a decision finding the infringement of Article 101 TFEU, but most importantly, demonstrated various strengths of EU competition law analysis in tackling the issue of the power imbalance. The Commission undertook a detailed analysis of the current sports market, and of how SGBs leverage their bargaining powers to maintain control in different aspects of their activities, often to the detriment of weaker parties.

First of all, antitrust analysis is based on a complex approach. The problem of bargaining imbalance lies at the intersection of contract law and antitrust: competition law looks at market power and the degree of competition in markets as a whole, while contract law, in principle, focuses on contractual power

45 Baddeley (2020), p. 16.

46 Case 36/74 Walrave and Koch ECLI:EU:C:1974:140, para. 4; Case C-519/04 P Meca-Medina, ECLI:EU:C:2006:492, para. 22; Case C-49/07 MOTOE ECLI:EU:C:2008:376, para. 22.

47 A position that ‘invites abuse’ in the words of Advocate General Kokott in Opinion of AG Kokott in Case C-49/07, MOTOE, delivered on 6 March 2008, para. 88.

48 Decision of the Commission in case AT. 40208 – International Skating Union’s Eligibility rules, paras. 116, 173. See also Opinion of Advocate General Kokott delivered on 6 March 2008 in Case C-49/07 MOTOE ECLI:EU:C:2008:142, paragraph 98.

49 Decision of the Commission in case AT. 40208 – International Skating Union’s Eligibility rules, para. 21.

50 *Ibid.*, para. 22.

in individual transactions.[51] Therefore, antitrust approach seems better equipped for industry-specific bargaining abuses. When assessing an agreement or a decision, one takes into consideration not only a particular situation of the parties, but the sport-related context, including the objectives and necessities of the given industry as well as the actual economic characteristics inherent to its markets.[52]

Second, this approach does not aspire to establish bargaining parity but rather suggests the conditions necessary to ensure market functionality of a given industry. For example, neither Court of Justice in MOTOE nor Commission in the ISU challenged the right of SGBs to conduct economic activities alongside their regulatory functions.[53] Besides, the Commission admitted that these activities were of paramount importance to finance the social tasks through the mechanisms of financial solidarity.

Indeed, SGBs and athletes, despite numerous divergencies and the imbalance of powers, have many overlapping interests, notably the interest in good functioning of sport. The market for sports events would not exist without a regulatory framework.[54] Athletes benefit from this framework established by SGBs just like everybody else. The German *Bundesgerichtshof* formulated this idea in the following way:

> A predominant position of the federation [...] vis-à-vis the athlete [...] could only be deduced [...] if 'federations' and 'athletes' were seen as two 'camps' confronting each other and motivated by opposing interests, as may be the case in other areas, e.g., in disputes involving employers and employees. However, 'federations' and 'athletes' do not represent such opposing camps.[55]

While SGBs are 'competing units with very different individual interests', from a wider standpoint, they still share with athletes common goals and represent parallel interests in many cases.[56]

Therefore, the restrictions necessary to attain these common goals (attain integrity of competitions, health and safety of participants, formation of new generations of sportsmen and sportswomen)[57] might be accepted as serving the legitimate objectives.[58] That said, the effects restrictive of competition caused

51 Rutgers & Sauter (2021), pp. 345–346.

52 Case C-309/99 Wouters and Others [2002] ECLI:EU:C:2002:98, para. 97; Case C-519/04 P Meca-Medina and Majcen v Commission [2006] ECLI:EU:C:2006:492, para. 42.

53 Decision of the Commission in case AT. 40208 – International Skating Union's Eligibility rules, para. 173.

54 Case C-519/04 P Meca-Medina, ECLI:EU:C:2006:492, para. 45.

55 Judgment of the German Federal Court of Justice KZR 6/15 of 7 June 2016, paras. 32–36.

56 *Ibid.*

57 Case C-519/04 P Meca-Medina, ECLI:EU:C:2006:492, para. 43.

58 *Ibid.*, paras. 43, 45; Decision of the Commission in case AT. 40208 – International Skating Union's Eligibility rules, paras. 211, 219.

by a rule or a decision of an SGB should be inherent in the pursuit of the legitimate objectives.[59] The Commission sets a high standard for the assessment of the justifications provided by SGBs, in particular, where it is necessary to demonstrate an actual link between the restrictive measure and its role in attaining the objective.[60]

For example, the Commission did not accept the protection of the ISU's solidarity mechanism (embedded in the ISU Development programme) as the legitimate objective because, instead of mounting a vertical solidarity system (redistribution of financial resources generated by elite sport down towards the grassroots level), the programme implemented a system of horizontal solidarity (redistribution of financial resources between richer and poorer ISU members in order to subsidise competitions hosted by them).[61] In addition, compliance with the requirements of objectivity and transparency are vital for a justification to be accepted. In particular, the ISU failed to demonstrate how solidarity contributions were actually used to finance grassroots sports activities.[62]

Such a functional approach applied by the Commission allows to disentangle the measures genuinely serving the interest of athletes from excessively general objectives serving commercial aspirations of sports federations.

Finally, the anti-competitive effects of a measure adopted by an SGB should be proportionate to the objective.[63] The requirement of proportionality has been the Achilles' heel for many organisations because it not only exposes the bargaining abyss between SGBs and their members but increases this abyss even further. As Baddeley argues,

> [G]iven the unequal weight of parties in sports contention in general, courts must be critical too of the formulation and the scope of the rules applied which are not to exceed, as far as prohibitions and sanctions are concerned, the absolutely necessary for [achieving a legitimate objective] [...] and which must also leave room for [...] the application of principle of proportionality in each case.[64]

In the ISU case, the sanctions provided by the skating federation for participation in non-authorised events were found 'manifestly disproportionate' as they could potentially put an end to a career (in the case of a lifetime ban, provided in 2014 Eligibility rules) and 'excessively punitive' (in the case of a suspension for five to ten years, provided in the 2016 version of the Rules). In addition, the

59 Case C-309/99 Wouters and Others [2002] ECLI:EU:C:2002:98, para. 97.
60 Decision of the Commission in case AT. 40208 – International Skating Union's Eligibility rules, paras. 211–250.
61 *Ibid.*, para. 246.
62 *Ibid.*, para. 247. See more in Kornbeck (2019), pp. 74–76.
63 Case C-519/04 P Meca-Medina, ECLI:EU:C:2006:492, para. 42.
64 Baddeley (2020), p. 16.

ineligibility periods were assessed not in abstract but in application to the realities of skating sport with its short careers.[65] Finally, not only the duration of suspension but also the way of application of these sanctions (no pre-established, clear and transparent criteria) were indicative of disproportionality. In line with all the Commission's findings, the ISU's Eligibility rules were subject of considerable modifications (from 2014 to 2016 to 2018 rules) and became much more detailed. In the latest version, skaters can find more guidance as for the risks associated with their commercial activities.

Another part of the case tackled the question of the procedural guarantees of athletes: do they have a *workable* possibility to access justice in the case of anticompetitive behaviour of an SGB?

As the General Court reminded, once an infringement of competition law was found, in line with a well-established case law of the Court of Justice, 'any person [including organisers who are third parties] is entitled to bring proceedings before a national court and claim compensation for the harm suffered where there is a causal link between that harm and an agreement or practice'.[66] Alternatively, anyone may also lodge a complaint with a national competition authority or the Commission, and, if necessary engage further enforcement mechanism.[67]

Indeed, EU antitrust system seems well placed to review the anticompetitive practices of sports organisations. Its institutions have strong position vis-à-vis Swiss-based associations. EU represents the principal market for most Olympic sports disciplines (with some exceptions).[68] EU law system is fully independent and provides sufficient expertise: the General Court emphasised that, when hearing a case on damages incurred as a result of anticompetitive rules by a sports federation, 'the national court is not bound by the CAS's assessment of the compatibility of [SGB's rules] with EU competition law'.[69]

This position should nevertheless be taken with a grain of salt. Even with the judgment of the General Court, it is difficult not to agree with the logic behind the Commission's reasoning: the exclusive jurisdiction of the CAS, even if legitimate in itself, does have a reinforcing effect on the policies imposed by the SGB[70] and there is a close linked between them as the arbitration clause is the

65 Decision of the Commission in case AT. 40208 – International Skating Union's Eligibility rules, paras. 186, 208.

66 Case T-93/18 International Skating Union v Commission [2020] ECLI:EU:T:2020:610, paras. 157–159; Case C-557/12 Kone and Others [2014] ECLI:EU:C:2014:1317, para. 22; Case C-295/04 Manfredi [2006] ECLI:EU:C:2006:461, paras. 60–61; Case C-453/99 Courage and Crehan [2001] ECLI:EU:C:2001:465, para. 26.

67 Case T-93/18 International Skating Union v Commission [2020] ECLI:EU:T:2020:610, para. 160.

68 Shields v. Fed'n Internationale de Natation, 419 F. Supp. 3d 1188, 1213 (N.D. Cal. 2019). USA is the major market for swimming.

69 Case T-93/18 International Skating Union v Commission [2020] ECLI:EU:T:2020:610, para. 159.

70 Decision of the Commission in case AT. 40208 – International Skating Union's Eligibility rules, para. 286.

procedural rule according to which the substantive rules can only (or most likely to) be appealed before the CAS.[71] Therefore, instead of being the tool mitigating the bargaining imbalance, the CAS clause represents another manifestation of the same imbalance.

3.6 Conclusion

The protection of athletes' rights undoubtedly deserves more attention from the antitrust authorities. Coercive policies of SGBs often significantly restrict commercial opportunities of individuals who try to make a decent living from their vocation, just like others. The structural, legal, economic and social dimensions of bargaining imbalance limit considerably their field of action and increase the degree of dependence from sports federations. Even if solving imbalance issues is not a direct concern of antitrust, it looks beneficial for all stakeholders: protection of the commercial freedom of athletes would naturally bring more competitiveness and opportunities to the market for organisation and commercial exploitation of sports events.

The (still ongoing) ISU case[72] brings along certain advancements in this regard by putting emphasis on the financial component of sports careers of individuals, the chronic unilateralism of decision-makers, and the lack of transparency and accountability of big associations.

It is also interesting to see the interaction between the reasoning of the Commission and the position of the General Court. The latter is more concise, but one can see in its judgment a powerful statement. From the first sight, there is big reluctance about touching upon a delicate issue of CAS arbitration. But the words of the Court can be interpreted as a manifestation of self-sufficiency of the antitrust enforcement system and the full readiness to handle eventual bargaining abuses of sports federations. Would this determination inspire the EU legislator too?

Bibliography

Agafonova, R. (2019) International Skating Union versus European Commission: Is the European sports model under threat? *International Sports Law Journal*, 19, 87–101.

Baddeley, M. (2020) The Extraordinary Autonomy of Sports Bodies Under Swiss Law: Lessons to be Drawn. *International Sports Law Journal*, 20, 3–17.

Feldman, G. (2018) Collective Bargaining in Professional Sports: The Duel between Players and Owners and Labor Law and Antitrust Law. In: McCann, M.A. (ed.) *The Oxford Handbook of American Sports Law*. Oxford: Oxford University Press, 209-205.

Freeburn, L. (2021) Forced Arbitration and Regulatory Power in International Sport – Implications of the Judgment of the European Court of Human Rights in Pechstein and Mutu v. Switzerland. *Marquette Sports Law Review*, 31:2, 287–323.

71 *Ibid.*, para. 280.

72 Case before the Court of Justice C-124/21 P.

Galanter, M. (1974) Why the 'Haves' Come out Ahead: Speculations on the Limits of Legal Change. *Law & Society Review*, 9:1, 95–160.

Helveston, M. & Jacobs, M.S. (2014) The Incoherent Role of Bargaining Power in Contract Law. *Wake Forest Law Review*, 49, 1017–1058.

Hondius, E. (2004) The Protection of the Weak Party in a Harmonised European Contract Law: A Synthesis. *Journal of Consumer Policy*, 27: 245–251.

Kornbeck, J. (2019) Specificity, Monopoly and Solidarity in the European Commission's ISU (International Skating Union) Decision: Anything New Under the Sun? *Journal of European Competition Law & Practice*, 10:2, 71–79.

Niedermaier, T. (2015) The Athlete as the 'Weaker' Party. In: Geisinger, E. & Trabaldo-de Mestral, E. (eds) *Sports Arbitration: A Coach for Other Players?* Huntington, NY: Juris-Net, 145–158.

O'Leary, L. (2017) *Employment and Labour Relations Law in the Premier League, NBA and International Rugby Union*. The Hague: T.M.C. Asser Press.

Rigozzi, A., Hasler, E. & Quinn, B. (2013) The 2011, 2012 and 2013 Revisions to the Code of Sports-related Arbitration. *Jusletter*, https://jusletter.weblaw.ch, 3 juin 2013

Rösler, H. (2010) Protection of the Weaker Party in European Contract Law: Standardized and Individual Inferiority in Multi-Level Private Law. *European Review of Private Law*, 18:4, 729–756.

Rühl, G. (2014) The Protection of Weaker Parties in the Private International Law of the European Union: A Portrait of Inconsistency and Conceptual Truancy. *Journal of Private International Law*, 10:3, 335–358.

Rutgers, J. & Sauter, W. (2021) Promoting Fair Private Governance in the Platform Economy: EU Competition and Contract Law Applied to Standard Terms. *Cambridge Yearbook of European Legal Studies*, 23, 343–381.

Szymanski, S. & Ross, S.F. (2007) Governance and Vertical Integration in Team Sports. *Contemporary Economic Policy*, 25:4, 616–626.

4

THE SUPERLEAGUE CONCEPT IN EUROPEAN FOOTBALL IN THE LIGHT OF EU COMPETITION LAW

Dennis Cukurov

4.1 Introduction

The intersection of sports and competition law is enjoying increasing popularity. Cases like *Bosman*, *Meca-Medina* and *ISU* exemplify the increased importance of sports in competition law and vice versa, as well as the recognition of the respective legal issues as a distinct field of application of law. The newest sports case of the Court of Justice of the EU (CJEU) concerning the European Super League (ESL) proposal is not only of concern to lawyers but also to associations, clubs, fans and investors. The underlying facts illustrate both the commercialisation of sports and the competition law limits applicable to stakeholder activities in the sport business. This is reason enough to take a closer look at the Superleague concept and how competition law can help shaping the future of sports.

The purpose of this chapter is not to provide an exhaustive competition law assessment of all conceivable Superleague models, but to explain the Superleague concept in general and to highlight selected issues of that concept from a competition law perspective. The article does not address the question of whether the measures taken by the associations, namely FIFA and UEFA, to prevent the introduction of Superleagues violate EU competition law. Rather, it focuses on the antitrust issues arising from the hypothetical cooperation of the clubs.

In Section 4.2, the Superleague concept, including the developments that have taken place to date, will be explained, and a model will be selected for assessment under Article 101 TFEU, which will follow in Section 4.3. Section 4.4 will outline some suggestions on what an EU competition law compliant league system could look like – one which could meet both the demands of the top clubs and preserve the principle of 'one association per sport.' Finally, the article will draw a conclusion (Section 4.5).

DOI: 10.4324/9781003305989-4

4.2 The Superleague concept and the concrete model underlying this article

4.2.1 Definition

The term 'Superleague' is well known to the general public, but not yet defined. For the purposes of this chapter, it is assumed that a Superleague is defined as a special sports league that is (i) not part of the established league structures that belong to the existing world and continent-wide associations, and which, unlike other alternative leagues,[1] is (ii) only composed of the very best clubs and athletes within the respective sport. Such a league is not meant to constitute a second championship in a territory that already has a league, but to establish a completely new competition.

4.2.2 Historical outline

The Superleague concept as such is already a few decades old. In fact, the first ideas and efforts in European football date back to the 1980s.[2] The following is a non-exhaustive overview of the projects that have been developed in the past (all relating to professional football):

- The first notable project was initiated in the late 1990s. Media Partners International (MPI), an international rights marketing company, wanted to introduce and operate two new European leagues (Super League and Pro-Cup). The plans for this project were so advanced that it was notified to the European Commission (Commission) in 1999.[3]
- UEFA responded to MPI's plan by modifying its system: it fundamentally restructured its Champions League by changing the format and increasing not only the number of participants from 24 to 32 but also the pay-outs to the clubs.[4] This seemed to satisfy the clubs that were interested in introducing the new leagues back then. The MPI project was cancelled and the notification to the Commission was withdrawn; no decision was taken on the matter.
- In 2000, a Spanish telecommunication company intended to establish a Superleague.[5] Two years later, reports were published about a Superleague initiative (European Golden Cup) by several Spanish entrepreneurs.[6] None of these plans were executed.

1 This would include amateur leagues.
2 Mittag (2018), p. 197.
3 Commission, Notification of a number of agreements concerning the European Football League (Case No IV/37.400 – *Project Gandalf*), OJ C 70, 13 March 1999.
4 Pijetlovic (2015), pp. 59 et seq.; Mittag (2018), p. 202.
5 Mittag (2018), p. 201.
6 Goodbody, J. (2002) Champions League Challenged. *The Times, 21 December 2002, UK, p. 27.*

- Later, seven top clubs ('Big Seven'[7]) allied to form a Superleague, which would have resulted in the participating clubs leaving their respective national leagues and associations.[8]
- In autumn 2018, apparently on the initiative of Real Madrid, a document was drafted for a total of 16 clubs to agree to. This document is believed to have been aimed at creating a Superleague starting in the 2021/22 season.[9]
- In October 2020, it was reported that some of the top clubs from Germany, Spain, France, England and Italy had held discussions about the creation of a Superleague (European Premier League).[10] They were said to be planning to launch a new Superleague with the help of a major bank, which was willing to provide six billion US dollars, as well as other investors.[11]
- In January 2021, a working paper was discussed that included 20 top clubs (15 fixed clubs, five additional clubs elected annually) and a hybrid league format.[12] Following this, FIFA and its continental associations threatened not to recognise a Superleague and that clubs or players participating in it would not be allowed to take part in any competition organised by FIFA or its continental associations.[13]
- In April 2021, news were coming thick and fast: while UEFA was once again drafting and adopting a Champions League reform favourable to the top clubs, 12 clubs[14] announced that they had agreed to create the ESL. The intention – as envisaged in January 2021 – was to introduce a semi-open league with 15 fixed and five additional starting slots, to be played parallel to the national leagues.[15]
- The announcement of the ESL plan sparked major fan protests.[16] UEFA stated that it would exclude clubs and players from competitions such as

7 AC Milan, Arsenal, Barcelona, Bayern Munich, Juventus, Manchester United and Real Madrid.

8 *Der Spiegel* (2018) Dirty Deals. November 2018 (No. 45), Germany, pp. 90 et seq.

9 *Ibid.*, p. 90.

10 Kleinman, M. (2020) Top English Clubs in Bombshell Talks to Join European Premier League. *Sky News* online, 20 October 2020, UK. https://news.sky.com/story/top-english-clubs-in-bombshell-talks-to-join-european-premier-league-12109175.

11 *Ibid.*

12 Ziegler, M. (2021) European Superleague Would Have Six Premier League Teams – Each Paid up to £310m to Join. *The Times* online, 21 January 2021, UK. https://www.thetimes.co.uk/article/european-super-league-would-have-six-premier-league-teams-each-being-paid-up-to-310m-to-join-63prbtbfl.

13 Wallace, S. (2021) Fifa Threatens World Cup Bans for Any Players Competing in Breakaway European Super League. *The Telegraph* online, 21 January 2021, UK. https://www.telegraph.co.uk/football/2021/01/21/footballs-confederations-warn-players-involved-european-super/

14 Barcelona, Real Madrid, Atlético Madrid, Juventus, AC Milan, Inter Milan, Manchester United, Manchester City, Arsenal, Chelsea, Liverpool and Tottenham.

15 Panja, T. (2021) Top European Soccer Teams Form Breakaway League. *The New York Times* online, 18 April 2021, US. https://www.nytimes.com/2021/04/18/sports/soccer/super-league-united-liverpool-juventus-madrid.html.

16 Panja, T. (2021) Super League Collapses as Premier League Teams Walk Away. *The New York Times* online, 20 April 2021, US. https://www.nytimes.com/2021/04/20/sports/soccer/super-league-collapse.html.

the European Championship if they were participating in the ESL.[17] As a result, only a few days after the ESL plan was announced, almost all of the participating clubs withdrew from the project.[18] The remaining three clubs (Real Madrid, Barcelona and Juventus) recognised that the establishment of the ESL could not be completed as planned, but were not willing to abandon the idea as such. They filed a lawsuit against FIFA and UEFA before a Spanish court, which later referred the matter to the CJEU, in order to clarify whether the two football associations FIFA and UEFA violated European competition law by blocking the introduction of a Superleague in football.[19] Thus, at least Real Madrid, Barcelona and Juventus seem to remain interested in establishing the Superleague concept.

4.2.3 Variety of possible models and the Superleague model underlying this chapter

In principle, any legal limits aside, the clubs are entirely free in designing their new league. They can decide which features their product should have. There are two main league features to consider:

- Should multiple membership be possible or should the clubs be prohibited from competing in other leagues, i.e. should they play exclusively in the Superleague to be established?
- Should the new league be closed or open, i.e. should promotions and relegations be possible?

These two questions alone result in four possible combinations. Since a league cannot only be closed or open, but also semi-open, the number of possible combinations increases. Of course, not all conceivable constellations can be examined here. Thus, the discussion below is based on a closed and exclusive league model, assuming that such a model comes closest to the wishes of the clubs that (still) want to introduce a Superleague.

4.2.4 Need for a Superleague due to current circumstances?

Before going into the legal considerations, it is important to briefly point out where the intention of establishing a Superleague comes from and whether or not a Superleague is just the logical consequence of and possibly the solution to the continuing lack of suspense in Europe's top football leagues.

In the European top leagues, it is the top clubs that decide the championship among themselves year after year.[20] From 2011 to 2020, Juventus won the Italian championship nine times in a row; so did Bayern Munich in Germany from 2012

17 *Ibid.*
18 *Ibid.*
19 See Case C-333/21, *ESL Company*.
20 Cf. Heermann (2015).

to 2021. Further, it is certainly not unusual for smaller clubs to be 'blown out' by the top clubs. Looking at Bayern Munich, for example, big wins are more or less the norm. In the 2021/2022 Bundesliga season, Bayern Munich often won by a difference of four or more goals.[21] In the Premier League, La Liga and Ligue 1, too, the top clubs have been dominating for decades.

With this in mind, the 'lack of suspense' can become an economic problem. This is because suspense is often considered an essential factor for viewers' interest ('uncertainty of outcome' hypothesis) and their willingness to pay.[22] Although not uncontroversial,[23] it can be assumed that viewers prefer uncertainty and some degree of competitive balance.[24] Thus, if there is no competitive balance in a league, viewers may lose interest in it.[25]

Now, in order to keep the product (the league) attractive, consideration needs to be given to whether measures should be taken to tackle the emerging boredom. In this light, the establishment of a Superleague could be a possible way forward. The top clubs could be taken out of the national leagues, helping to revive some of the suspense they have long lost.[26]

4.3 Antitrust assessment: would the creation of a Superleague violate Article 101 TFEU?

4.3.1 Anti-competitive aspects of the clubs' cooperation

From an antitrust point of view, any cooperation between the top clubs for the purpose of introducing and running the new league would require closer attention.[27] This includes all agreements between the clubs, whether written or verbal.

Competition could be restricted by the interaction as such ('abstract level') and, in particular, by all agreements aimed at establishing and operating an exclusive/closed league ('concrete model'). With the founding agreement, the clubs, as independent companies, would make a joint decision to jointly offer

21 As of 30 March 2022: 5:0 v. Hertha Berlin (28 August 2021); 7:0 v. Bochum (18 September 2021); 1:5 v. Leverkusen (17 October 2021); 4:0 v. Hoffenheim (23 October 2021); 0:5 v. Stuttgart (14 December 2021); 4:0 v. Wolfsburg (17 December 2021); 0:4 v. Cologne (15 January 2022); 4:0 v. Union Berlin (19 March 2022).

22 For the uncertainty of outcome hypothesis, see, e.g., Neale (1964), pp. 1 et seq.; Szymanski (2003), pp. 1155 *et seq*. See also Monti (2000), p. 4.

23 See, e.g., Szymanski (2003), p. 1156; Vrooman (2007a), p. 311; Ross (2013), p. 319; Heermann (2020), pp. 310 *et seq*.

24 For an overview of the evidence, see Szymanski (2010), pp. 26 *et seq*.

25 Cf. Buzzacchi, Szymanski & Valletti (2003), p. 168.

26 Cf. Hoehn & Szymanski (1999), p. 224.

27 There is no doubt (any longer) that EU competition law is applicable in the sports sector, also with regard to sporting rules, see, e.g., Podszun (2021), pp. 139 et seq.; Whish and Bailey (2021), p. 142. See also Kornbeck (2017), pp. 72 et seq.; Pijetlovic (2017), p. 100; Weatherill (2021), pp. 9 *et seq*.

a product. The permanent exclusivity would restrict the economic autonomy of the clubs concluding the founding agreement, as these would no longer be free to participate in other football competitions, whether at the European or the national level. Rather, they would be tied to a single league and the related economic activities.

Permanent exclusivity would also have a negative external effect: UEFA and potential competitors, i.e. those who might want to introduce other European top football competitions, such as another Superleague, would face barriers to market entry due to the exclusivity of the existing Superleague. They would no longer be able to recruit the clubs that have agreed on forming their own league.

Closedness as the second league feature would also have to be regarded as a restriction of competition by object. The founding clubs would not be exposed to any competition with regard to their Superleague starting places. This would strongly contravene the principle of competition and foster enormous inefficiencies: If the competitive pressure were taken away from the top clubs, they would run the risk of using their resources inefficiently in the long run. Consequently, prices could rise and the quality of the products, after a possible significant improvement at the beginning, could decline.

Moreover, the other European clubs would not have the opportunity to qualify for the new football league. This would, in turn, result in restrictions of their economic options, and lead to market foreclosure.[28] Also, the potential organisers of alternative Superleagues would only have limited possibilities to compete with the Superleague, which would be due to the nature of the Superleague founding agreement and its closed nature. Assuming that a Superleague would create a new, independent market and regardless of whether alternative providers would quickly enter such a market, it would have to be taken into account that the league being permanently composed of clubs such as Real Madrid and Juventus would enormously reduce the interest in any other Superleague. As a consequence, this closed league would likely be commonly regarded as *the* Superleague. This would lead to serious difficulties for potential competitors in attracting spectators and advertising and media partners, except for the (die-hard) fans of the clubs they can attract for their offering. If no alternative Superleague was formed because of the closed Superleague, there would be no European competition running at a comparable level.

4.3.2 Approaches to justification

The above restrictions could be justified, i.e. not be subject to Article 101(1) TFEU or exempt under Article 101(3) TFEU, on the basis of the specific design and related advantages of a Superleague.

28 Cf. Parrish (2003), p. 133. But see Hornsby (2001), p. 167, who points out that 'forcing access to a "closed league" cannot be justified by recourse to the competition rules' if alternative leagues are conceivable.

4.3.2.1 Assessment of the cooperation as such

The cooperation as such, i.e. the mere joint decision of independent companies (the clubs) to jointly offer a product (the league), could be considered as justified.

A sports league is a joint product that no club can offer on its own.[29] A certain degree of cooperation is necessary to be able to create the product.[30] Irrespective of the specific model examined here, the decision to establish a football Superleague would therefore fulfil the requirements of the test that the CJEU developed in *Meca-Medina*[31] in 2006 (Meca-Medina test).[32] The cooperation would have a legitimate objective, because without cooperation, there would be no league at all, and without football leagues, there would be no league football. The restrictions of competition resulting from the cooperation would also be necessary and proportionate. Less restrictive alternatives are not conceivable.

The requirements of Article 101(3) TFEU would also be met. Only if the clubs cooperated the product 'Superleague' could be offered to consumers. The (mere) decision to form a league would also be indispensable for the existence ('production') of the league, and would not eliminate (but rather create) competition.

4.3.2.2 Assessment of exclusivity and closedness

The conditions of exclusivity and closedness, on the other hand, could not be justified by the fact that a Superleague as a product could not otherwise be produced and offered. This is because the organisation of leagues in sports is not conditional on having exclusive participants and being closed. On the contrary, sports leagues in Europe are usually non-exclusive and open.

In principle, however, one could argue that stimulating competition and improving the competitive balance could be a justification for an exclusive and closed league. This is examined in detail below.

4.3.2.2.1 The Meca-Medina test

The first requirement of the Meca-Medina test is a 'legitimate objective,' the exact definition and limits of which have not been clarified yet. A proper interpretation of this term, however, should be a narrow one.[33] The main reason is that it is crucial to protect effective competition, not to apply generous standards of justification to enable anti-competitive behaviour in the sports sector. Thus, legitimate objectives should only be those that are directed at the existence or functioning of sports or a particular sport.

29 Neale (1964), pp. 2 *et seq.*
30 Kesenne (2015), p. 811.
31 CJEU, decision of 18 July 2006, Case C-519/04 P, *Meca-Medina and Majcen.*
32 To be precise, in *Meca-Medina*, the CJEU for the first time applied the three-step test developed in *Wouters* (CJEU, decision of 19 February 2002, Case C-309/99) to a sports-related case.
33 Cukurov (2021), pp. 189 *et seq.*

Here, the stimulation of competition could not be considered as a legitimate objective within the meaning of the Meca-Medina test. Neither the breaking of UEFA's monopoly nor the expansion of the offer affect the existence or functioning of European football. To date, European club football has functioned without an exclusive and closed Superleague.

An improvement of the competitive balance in European club football could also not be regarded as a legitimate objective. Competitive balance in general cannot qualify as a legitimate objective within the meaning of the Meca-Medina test, as improving competitive balance has no impact on the existence or functioning of club football. It merely promotes its commercialisation.

4.3.2.2.2 Article 101(3) TFEU

If the Meca-Medina criteria are not met, justification can still be based on an exemption pursuant to Article 101(3) TFEU. This would require (i) the cooperation to lead to efficiencies (ii) in which consumers would have a fair share, (iii) the restriction of competition to be indispensable to the attainment of these benefits, and (iv) for competition to not be eliminated as a result.

4.3.2.2.2.1 Stimulating competition as an efficiency gain?

At first glance, the stimulation of competition could be classified as an efficiency gain. The disruption of UEFA's monopoly regarding the organisation of football events by the entry of another organiser and the resulting addition to the range of football events available creates benefits for competition. However, in the context of sports, it must be noted that the addition of another provider does not necessarily lead to an improvement for consumers. A fragmentation of club football would probably have the opposite effect. This is because there is a basic human need to determine the best,[34] and a concept with one league and one champion comes closest to this need. The introduction of a Superleague would not be of much use to consumers if, after its introduction, the same sporting conditions remained the same and only the organiser and the name of the competition changed. Even if the addition of another provider were to be classified as a significant efficiency gain, this efficiency gain would in any case not be sufficient to compensate for the restrictions of competition. The exclusion of all other clubs and the entry barriers that other organisers would face with an exclusive and closed Superleague would likely significantly outweigh the mere stimulation of competition in an already well-functioning market.

4.3.2.2.2.2 Improving competitive balance as an efficiency gain?

The improvement of the competitive balance in European club football could only be considered to be an efficiency gain for the purposes of EU competition

34 See Cukurov (2021), pp. 72 *et seq.*

law if a Superleague would positively affect the situation in the football leagues in Europe. It could not be considered an efficiency gain if the situation remained more or less unchanged. However, the latter is more likely to occur, as the following statistical analysis suggests.[35]

For the sake of argument, it shall be assumed that the following clubs would play in a Superleague: Real Madrid, Barcelona, Atlético Madrid, Bayern Munich, Borussia Dortmund, Leipzig, Juventus, Roma, AC Milan, Liverpool, Chelsea, Manchester City, Manchester United, Arsenal, Paris, Monaco, Ajax, FC Porto, Shakhtar Donetsk and Zenit (Model Superleague, MSL).[36] Their performances in UEFA's competitions (UEFA Club Coefficients) and, for the national leagues, the accumulated points shall serve as comparative values.[37] The coefficient of variation (CV) and the concentration ratio (CR) shall serve as objective comparison parameters.

The CV is a statistical parameter that indicates the dispersion of the results in a sample around the arithmetic mean. It does not depend on the unit of measurement of the comparative values. The higher the CV, the greater the imbalance of the league.

CR is a key figure for the absolute concentration. It indicates the share of the largest feature carriers in relation to the total value of the selected feature. CR_5 thus indicates the share of the five largest feature carriers. To put it in terms of sports leagues: the higher the value, the more dominant are the five best teams in the league.

This analytical set-up leads to the following results for the last three seasons before[38] the COVID-19 pandemic (Table 4.1).

TABLE 4.1 Competitive balance in MSL (2016–2019)

MSL	*18/19*	*16–19*
CV	0.4211	0.4811
CR_5	0.3737	0.3885

35 For an in-depth analysis on the basis of various comparison parameters, see Cukurov (2021), pp. 249 *et seq*.

36 These are clubs that have been associated with the Superleague idea as well as clubs outside the top 5 leagues that have performed well in European competitions over the last decade. Tottenham and Inter Milan were never serious candidates for a Superleague until April 2021, and were therefore not considered.

37 All figures available at https://www.transfermarkt.com/ and https://www.uefa.com/nationalassociations/uefarankings/.

38 Sporting competition was distorted by the COVID-19 pandemic and the 'ghost games', see, e.g., Fischer & Haucap (2020). Even today, many stadiums in Europe are not at full capacity.

A look at Europe's top leagues in recent years shows that the MSL figures are not better, but strikingly worse (Table 4.2).

TABLE 4.2 Competitive balance in Europe's top five leagues (2016–2019)

	Bundesliga		*Primera División*		*Ligue 1*		*Premier League*		*Serie A*	
	18/19	*16–19*	*18/19*	*16–19*	*18/19*	*16–19*	*18/19*	*16–19*	*18/19*	*16–19*
CV	0.3623	0.3204	0.2701	0.3361	0.3130	0.3285	0.3930	0.3791	0.3568	0.3779
CR_5	0.3941	0.3839	0.3408	0.3613	0.3544	0.3653	0.3817	0.3851	0.3644	0.3775

When looking at the teams that finished in the top five places in the European top leagues (top 5) and analysing which clubs would have finished in the top five had the Superleague clubs not been in the mix, it is quite obvious that other clubs would have taken over the dominant roles, especially in England and Italy. So in this respect, too, hardly anything would have changed (Tables 4.3 and 4.4).

TABLE 4.3 Alternative top 5 Premier League clubs (2016–2019)

Premier League	*Champion*	*Other teams in top five*	*Alternative champion*	*Alternative other teams in top five*
16/17	Chelsea	Tottenham	Tottenham	Everton
		Manchester City		West Ham
		Liverpool		Southampton
		Arsenal		West Brom
17/18	Manchester City	Manchester United	Tottenham	Burnley
		Tottenham		Everton
		Liverpool		Leicester
		Chelsea		Crystal Palace
18/19	Manchester City	Liverpool	Tottenham	Watford
		Chelsea		West Ham
		Tottenham		Wanderers
		Arsenal		Everton

Admittedly, the above analysis is of a purely theoretical nature as it seeks to compare alternate scenarios that might occur *if* a Superleague were to be established (i.e. if a new feature was added which entails certain dynamics) while relying on past data that was gathered in absence of such a league (i.e. data relating to static, historic events). However, it is an indication that removing the current top clubs from their respective leagues and grouping them together in a Superleague would likely repeat the pattern of concentration in both the national leagues and the Superleague – as the latter would also be prone to the dominance of the narrow tier of elite clubs which tend to repeatedly win Europe's current top football tournament, i.e. the Champions League. In the absence of any contradictory analyses, it can thus be assumed that the competitive balance would not be improved by a Superleague and that it would therefore not provide efficiency gains.

TABLE 4.4 Alternative top 5 Serie A clubs (2016–2019)

Serie A	*Champion*	*Other teams in the top five*	*Alternative champion*	*Alternative other teams in the top five*
16/17	Juventus	Roma Napoli Bergamo Lazio	Napoli	Lazio Bergamo Inter Milan Fiorentina
17/18	Juventus	Napoli Roma Inter Milan Lazio	Napoli	Lazio Inter Milan Fiorentina Bergamo
18/19	Juventus	Napoli Bergamo Inter Milan AC Milan	Napoli	Bergamo Inter Milan Torino Lazio

4.3.3 Result of the antitrust assessment

In the author's view, the Superleague model assessed here could not be justified. Although the cooperation for the purpose of establishing a league does not raise any concerns under EU competition law, the cooperation to establish an exclusive and closed Superleague would not be compatible with Article 101 TFEU.

4.4 Proposal for a genuine European league system

4.4.1 The underpinning and the goal: 'soft detachment' and 'Europeanisation'

If an exclusive and closed Superleague cannot be established for competition law reasons, but the top clubs do not want to accept the current situation, what is the (competition law-compliant) alternative? The alternative is the integration of a Superleague into the existing league systems.

The top clubs could opt for an approach of 'soft detachment'[39] by creating a league that would be integrated into the established league systems by means of a promotion and relegation mechanism. This could serve the interests of UEFA, the top clubs as well as other European clubs, including those in the lower leagues.

Specifically, the clubs establishing the Superleague could involve UEFA, entrusting it with the (time- and work-intensive) task of providing the organisational rules, creating a level playing field, without losing control over the event

39 For a possible distinction between 'soft break-away' and 'hard break-away,' see Boyes (2016), pp. 30 *et seq.*

and distribution of profits. UEFA would probably not be averse to such cooperation, as this would serve its interests by maintaining its influence in European club football and the 'one association per sport' principle.

The interests of the top clubs could be served as well, despite the identified competition law limits. An *un*limited participation guarantee in the Superleague would be problematic under competition law. It would have similar foreclosing effects as the establishment of a closed league and could not be justified because it would not have the objective of maintaining the existence or functioning of the league. However, a limited participation guarantee should be workable. If a participation guarantee is limited to five years, market access would appear to be sufficiently preserved.[40]

Finally, the opportunity for promotion to a top European league would have at least some positive effects for the lower leagues. Their clubs would have the opportunity to be promoted to the top European league by being integrated into an overall system. Since the top clubs would play in the top European league, they would not hinder the smaller clubs from winning national championships and being promoted to the European league. Furthermore, the chances of signing (young) top players would improve after a promotion, so that it would not be impossible for a promoted club to stay and compete in the top European league for several years.

This would have a broader benefit as well: A Superleague integrated into the existing systems could further advance the process of 'Europeanisation,' which, from a legal point of view,[41] was pushed forward by EU law and above all by the *Bosman* decision[42] of the CJEU.

'Europeanisation' would be beneficial for two reasons: (i) the organisation of more European matches could lead to a better realisation of the full European market potential, and (ii) there would be more high-class matches that could arouse the interest of new spectators or increase the interest of already convinced spectators (fans). The reason is that games at the European level usually have a larger audience because of the involvement of different countries (compared to national football matches, for which the audience is usually much smaller).

4.4.2 The proposal

The following proposal[43] seems to be a reasonable compromise:

Instead of the Champions League and Europa League, two new competitions could be introduced: League A and League B. The Champions League and

40 The idea behind this is that the Vertical Block Exemption Regulation (VBER) considers exclusivity for terms of up to five years to be unproblematic if the market shares of the parties involved are below 30%.

41 Of course, this process is also influenced by many other factors, such as macro-level trends, populism and Brexit, which Kornbeck (2022), p. 244, explicitly points out.

42 CJEU, decision of 15 December 1995, Case C-415/93, *Bosman*.

43 Based on Hoeksma (2000), pp. 10 et seq., Vrooman (2007b), pp. 348 *et seq.*, and Kesenne (2007), pp. 393 *et seq.*

Europa League would be discontinued. European matches would then only be possible in League A and League B. League A would be organised and marketed by the top clubs themselves. UEFA would only be responsible for the organisational framework, in particular setting up and enforcing the rules of the game. League A would be Europe's top tier league, League B would be Europe's second tier league. The national leagues would be connected directly below.

League A could be structured as a semi-open league. The founding clubs, for example, the Big Seven, could have five-year licences that prevent relegation to League B even in the event of poor performance. At the end of every five years, these licences would be renewed or reissued, for example, on the basis of sporting success. This would ensure that the top clubs received the desired planning security. At the same time, not too many starting places in League A would be permanently blocked.

The integration into the well-established league structures could prevent the creation of parallel systems that would make the comparability of sporting performances more difficult. Such a system, however, presupposes UEFA's willingness to cooperate. It would have to give up its position as the sole organiser of European football competitions and, as far as League A is concerned, limit itself to association activities only. UEFA could, however, be the organiser of League B.

League A could consist of 20 clubs and be played in a hybrid format with 38 match days followed by playoffs. The playoffs would have the decisive advantage that the suspense would be maintained even if a League A club got far ahead early in the regular season. This would presumably keep the spectators' willingness to pay high.

The playoffs could consist of a total of three rounds: the quarter-finals (the first-place team against the eighth-place team, the second-place team against the seventh-place team, the third-place team against the sixth-place team, the fourth-place team against the fifth-place team), the semi-finals and the League A final. These three rounds could be played without second legs on neutral ground.[44] The winner of the final would become European champion.

The last four clubs after the regular season could be relegated to League B. Since the openness of the leagues in European football, as argued above, is a fundamental requirement under EU competition law, at least four clubs should be relegated in order to keep the fluctuation high and give the clubs in the lower leagues more chances to be promoted to the highest league.

The subordinate League B could also consist of 20 clubs, also with a regular season in round robin format and playoffs. The semi-finalists of the playoffs could be promoted to League A. Again, four clubs should be relegated to the subordinate national leagues (Bundesliga, Primera División, Ligue 1, Premier League, Serie A, etc.).

44 As in the 2019/2020 Champions League season.

A new competition could be held at the end of each season – the Champions Cup (playoffs without second legs on neutral ground). Only the champions of the first leagues of the 55 UEFA associations would be eligible to participate in this tournament. The opponents could be drawn by lot. In the first round, nine clubs would then receive 'wild cards' and automatically advance to the second round.

In addition, national cup competitions (DFB Cup, etc.) would continue to exist. This would give internationally less successful clubs the opportunity to compete with the top clubs of their national associations.

This restructuring would entail losses for all those football clubs that regularly play in the Champions League and the Europa League, but would only compete in the national leagues and initially not play any European matches. Their losses could be compensated by solidarity payments, which the top clubs would have to bear. It is fair to assume that the expected sales in Leagues A and B would easily allow for such adjusted solidarity payments (Table 4.5).

TABLE 4.5 Proposal for a future European football league system

League A	
Best 8 teams qualify for playoffs Last 4 teams are relegated to League B	Playoffs (8 teams) Winner is the 'European champion'
League B	
Best 8 teams qualify for playoffs Last 4 teams are relegated to national top tier leagues	Playoffs (8 teams) Teams in semi-finals are promoted to League A
55 European top-tier leagues	
55 national champions (best teams after regular season) play a knockout tournament (Champions Cup)	Winner is the 'Champion of the European national leagues' Teams in semi-finals are promoted to League B
European lower leagues (connected to national top tier leagues through promotion-relegation system)	

4.5 Conclusion and outlook

Irrespective of whether the associations may prohibit the clubs from establishing their own Superleague, or whether measures aiming at this are compatible with EU competition law, any cooperation between the clubs for the purpose of establishing an exclusive and closed Superleague has to be considered critically under competition law. In the author's view, the specific model outlined above would constitute a restriction of competition and could not be justified. In particular, the competitive balance would not improve in view of the above results.

However, the current lack of suspense in Europe's top leagues calls for change. If nothing changes, the market volume could decrease, as spectators (and other stakeholders such as broadcasters, sponsors, etc.) might not be willing to pay more or only be willing to pay less in the future. The top clubs' dissatisfaction, which is evident in the efforts to establish a Superleague, is also an indicator that change is inevitable. Therefore, the associations are under pressure to act and for this reason would be well advised to initiate fundamental changes.

The author proposes a 'Europeanisation' of football. On the one hand, this would meet the interests of the top clubs, as they could organise Europe's highest league themselves. On the other hand, the associations would retain their sovereignty over the sport and oversee all other leagues below the European top league.

With the proposed concept, suspense could rise again, not only at the top but also at the national level, where clubs that have been average performers in the recent past could (once again) play for trophies and, due to the promotion and relegation system, push all the way to the top. Such a system would fuel competition and keep markets open, ultimately putting sporting success first.

Bibliography

Boyes, S. (2016) Don't Take Away my Break-Away: Balancing Regulatory and Commercial Interests in Sport. *Nottingham Law Journal*, 25, 28–38.

Buzzacchi, L., Szymanski, S. & Valletti, T.M. (2003) Equality of Opportunity and Equality of Outcome: Open Leagues, Closed Leagues and Competitive Balance. *Journal of Industry, Competition and Trade*, 3:3, 167–186.

Cukurov, D. (2021) *Kartellrechtliche Zulässigkeit von Superligen im Fußball*. Baden-Baden: Nomos.

Fischer, K. & Haucap, J. (2020) Does Crowd Support Drive the Home Advantage in Professional Soccer? *Dice Discussion Papers*, No. 344, Heinrich Heine University Düsseldorf, Germany.

Heermann, P.W. (2015) Sportlich ausgeglichene Wettbewerbe durch Kartellrecht? *Wirtschaft und Wettbewerb*, 12/2015, 1187.

Heermann, P.W. (2020) Rechtfertigung einer Zentralvermarktung der Fußballübertragungsrechte nach Art. 101 Abs. 3 AEUV im Wandel der Zeit. In: Ahrens, H.-J., Büscher, W., Goldmann, M. and McGuire, M.-R. (eds) *Praxis des Geistigen Eigentums: Festschrift für Henning Harte-Bavendamm zum 70. Geburtstag*. Munich: C.H. Beck, 303–317.

Hoehn, T. & Szymanski, S. (1999) The Americanization of European Football. *Economic Policy*, 14:28, 203–240.

Hoeksma, J.A. (2000) The Future of Professional Football in Europe. *International Sports Law Journal*, May 2000, 8–11.

Hornsby, S. (2001) "Closed Leagues": A Prime Candidate for the "sporting exception" in European Competition Law? *International Sports Law Review*, 2 (June), 161–167.

Kesenne, S. (2007) The Peculiar International Economics of Professional Football in Europe. *Scottish Journal of Political Economy*, 54:3, 388–399.

Kesenne, S. (2015) The Single Entity Status of a Sports League. *Journal of Sports Economics*, 16:8, 811–818.

Kornbeck, J. (2017) Specificity, Monopoly and Solidarity in the European Commission's ISU (International Skating Union) Decision: Anything New Under the Sun? *Journal of European Competition Law & Practice*, 10:2, 71–79.

Kornbeck, J. (2022) Conclusion: Sport regulation between Brussels Effect and Brexit Dividend. In: Kornbeck, J. (ed) *Sport and Brexit: Regulatory Challenges and Legacies*. Abingdon: Routledge, 224–248.

Mittag, J. (2018) Aufstieg und Auflösung der G14: Episode oder Paradebeispiel der Konfliktregulierung europäischer Sportpolitik? In: Mittag, J. (ed) *Europäische Sportpolitik: Zugänge – Akteure – Problemfelder.* Baden-Baden: Nomos, 195–215.

Monti, M. (2000) A level playing field in sport and in sport business. *International Sports Law Journal*, May 2000, 4–6.

Neale, W.C. (1964) The Peculiar Economics of Professional Sports. *The Quarterly Journal of Economics*, 78:1, 1–14.

Parrish, R. (2003) *Sports Law and Policy in the European Union.* Manchester: Manchester University Press.

Pijetlovic, K. (2015) *EU Sports Law and Breakaway Leagues in Football.* The Hague: T.M.C. Asser Press.

Pijetlovic, K. (2017) EU Sports Law: A Uniform Algorithm for Regulatory Rules. *International Sports Law Journal*, 17:86, 86–100.

Podszun, R. (2021) Anwendbarkeit des Kartellrechts auf die Regulierung von Spielervermittlern durch Sportverbände. *Neue Zeitschrift für Kartellrecht*, 3/2021, 138–147.

Ross, S.F. (2013) Competition Law and Labor Markets. In: Nafziger, J.A.R. and Ross, S.F. (eds) *Handbook on International Sports Law.* Cheltenham: Edward Elgar Publishing, 311–338.

Szyszczak, E. (2007) Competition and Sport. *European Law Review*, 32:1, 95–110.

Szymanski, S. (2003) The Economic Design of Sporting Contests. *Journal of Economic Literature*, 41:4, 1137–1187.

Szymanski, S. (2010) The Economic Design of Sporting Contests. In: Szymanski, S. (ed.) *The Comparative Economics of Sport.* Basingstoke: Palgrave Macmillan, 1–78.

Vrooman, J. (2007a) Economics of Sport: Editor's Introduction. *Scottish Journal of Political Economy*, 54:3, 309–313.

Vrooman, J. (2007b) Theory of the Beautiful Game: the Unification of European Football. *Scottish Journal of Political Economy*, 54:3, 314–354.

Weatherill, S. (2021) The EU as a Sports Regulator. Forthcoming in Nafziger, J. & Gauthier, R. (eds) *Handbook on International Sports Law.* 2nd edition. Cheltenham: Edward Elgar Publishing). *SSRN Papers.* https://ssrn.com/abstract=3872699

Whish, R. & Bailey, D. (2021) *Competition Law.* Oxford: Oxford University Press.

5

THE APPLICATION OF ANTITRUST LEGISLATION BY SWISS COURTS IN CASES INVOLVING INTERNATIONAL SPORTS GOVERNING BODIES

Margareta Baddeley

5.1 Questions raised

Although a small country not belonging to the European Union (EU), Switzerland often draws international attention to itself in matters relating to competition sport as the host country to many international sports governing bodies (ISGBs), amongst them the most powerful ones: the International Olympic Committee (IOC), Fédération Internationale de Football Association (FIFA), Union of European Football Associations (UEFA) and Court of Arbitration in Sport (CAS).

Competition sport creates litigation before competitions as well as on and beyond the playing field, with the final decision usually taken on the basis of the ISGBs' regulations by national or international sports bodies. These regulations generally provide for appeals within the SGBs or to outside judicial bodies, nowadays frequently the CAS or other arbitral tribunals (although procedures in ordinary State courts are possible). Such decisions can then be challenged in higher courts or before other public authorities, on a national or supra-national level, with the European Union (EU) authorities and the European Court of Human Rights (ECtHR) playing an important role. As concerns Swiss law, decisions of SGBs can be submitted successively to three judicial instances in regular procedures, but decisions by CAS can be challenged in most cases only before the Swiss Federal Tribunal (SFT), the highest Swiss court, and subsequently before the ECtHR.

Reviews by national and supra-national authorities have led to important changes in the regulations of the ISGBs not compliant with mandatory law. Some of the decisions of the EU authorities have sent shock waves through the sporting world and have proven that mandatory law, and therefore also EU antitrust law, the core subject of this publication, is also applicable to sports under the regulations of

DOI: 10.4324/9781003305989-5

the ISGBs.[1] By contrast, and rather astonishingly, cases decided by the SFT might have given the opposite impression. And this impression is not wrong.

This phenomenon is the result of three essential factors: the legal status of the ISGBs as associations under Swiss law and the quasi-absence of supervision by public authorities of regulations of ISGBs (Section 5.2), the priority given by law to self-regulation by the ISGBs combined with the general leniency of courts in favour of associations, especially in sports (Section 5.3) and, finally, the hands-off regime enshrined in Swiss international private law as regards the review of arbitral awards (Section 5.4). The result of these developments will be summed up in the last section of this contribution (Section 5.5).

5.2 The legal status of the ISGBs set up under Swiss law as associations or foundations and their supervision by public authorities

Swiss law does not provide a special legal status for sports regulatory bodies and does not contain special provisions for such bodies. Not being set up by States and not executing state functions by delegation, ISGBs in Switzerland are *not* international organisations.[2] They resemble to a certain degree international *non*-governmental organisations (NGOs).[3] Therefore, ISGBs and other entities active in sports can be constituted (only) under one of the **legal forms** provided by **private law** and are subject to the relevant provisions of law.

The ISGBs established in Switzerland are nearly exclusively **associations** as per Articles 60 seq. Swiss Civil Code (SCC),[4] with their titles most of the time including the terms 'association' (e.g. International Boxing Association), 'fédération' (e.g. Fédération Internationale de Football Amateur, International Ice Hockey Federation) or 'union' (e.g. Union Cycliste Internationale, Union of European Football Associations). Physical persons or legal entities can be (founding) members of associations. The ISGBs' members are generally the next lower

1 See in this regard, J. Kornbeck's introduction to this book, as well as Kornbeck (2018); Heermann (2019b); Del Fabro Marco (2018).

2 The statement in the statutes of some ISGBs that they are 'international … organisations' might be misleading in this respect. As to WADA, see fn. 8. The private law nature of (I)SGBs does not exclude support of different kinds by public authorities to promote (youth, competition, clean, etc.) sports and sporting events. The qualification of ISGBs as private law entities is important also in other fields of law, especially as concerns tax law and penal law; cf. Cassani & May (2017), pp. 353 f. ; Mbenge (2017), p. 427.

3 As the SFT states in its decisions 129 III 445, par. A.a. (IOC), 138 III 322, par. A.a. (FIFA). SFT decisions are in French, German or Italian and can be consulted on https://www.bger.ch/fr/index/juridiction/jurisdiction-inherit-template/jurisdiction-recht.htm). Decisions marked as shown above, f. ex. 129 III 445, are lead decisions; decisions of lesser importance are presented by a number, which includes the year of the submission of the cause to the SFT (f. ex. 4A_260/2017).

4 Cf. https://www.fedlex.admin.ch/eli/cc/24/233_245_233/en. All Swiss legislation can be consulted on this website in French, German and Italian, some also in English.

sports bodies, i.e. the continental SGBs or, if such entities do not exist, the national SGBs; the statutes can also provide for other entities or persons to be admitted as members. By exception, the 119 members of the **IOC** are all natural persons.[5] The organisation set up by the IOC is nevertheless comparable to those of the other ISGBs since the Committee acts as the 'supreme authority' of other regulatory bodies, which are mostly legally independent entities, but 'recognised' by it (National Olympic Committees, the organising committees of the Olympic Games, the international federations, the Word Anti-Doping Agency [WADA], the International Council of Arbitration of Sports [ICAS] etc.).[6] The resources of ISGB associations are produced by their members and the lower echelons of the pyramids (yearly fees, licence and participation fees, other dues) and – especially for the ISGBs in popular sports – by their commercial income, most importantly from media rights.

Two major actors in international sports amongst the most powerful ISGBs in Switzerland are **foundations** under Articles 80 seq. SCC: ICAS and WADA. The **foundation ICAS** is the umbrella organisation of the **CAS**.[7] CAS and ICAS have their seat in Lausanne, and for procedural purposes, all CAS-rulings, including the 'ad hoc' awards of the panels acting at the different locations outside Switzerland during the Olympic Games are formally issued in Switzerland, with the SFT as the only instance for appeals. The **WADA** is also a foundation set up in Lausanne in 1999 by governmental agencies and ISGBs under Articles 80 seq. SCC.[8] Foundations are generally established by physical or legal persons to dedicate assets to specific aims spelled out in the statutes (e.g. the fight against doping, the development of youth sports or the creation of sports infrastructure). Foundations have no members, their organisation is determined by the constituent(s) in the foundation deed and the internal bye-laws. They are run by the 'supreme organ' and other bodies as determined by the foundation deed and are under the supervision of a federal or cantonal authority. The initial endowment

5 Cf. art. 15 and 16 of the Olympic Charter (OC) which fulfils the function of statutes (https://olympics.com/ioc/documents/international-olympic-committee/olympic-charter). The IOC enjoys some privileges granted by the federal and cantonal authorities as to the status of foreign personnel and gets support of different kinds from relevant public authorities, but this does not change its legal status.

6 See section 3 on the Fundamental Principles of Olympism, as well as part 1, sec. 3 OC.

7 CAS was set up initially by the IOC as a financially and organisationally dependent entity, operational as of 1984. Responding to criticism by the SFT – in the lead decision *Gundel v FEI*, SFT 119 II 271 (1993) – of the organisational and financial proximity of the IOC, ICAS was created in 1994 in order to handle the running and the financing of CAS independently of the IOC. Half of the cost of the CAS is nevertheless financed by the ISGBs, with the other half covered by the fees paid by the parties in arbitration proceedings; subsidies are granted by public authorities for ICAS' and CAS's offices. For more details, cf. https://www.tas-cas.org/en/general-information/history-of-the-cas.html, and https://www.tas-cas.org/fileadmin/user_upload/ICAS_2020_Annual_Report_and_Financial_Statements_.pdf.

8 WADA is still financed partly by governments. Its headquarters are presently in Montreal, but an office remains in Lausanne, Switzerland (https://www.wada-ama.org/en/who-we-are).

by the constituent(s) can be complemented during the lifetime of the foundation by the constituent(s) or other sources. Both WADA and ICAS/CAS are examples of foundations with large inflows of funds every year. The regulations of ICAS and CAS, as well as the doping rules established by WADA, are recognised in all international sports affiliated to the IOC.

Associations and foundations are entities with **full valid legal status**, empowered to

- determine their internal structure, organisation and governance,
- set up, own or recognise other legally independent entities (including commercial companies), a faculty widely used in the sports world, and
- conduct business with other ISGBs or any other private or public person or entity.

The rules and activities of associations and foundations are subject to **regular law**, which also means that they are subject to the **mandatory provisions of law** on setting up and running the entity. The content and the enforcement of mandatory law determine the autonomy of ISGBs, which is large under Swiss law as will be shown in this section and in Sections 5.3 and 5.4.[9]

As concerns the **setting up of the regulations of the ISGBs and their subsequent modifications**, it should be emphasized that **controls by public authorities** are nearly absent. The regulations of associations which are not registered in the Commercial Register are not subject to any control by any public authority and do not need to notarize their statutes. Registration is required for some associations and for all foundations,[10] leading only to a summary control of the statutes and other required documents by the Registrar's office as to the presence of the mandatory contents. Importantly, the compliance with Swiss and foreign antitrust law of rules pertaining to the sporting activities, e.g., on transfers and qualification of players or teams, will therefore not be checked by any authority, neither at the setting up of an association nor afterwards when rules are changed during the life of the association.

The **legal situation** is therefore the following: regulations of ISGBs, as long as not set aside by a court, usually in the case of litigation between stakeholders of the sporting world, or invalidated by a competent public authority, will stand and apply to their internal bodies and to their members. They will be passed on by the members to their own members (**trickling down effect** within the pyramid). By incorporation into contracts with third parties or by referral in the documentation of third parties, the ISGBs' regulations will also govern many

9 For more detail than can be given in this chapter on the autonomy of ISGBs in general, cf. Baddeley (2020).

10 Registration is mandatory for all foundations and a condition for becoming a legal entity, while associations are valid legal entities as soon as their statutes are drawn up by the founding members (cf. Articles 60 SCC vs. 81 & 52 SCC). There exists no official register listing associations whether they are entered in the Commercial Register or not.

other situations of the sports world and apply to the persons and entities implied (**spill over effect**).

This state of affairs might give the impression that ISGBs are allowed altogether to ignore mandatory law and that they evolve in an **extra-legal space**, affording them immunity from State law. This impression is enhanced by the global span of the activities governed with great efficiency by the ISGBs and by the participants in each of the sports bodies pyramids, and make international sport a **special phenomenon in international social relations**. The regulations of sports bodies are on the one hand subject to various national laws, but on the other hand do not need, in most cases, enforcement by States' organs.[11] It follows unsurprisingly that the economic and political power of ISGBs, combined with the large autonomy granted many of them by virtue of their legal status under Swiss law makes ISGBs reluctant to submit to ordinary national law or even supra-national law which does not satisfy, in their eyes, the needs of the organisation of their sport.

The ISGBs have nevertheless been shown by **national and supranational public authorities** that, while they benefit from a certain leniency and comprehension of the specificities of high performance and international sport, mandatory law – amongst others antitrust law – applies to them too in the final count. The ISU case,[12] and its predecessors, the *Walrave, Dona, Bosman* and *Meca-Medina and Majcen* cases,[13] on the European level, and Swiss cases – *Perroud*,[14] *Grossen*[15] and *Gasser*[16] – leave no doubt as to this reality. Section 5.3 will explain the approach of Swiss courts and the latitude left for ISGB's self-regulation under Swiss law.

5.3 The challenges of decisions of ISGBs in Swiss courts: the importance of the liberal Swiss association law and of the approach of Swiss courts to sport

ISGBs decisions can be **challenged in ordinary courts** by their members, but also by 'indirect members,' i.e. the members of the members (lower-level SGBs, clubs, athletes), as per **Article 75 SCC**. The case can be brought for inobservance

11 Rigozzi (2005), pp. 71 ff.; see also the Dieter Baumann case (2000–2002), pp. 93 f., for an example of the multiple sports and public authorities intervening in high level sports.

12 Cf. Kornbeck (2018) as well as Heermann (2019a), pp. 1563 ff. with references; Kornbeck (2020), pp. 218 ff., comparing this decision with several others, in particular the FIA-decision of 2001 (pp. 210 ff.).

13 These decisions are summarised and put into perspective with the *TopFit* decision of the Court of Justice of the European Union, 13.6.2019, by Hessert & Dunjic (2021), pp. 187 ff., as well as by Rusa Agafonova in her contribution to this publication. See also Cherkeh, Daumann & Renz (2021).

14 SFT 102 II 211 (1976 – invalidity of excessive engagements).

15 SFT 121 III 350 (1995 – principle of good faith and loyalty in contractual relationships and beyond for parties subject to the rules of the SGBs).

16 References and a discussion in Baddeley (2020), pp. 7 ff.; Baddeley (1994), pp. 275 ff.

by the ISGB of its proper regulations – including the rules of WADA or other external bodies incorporated in the regulations or referred to by them – or of mandatory State law. International cases can be challenged on grounds given in the International Private Law Act (PILA)[17]. Each case, except for challenges of arbitral awards (as discussed in Section 5.4), will be heard as to its procedural and substantive merits by a first instance cantonal court, the decision of which can be appealed in a second level cantonal court, whose decision can, in turn, be challenged in most cases before the SFT as the final Swiss review court, with a further appeal to the ECtHR possible. Such ordinary proceedings are possible also if the ISGB's regulation has been applied in a relationship based on **other provisions than the association law**, f. ex. employment law. Procedures before **other public authorities**, including the antitrust authorities, are possible as well.

The court will determine the applicable (national or supra-national) law and review the challenged decision in this light. Under Swiss association law, the **authority of the judge** as to the merits of the case submitted derives from and is determined by **Article 63 SCC**: primarily, the **regulations of the ISGB** will be the basis for the review of the challenged decision. Swiss State law will apply only in a subsidiary function or to replace autonomous rules infringing **mandatory provisions** of association law or other legal provisions.

The most important rules of mandatory law for ISGBs are the following:

– Article 60 SCC provides that the **overall purpose** of ISGBs set up as associations must be 'ideal,' i.e. not profit-oriented. This condition is generally met by the ISGBs despite of the commercial business conducted by them, since the proceeds of their commercial activities are used to fulfil their overall non-economic statutory purpose which is to organise and further their sport and their members, and to promote the ideals of sports in general.
– As to the other provisions of the ISGBs' statutes, drawn up by the founding members or modified subsequently by the General Assemblies, few **constraints** derive from the law as to their structure, their organisation and the relation of the ISGB with its members: the **General Assembly of Members** is by virtue of Article 62 SCC necessarily the supreme organ of the association; several provisions impose minimal standards for **bookkeeping and auditing**; members have a right to **unencumbered exit** from the association and **to vote** in the General Assembly (but the voting rights may be different for the different categories of members).
– The most important mandatory provision of the SCC, is the **right of members to challenge decisions of the association 'in court'** for violations of the association's own regulations or mandatory law. This right as guaranteed by **Article 75 SCC** cannot be waived by the rules of the ISGB or by a

17 Cf. https://www.fedlex.admin.ch/eli/cc/1988/1776_1776_1776/en.

convention other than by a valid arbitral clause in the statutes or an arbitration agreement providing for arbitral proceedings equivalent to proceedings before State courts.

- Besides association law, the mandatory provisions of other legal texts (**Article 27 f. SCC** and laws on personality rights, employment contracts, torts law etc.) aim at protection the **essential rights of members or other persons implied**, such as due process, the unenforceability of excessive engagements by subordinate persons and entities, and the invalidity of sanctions causing excessive restraints of the persons or entities punished.
- ISGBs are subject to **penal law** and **tax law.**[18]
- **Competition and antitrust law** applies to the ISGB's commercial activities or to their rules concerning the commercial activities of third parties reducing and restraining competition, albeit taking into account the specificities of sports.[19,20]
- **Foreign law, including its mandatory provisions** may be applicable, following the provisions of private international law, to cases submitted to Swiss courts. Regarding **EU law**, it has to be kept in mind that Switzerland is not a member of the European Union although its laws are often compatible with EU law. EU law, including the principles and provisions of **antitrust legislation** will therefore only be applied on the basis of bilateral agreements or if the law applicable to a case is EU law.[21]

The mandatory law described above leaves the ISGBs considerable room for **self-regulation** of all matters relating to the organisation of their specific entity and their sport.[22] This power is amply used by the ISGBs for issuing the rules of the game and the competitions, on qualifications of athletes, concerning support personnel, clubs and materials, for the classification of results, but also for the suppliers, providers of publicity and sponsoring, ticket sales, media companies, entities involved in the measuring of performance, security and the IT equipment etc.

18 See Cassani & May (2017), pp. 351 ff., as to the application of the provisions on corruption of the competition law (below fn. 19) to ISGBs, especially FIFA and the IOC, over the years. Heermann (2019b), see namely N 20 ff. in detail as to the special treatment discussed and sometimes granted sports organisations. Being subject to tax law also means that ISGBs may qualify for tax exemptions due to the public interest of their activities.

19 The Swiss rules applicable are primarily the Federal Act on Cartels and other Restraints of Competition (Cartel Act) of Oct. 6, 1995 (current version in French, German, Italian and English: https://www.fedlex.admin.ch/eli/cc/1996/546_546_546/en), and the Act on Unfair Competition (Unfair competition Act) of Dec. 19, 1988 (current version in French, German and Italian: https://www.fedlex.admin.ch/eli/cc/1988/223_223_223/fr).

20 As outlined, e.g., in Cherkeh, Daumann & Renz (2021), pp. 179 ff. For the detailed discussion of the application of Swiss antitrust provisions by antitrust authorities and the SFT see SFT 2C_44/2020, 3.3.2022 (publishing sector).

21 Bellamy & Child (2013), N 16.103.

22 Very clear on this subject and on the respective roles of the ISGBs and the courts: SFT 144 III 120 (2018), par. 5.3, and 4A_116/2016, 13.12.2016, par. 4.2.3 (violation of EU antitrust law).

The **autonomy** of sports bodies goes **further** however than what the simple application of the mandatory law allows and that is granted to associations in other fields of activity, thanks to **the interpretation of the law by Swiss courts**. This came about initially because sport has historically been viewed as leisure and such activities were not meant to be governed by law. This vision resulted in a self-imposed restraint by judges who will not review decisions taken on the basis of the 'rules of the game,' considered as irrelevant in law. In the early days of sports law cases before courts, all rules concerning the organisation of their sports by the SGBs, including transfer and sanctioning rules, were refused review in Swiss court.[23] With the emergence, especially as of the 1980s, of professional sports and sporting activities becoming business for athletes, clubs, SGBs and other stakeholders, attitudes amongst judges changed. Today, only a remnant of the 'rules of the game' still stands, i.e. the rules applied on the playing field by referees and the like, during the duration of one game, cannot be submitted to courts for review.

Jurisprudence of the 1970s and 1980s **has corrected some legal flaws of the regulations of sports bodies**, mostly concerning procedures and transfer issues, which violated personality rights and workers' rights. The principles spelled out in the individual procedures have led not only to the setting aside of some specific decisions, but usually resulted also in the modification of their rules by the (I)SGBs. This effect of the judicial review could have given antitrust law, although rarely the basis for the argumentation of the parties in litigation up until 1990, more visibility over time in the procedures before Swiss courts. But this did not happen due to the move of conflict resolution in sports away from State courts to arbitration.

5.4 The impact of arbitration on the application of law in the decisions and regulations of the ISGBs

Nowadays, most litigation in sports involving ISGBs and other important actors is dealt with by arbitration rather than by ordinary court proceeding. **Arbitration clauses** in favour of CAS and other arbitral bodies[24] set up by ISGBs and other sports regulatory bodies are mostly **integrated in statutes and contracts**. The SFT generally recognises the validity of the submission of the parties to these clauses under the condition of the **independence and impartiality** of the arbitrator or the arbitral panel in each specific case. The SFT has confirmed several times that it holds this condition as fulfilled as concerns CAS and the CAS panels in general.[25] The ECtHR has agreed with the SFT's vision in the

23 Rigozzi (2005), pp. 403 ff., 421 ff., with references to jurisprudence and legal opinions; Baddeley (1994), pp. 112 ff., 344 ff.

24 E.g. the Basketball Arbitral Tribunal BAT, with its seat in Geneva (https://www.fiba.basketball/bat).

25 Therefore, the requirement of Article 75 SCC guaranteeing members of associations a review of the association's decisions by a proper jurisdictional authority is satisfied, cf. SFT 144 III 120 (2018 – TPO case); SFT 129 III 445 (2003 – Lazutina). In the recent Sun Yang case (SFT

Pechstein affair.[26] Critical voices pointing out problem spots (forced arbitration, the closed list of arbitrators, the overpowering influence of the ISGBs, the inadequacy of arbitration involving athletes and clubs opposing national SGBs or ISGBs, the powers of the Secretary General of CAS, inadequate rights of appeal under PILA) have existed ever since CAS started its operations and have not ceased despite some (insufficient) improvements over the years, but are not considered justified by the SFT.[27]

As to the question raised in this chapter, whether or not mandatory national or EU laws, in particular antitrust regulations, are enforced in these proceedings, the answer is determined by the CAS rules as to the applicable law (1), the awards of the panels (2) and, in the final phase, the review of CAS awards by the SFT (3).[28]

1 As to the **applicable law** in CAS procedures, the rules are complex and differ depending on the specific procedure requested. In the Ordinary procedures of CAS panels (R38 seq. CAS-Code), the parties choose the applicable law (R45 CAS-Code), which can also be – and very often is – the regulations of the ISGB concerned or *ex aequo et bono*; Swiss law is applied in the absence of a choice by the parties and in a subsidiary function. In Anti-doping procedures (A20 ADD-Rules) parties may choose 'the applicable anti-doping regulation or the laws of a particular jurisdiction'; in the absence of such a choice by the parties, Swiss law is applicable. The regime is less liberal in the Appeal Arbitration Procedure (R47 seq. CAS-Code) with the regulations of the ISGB concerned *primarily* applicable (R58 CAS-Code, A2 ADD-Rules). Finally, applicable law in *ad hoc* arbitral proceedings during the Olympic Games is determined by the panel which chooses the most appropriate, in its views, of 'the Olympic Charter, the applicable regulations, general principles of law and the rules of law' (Article 17 of the Arbitration Rules for the Olympic Games). These rules comply with the Articles 187 and 189 f. PILA.

4A_318/2020, 22.12.2020), however, one arbitrator did not fulfil the requirement of impartiality and should have been rescinded; the award was annulled by the STF on the basis of Article 190 par. 2.a PILA.

26 Pechstein and Mutu v. Switzerland, ECtHR (2018), Nos. 40575/10 and 67474/10, par. 124 ff. However. Germany owes C. Pechstein indemnity of the violation of her right to a public hearing. Subsequently, the German Constitutional Court has gone further and has annulled the sentence for violation of due process (cf. 1 BvR 2103/16. 3.6.2022: *Causa sport* 2022.174 seq.). mentioning also the violation of antitrust law (par. 4 bb).

27 Heermann (2019a), pp. 1562 ff.; Freeburn (2021), pp. 293 ff., 297 ff., 303 ff. and 315 ff. See also Baddeley (fn. 9), a remark by chief editor Scherrer (2020), pp. 495 f., summing up the arguments, and Rigozzi (2005), pp. 727 ff. See also the German Constitutional Court's Pechstein decision (fn. 26), and the remarks by K.Ludwig, Causasport 2022, 185–187.

28 Execution of foreign awards could also lead to a review by Swiss courts (art. 194 PILA). This is, however, of lesser relevance in sports since many of the decisions by ISGBs and of the arbitral authorities do not need the State's assistance for the execution of their decisions or of decisions of review bodies. In particular punitive suspensions, bans, withdrawals of licenses, and even fines, can generally be enforced without needing the support of State authorities (see e.g. https://www.fiba.basketball/bat).

2 It results from these rules that **CAS awards** will generally be based on the **regulations of the ISGBs**, including the WADA-Code,[29] and that Swiss law will be applicable in many procedures as the most appropriate law or in a subsidiary function, since the ISGB involved is domiciled in Switzerland. Nevertheless, applicable law has to be checked in each case; depending on the type of procedure before CAS and the contents of the regulations applied, very little room or even none might be left for the application of Swiss or other State law.[30] **EU antitrust law** which is not already integrated in the regulations of the ISGBs, e.g. as a response to a decision by European authorities, as was the case after the Bosman case, can be taken into account by CAS as subsidiary or overriding mandatory law.[31] However, it is up to each party to prompt the panel to discuss all relevant arguments including mandatory EU law, by spelling them out in their submissions. This is most important to note in view of the limited jurisdiction of the SFT as (the only) review instance (point 3).

In the case of an arbitral court established by an (I)SGB in a **different jurisdiction**, the validity of arbitration and the specific award, as well as the means of appeal depend on the national legislation by which national or EU antitrust law might be applicable.[32]

3 CAS awards are usually qualified as international awards under the provisions of **Chapter 12, Articles 176 ff. PILA** and are therefore subject to a **review by the sole SFT**.[33,34] Swiss arbitration law aims at attracting international arbitration proceedings to Switzerland by its liberal rules as

29 Brägger (2019), p. 18; Freeburn (2021), pp. 300 ff.; Rigozzi (2005), pp. 598 ff.

30 As discussed by Brugger (2020), pp. 22, 27 f., and Freeburn (2021), pp. 300 ff., 318 ff. CAS awards may confirm the decision of the (I)SGB and nevertheless contribute by the remarks of the panel recommending improvements of the regulation applied; cf. concerning the UEFA financial fair-play rues, Peter/Arn (2017), p. 441.

31 SFT 144 III 120, par. B.b.a. (2018 – *Seraing v FIFA*). The second option requires, as spelled out in the CAS ruling in the TPO-case 2016/A/4490, the conditions of legality, adequacy and proportionality to be fulfilled. For the reluctance of CAS in this respect in a high profile case in tennis, see Baddeley (2006), p. 374.

32 See e.g. Beschluss des Oberlandsgerichts Frankfurt a.M., 23.6.2020, in Causa Sport 2020, 458 seq., pp. 468, 469, with a critical review by Bechtel (2020); Landrove (2017), pp. 395 seq., 400 f. For references to commercial arbitration, cf. Bellamy & Child (2013), N 16.099 ff.

33 Article 119a of the Federal Act on the SFT (https://www.fedlex.admin.ch/eli/cc/2006/218/fr). If all parties are domiciled in Switzerland, the Swiss Code of Civil Procedure (CCP) applies, with less stringent rules for the review of awards. These rules empower the review court in particular to set aside awards containing arbitrary decisions by the panels, not only those violating public policy. For an example of such rather rare cases in sports: Platini vs. FIFA (SFT 4P.105/2006, 4.8.2006), commented by Haas (2020). Parties to international arbitration can also agree on the review procedures of the CCP, but this only happens exceptionally and is of no practical relevance in sports.

34 Even this limited review of arbitral award by the SFT can be waived by agreement of the parties, as spelled out in Article 192 PILA. However such waivers are not admitted by the SFT in the cases of the sports world; SFT 133 III 235, par. 4. This exception was introduced by the SFT in recognition of the dominant position of ISGBs facing an athlete or a lower entity of the pyramid or in a contractual relationship in many cases and of the fact that many confirmed ISGB

concerns the arbitral procedures and the very high hurdles for an arbitral award to be set aside by a State review court. No special rules for arbitration in sports are provided in the law despite of the quite different circumstances of the cases usually submitted compared to other types of arbitration.

The SFT does not act as an appeals court. The grounds on which a party's appeal of an award might be brought are listed in Article 190 par. 2.a-e PILA which leaves no room for a larger interpretation allowing other grounds.[35] The **non-application or wrong application of rules of the law**, including the European Convention of Human Rights, the Swiss Constitution and international treaties[36] or of any other provision of law may only be argued in the light of Article 190 par. 2.e PILA. This means that an award infringing the law, be it mandatory or even supra-national law, will only be annulled if its overall result amounts to a violation of **public policy**. The SFT holds that this is given if, and only if, 'the award disregards those essential and widely recognised values which, according to the prevailing values in Switzerland, should constitute the foundation of any legal order'.[37] Such a result does not flow necessarily from violations of **European competition and antitrust law** in commercial and in sports matters, as examined in detail by the SFT; therefore it is probable that it will not be held contrary to public order if awards apply rules not respecting EU antitrust law.[38] Decisions violating mandatory EU law will in such cases remain valid.

Infringements of antitrust law can nevertheless be brought up in the submission to the SFT to be included in the SFT's evaluation of the merits of the case if the argument has been raised before the CAS; the applicant must develop in sufficient detail why the CAS decision fulfils one or several of the grounds of

decisions will not be subject to any further judicial review since they can be executed within the sports pyramid without the need of help from public authorities (suspensions, …; see also fn.28).

35 SFT 4A_476/2020, 5.1.2021, par. 4 ; SFT 4A_612/2009, 10.2.2010, par. 2.4 (Pechstein). Procedural flaws (validity of the arbitration, the constitution of the panel, the possible impairment of one or several members of the panel and the procedure before the panel) must be taken up with the panel without delay as they arise during the arbitral proceedings (Articles 178, 180 f., 182 par. 4, 186 par. 2 PILA). Raised too late, such issues cannot be grounds for the SFT to set the award aside, but the SFT, if it deems it to be an important question, expresses its opinion in an *obiter dictum*. See e.g. the Pechstein case, par. 4 on the desirability of public hearings (cf.fn. 26).

36 SFT 4A_612/2009, 10.2.2010, par. 2.4 (Pechstein). Pfisterer (2021), Art. 190 N 52, N 104.

37 Bellamy & Child (2013), N 16.102, discussing SFT 132 III 389, concerning a case of commercial arbitrage.

38 SFT 144 III 120 (2018 – Seraign). Cf. in a non-sports-related case : SFT 132 III 389, par. 3.2, with a discussion of this position, also in view of the relation of the jurisdictions of the SFT and the EU Court of justice in par. 3.3. The application of Swiss antitrust law is subject to the above mentioned conditions if this argument is raised in a challenge to an award; cf. the overview of the situation by Deck (2021), however, without any mention of cases concerning the sporting world submitted to the Swiss antitrust authorities. Bucher (2011), Art. 190 N 141.

Article 190 PILA.[39] In the past, this has largely been omitted by applicants[40] who focus mostly on the validity of their submission to arbitrage, the independence and the impartiality of CAS, the violation of their right to be heard and of due process in general, and, as to substantive law, **the protection of personality rights**. It is true, alleging the violation of personality rights, rather than the infringement of antitrust law, appears to be more promising in many cases, especially if sanctions are contested, since this argument centres around the indisputable intrinsic rights of persons as to the protection by the State of their physical and psychological integrity and of their freedom of decision on the economic aspects of their lives. In the *Matuzalem v FIFA* case about the CAS panel confirming a very heavy fine and lifelong ineligibility of the player, the SFT held the (grave) violation of the economic freedom of the player to amount to a violation of substantive public policy and annulled the CAS award.[41] Arguments as to the infringement of antitrust legislation, had they been raised, would however probably not have carried sufficient weight in the view of the SFT.[42]

Strict rules for the review of awards aim generally to avoid that the advantages of arbitration are thwarted by extensive review of cases on antitrust grounds, but of course reduce, maybe even cancel out totally the **protection of the weaker stakeholders**, in particular athletes and smaller clubs, against otherwise forbidden practices of the sports organisations.[43] Facing these limits of the internal conflict resolution schemes in sports, parties to a litigation with ISGBs resort to other ways of challenging the regulations and decisions of sports bodies. As said above, especially decisions by the European authorities are sought; amongst the most famous recent examples one may mention the TPO-case

39 On the other hand, the SFT allows that, in its award, the panel may not discuss individually the violations argued by the parties, as long as they are taken into account indirectly (f. ex. STF 133 III 325, par. 5 – Cañas) The situation is similar in non-sports arbitration; see Pfisterer (2021), Art. 190 N 52, 104. On a different subject, the application by CAS of English law in the Mutu-case, for example, was not reviewed by the SFT.

40 SFT 4A_542/2021, 28.2.2022, par. 4. Commenting the inadequate argumentation by the parties in this respect in the Pechstein case: Scherrer (2016).

41 SFT 138 III 322 (2012); Matuzalem, a professional player, had been suspended for life and condemned, together with his club, to pay an € 11 mio. fine (plus interest). As per par. 4 of the SFT ruling, to be completely barred from exercising his profession, restricted Matuzalem's economic and personal freedom to a totally unacceptable degree for Switzerland; the acceptance by the player of the rules allowing the sanction was deemed an "excessive engagement" and declared invalid by virtue of Article 27 par. 2 SCC.

42 See also Heermann (2019a), pp. 1563 ff., for detailed developments on the non-application of EU antitrust rules by the SFT and the possibilities of EU review bodies to refer cases to EU authorities.

43 For Bronte Le-Fevre (2020), CAS is 'the sport industry's most valuable player' and absolutely necessary for international sports, but internal reform of the CAS is necessary to preserve its legitimacy (pp. 210 f.). Freeburn (2021), p. 321, argues that Switzerland fails in its duty to protect athletes' human rights. This is in my view especially true when sanctions result from autonomous regulations which are invalid under ordinary state law; cf. Baddeley (1996), pp. 139, 150 ff. It is, of course, up to the national legislators to provide more demanding rules for internal and international arbitration, as is the case e.g. in Germany; Heermann (2019a), p. 1564.

before the European Commission and Belgian courts, as well as the intervention of German courts in the case of Claudia Pechstein.

5.5 Conclusion

As it has been shown in this chapter, ISGBs in Switzerland are generally associations under Swiss law and as such are granted considerable autonomy to determine the rules applicable in their sports. The review by ordinary Swiss courts of the decisions of sports bodies applying these rules is limited. The review by the Swiss Federal Tribunal, on the basis of Article 190 par. 2 PILA, of decisions of ISGBs examined initially by an arbitral body, in particular by CAS, is subject to even less scrutiny and leads to the setting aside of the challenged award only if it infringes the law to a degree that amounts to the violation of Swiss public policy.

In the view of the SFT, infringements of antitrust law are not as such contrary to Swiss public policy. Therefore, the impression that EU antitrust law is (rarely) enforced by Swiss courts is correct. This derives certainly primarily from the considerable autonomy of ISGBs in the creation of their own regulations, and is greatly enhanced by the lack of control of these rules and their application in the light of mandatory national, supra-national and international law, both by ordinary and by arbitral courts, as well as by the SFT as review jurisdiction of CAS awards. In other words, there might not be another viable way to manage organised sport and to sort out litigation between its actors, but there is room for improvement and State courts can help to achieve this in matters relating to antitrust and in many other issues.

Application of mandatory State law and in particular antitrust law is of immense importance in sports due to the sums at stake for the different actors of the sporting world. Given the legal framework in Switzerland, the decisions by the ECtHR and the EU authorities are essential for the necessary corrections of the rules of ISGBs and other sports bodies which violate antitrust law. More light could also be shed on antitrust aspects of cases by CAS panels and the SFT, if the counsels of the parties raised questions pertaining to these subjects more frequently and in more detail.

Bibliography

Baddeley, M. (1994) *L'association sportive face au droit.* Geneva: Helbing & Lichtenhahn.

Baddeley, M. (1996) Le sportif, sujet ou objet? *Revue de droit Suisse* 115:2, 135–252.

Baddeley, M. (2006) The Puerta Case. *Causa Sport,* 6:3, 365–376.

Baddeley, M. (2020) The Extraordinary Autonomy of Sports Bodies under Swiss Law: Lessons to be Drawn. *The International Sports Law Journal,* 20:1, 3–17.

Bechtel, C. (2020), Das Ständige Schiedsgericht für die 3. Liga auf dem Prüfstand. *Causa Sport,* 17:3, 472–473.

Bellamy & Child (2013) *European Union Law of Competition*, ed. Rose, V. & Child, D., 7th ed. Oxford: Oxford University Press.

Brägger, R. (2019) Die neue "Anti-Doping Division" des Court of Arbitration for Sport (CAS) und weitere Änderungen im CAS-Code 2019. *Causa Sport,* 16:1, 11–20.

Bronte Le-Fevre, H. (2020) Ready, Set, Reform? The Future of Sports Arbitration. *International Arbitration Law Review*, 2020, 199–211.

Brugger, F. (2020) Nur spärliche Anwendung des deutschen Rechts in internationalen Sportschiedsgerichtsverfahren. *Causa Sport*, 17:1, 22–28.

Bucher, A. (2011) Art. 190 N 141, in *Commentaire romand, Loi sur le droit international privé – Convention de Lugano*, ed. Bucher (Basle 2011).

Cassani, U., & May, Ph. (2017) La corruption dans l'attribution des compétitions sportives. In: Leuba, A., Papaux van Delden, M.-L. & Foëx, B. (eds) *Le droit en question. Mélanges en l'honneur de la Professeure Margareta Baddeley*. Geneva & Zurich: Schulthess Verlag (Collection Genevoise), 351–378.

Cherkeh, R., Daumann, F. & Renz, M. (2021) The National League Principle as a Restraint of Competition in European Football. *Causa Sport*, 18:2, 174–184.

Deck, S. (2021) 25 Jahre Kartellgesetz. *jusletter* (weblaw, Zurich) 11.10.2021, N 31.

Del Fabro, M. (2018) Drei Jahre TPO-Verbot – die Verbände sind (weiterhin) gefordert. *Causa Sport*, 2/2018, 161–169.

Freeburn, L. (2021) Forced Arbitration and Regulatory Power in International Sport – Implications of the Judgment of the European Court of Human Rights in Pechstein and Mutu v. Switzerland. *Marquette Sports Law Review*, 31:2, 287–323.

Haas, U. (2020) Hohe Anforderungen an das Begründungsgebot. *Causa Sport*, 17:1, 19–21.

Heermann, P.W. (2019a) Sportschiedsgerichtsbarkeit 2019 – Eine Standortbestimmung. *Neue Juristische Wochenschrift (NJW)*, 72:19, 1560–1565.

Heermann, P.W. (2019b) Werbung mit Bezug zu Olympischen Spielen im Fokus des Kartellrechts und des sog. Olympiaschutzgesetzes, *Wettbewerb in Recht und Praxis (WuW)*, 7, 834–842.

Hessert, B. & Dunjic, I. (2021) Nationale Meisterschaften mit ausländischer Beteiligung im Lichte der EU-Rechtsprechung, *Causa Sport*, 18:2, 185–197.

Kornbeck, J. (2018) ISU-Fall entschieden: Loyalitätsklauseln als Kartellrechtsverstoß. *Zeitschrift für Sport & Recht (SpuRt)*, 25:1, 22–24.

Kornbeck, J. (2020) What can SGBs Do to Comply With Antitrust Rules While Maintaining the 'One Federation' Principle? *International Sports Law Journal*, 20:3–4, 203–226.

Landrove, J.C. (2017) Some Thoughts on a Procedural Issue Related to Third-Party Ownership in Soccer. In: Leuba, A., Papaux van Delden, M.-L. & Foëx, B. (eds) *Le droit en question. Mélanges en l'honneur de la Professeure Margareta Baddeley*. Geneva & Zurich: Schulthess Verlag (Collection Genevoise), 395–418.

Mbenge, M.M. (2017) Le sport, l'Etat et le droit international : Réflexions cursives sur la perception de l'Etat dans les statuts des organisations sportives internationales. In: Leuba, A., Papaux van Delden, M.-L. & Foëx, B. (eds) *Le droit en question. Mélanges en l'honneur de la Professeure Margareta Baddeley*. Geneva & Zurich: Schulthess Verlag (Collection Genevoise), 419–428.

Peter, H. & Arn, J. (2017) Gouvernance sportive: le système du fair-play financier de l'UEFA est-il correctement conceptualisé? In: Leuba, A., Papaux van Delden, M.-L. & Foëx, B. (eds) *Le droit en question. Mélanges en l'honneur de la Professeure Margareta Baddeley*. Geneva & Zurich: Schulthess Verlag (Collection Genevoise), 429–460.

Pfisterer, St. (2021) *Art. 190 N 52, N 104, in Basler Kommentar Internationales Privatrecht*, 4th ed. Basle: Schulthess.

Rigozzi, A. (2005) *L'arbitrage international en matière de sport*. Basle: Helbing & Lichtenhahn.

Scherrer, U. (2016) Was es mit der Gerechtigkeit in Rechtsprechungsverfahren auf sich hat. *Causa Sport*, 3/2016, 297–299.

Scherrer, U. (2020) Anm. der Red. *Causa Sport*, 17:4, 495–496.

6

SHOULD ORGANISING PREMIER-LEVEL EUROPEAN FOOTBALL BE A MONOPOLY? AND WHO SHOULD RUN IT? – AN ECONOMISTS' PERSPECTIVE

Oliver Budzinski and Arne Feddersen

6.1 Introduction

In early April 2021, twelve clubs agreed to form a mid-week pan-European football club competition, the Superleague, which would be in direct competition to the Champions League (UCL) organised by the Union of European Football Associations (UEFA). Besides a strong public backlash from football fans, UEFA, the Fédération Internationale de Football Association (FIFA), the English, Spanish and Italian football associations as well as the respective league organisations have immediately opposed and publicly condemned the project. In a subsequent press release, the above-mentioned governing bodies of football announced that the 12 involved clubs would be banned from playing in any competition at domestic, European or world level organised by those governing bodies if they pursue this idea further. Furthermore, the players from the 12 Superleague clubs were threatened that they could be denied the opportunity to represent their national teams.

In late April 2021, the clubs and the company (A22 Sports Management) behind the Superleague received legal protection from a Spanish commercial court. In mid-May 2021, the concerned court referred a preliminary question to the Court of Justice of the European Union (CJEU). Here, the question to be clarified is whether FIFA and UEFA have violated articles 101 and 102 of the TFEU and especially if UEFA's monopoly position as (1) the solely governing body, (2) the disciplinary institution and (3) income distributor is illegal according to European Union competition law. Furthermore, the court also investigates a potential abuse of a dominant position by UEFA through (a) actions to press the involved clubs to abandon the project, (b) issuing sanctions and (c) threatening to exclude the involved clubs from all UEFA competitions.

DOI: 10.4324/9781003305989-6

The aim of this analysis is to provide insights into the question whether UEFA (or other premier-level governing bodies in sports) can take on the three roles as sole regulator, operator and gatekeeper at the same time without infringing European competition law.

6.2 Monopolies, cooperation, and power in (sports) economics

6.2.1 A single premier-level league?

The crucial role of market competition is the decentralised coordination mechanism of demand and supply.[1] By discovering, generating and utilising coordination knowledge through decentral market interaction, the dynamic system 'market' – that is exposed to numerous forces driving individual demand and supply away from each other – contains an inherent force of coordinating individual demand and supply, i.e. bringing them together again.[2] According to current scientific knowledge, market competition is the only mechanism that can prevent demand and supply to drift permanently away from each other in an uncoordinated way. The decentralised coordination mechanism 'market competition' creates a number of welfare effects for society, in particular efficiency of (i) allocation (static welfare), (ii) innovation (dynamic welfare) as well as (iii) reactive capacity (evolutionary welfare). Furthermore, competition is simultaneously a precondition and a consequence of the individual freedom to act in economic affairs (freedom of consumption choice, freedom of supply). However, market competition is only workable and effective if anticompetitive arrangements and conduct by the market participants themselves is absent or prevented, for instance, by competition/antitrust policy combating the (ab-)use of market power as well as collusion among market participants that erodes competitive forces. Notwithstanding the need for freedom of consumption and supply choice, markets are social institutional arrangements and the design of the 'rules of the game' influence the market outcome.

While these fundamental insights hold true for the 'ordinary goods market,' the emergence of sports economics as a discipline is strongly connected to special characteristics of sports markets, distinguishing them from ordinary goods markets. These special characteristics do not primarily refer to the question whether sports markets are business and commercial in nature – those organised by professional leagues with billion-dollar turnovers are without doubt. Yet, there is a broad consensus that sports markets require a different level of cooperation among the competitors than ordinary markets:[3] in order to set up a championship or league as a marketable good, the competitors in the sports market must cooperate on, inter alia, the rules of the game, their enforcement, the schedule

1 Smith (1776); Hayek (1948).
2 Hayek (1978); Budzinski (2004); Kerber (2006); Kerber (2011).
3 Rottenberg (1956); Neale (1964).

etc. In economic language, this implies the need for a market-internal governance structure with market-internal institutions (rules of the game) that are enforced by a market-internal regulator.[4] This stands in contrast to ordinary goods market, which usually do not require such an additional layer between public regulation (as market-external institutions and regulators) and market participants/competitors. This special characteristic goes hand in hand with a notable difference in the incentive structure of sports market participants compared to ordinary markets: while competitors in ordinary markets may strive for a monopoly position (deterring all competitors), this makes no sense in a sports league or championship because the good itself – at the end of the day a form of entertainment for the consumers – can only be produced by sporting competition between different competitors. A monopoly by one competitor would erode the business of the monopolist. Since much of the scepticism in economics against cooperation among competitors (collusion) originates from monopolies being associated with severe consumer (fan) welfare loss and massive dynamic inefficiencies, the special characteristics of sports markets could be and are used as a justification to accept more cooperation among competitors in sports markets than in ordinary markets.

However, the need for a market-internal regulator who sets and enforces market-internal institutions merely shifts the monopoly problem to another level. While there is no economic logic for a sports team to monopolise a championship, i.e. being the sole competitor in it, the market-internal regulator (often called sports association) enjoys strong incentives to monopolise the market for championships. The majority of premier-level sports leagues and championships organises itself in a way that there is one single championship, tournament or league.[5] A monopoly of premier-level sports championship and leagues can be viewed to promote consumer (fan) welfare by

- offering a competition of the best talent (teams, athletes, etc.), i.e. the highest quality talent-wise (including athletic prowess);
- allowing to identify the very best, which is an important motivation for sports consumption;
- providing the highest competition intensity, i.e. the best competitive balance among competitors and thus the best quality in terms of uncertainty of outcome and tension/entertainment; and
- facilitating the building up of (specific) consumption capital.[6]

However, the commercial attractiveness of competing championships at the premier level, where some of the best talent competes here and some there, is

4 Budzinski & Szymanski (2015); Budzinski (2019).
5 Counter examples include commercial boxing, other martial arts, and to some extent motorsports.
6 Stigler & Becker (1977).

generally viewed to be considerably lower. Historic examples show that competing championships (so-called rival leagues) have mostly existed for only a few years and that then either the two rival leagues merged, or one league went bankrupt.[7] On the other hand, competition among premier-level leagues may also offer some advantages for consumer/fan welfare:[8]

- an increase in the number and frequency of premier-level sports events,[9]
- a decrease in prices for tickets and broadcasting,[10]
- a reduction of incentives and power to lobby for taxpayer money and public privileges and
- an increase in the variety of sporting rules and, at least for some consumer, increased attractiveness of the sport.

Nonetheless, monopolies of championship and league organisers are widely accepted – as it is in the EU with the so-called pyramidal structure of sports associations governing professional (and commercial) sports (as described, inter alia, in the EU White Paper on Sport[11]).

6.2.2 The market power of the governing sports association

However, all the things that speak in favour of having a single ('monopolistic') premier-level championship or league do not change a relevant problem that comes with it: the market-internal regulator (i.e. the competent sports association) enjoys significant market power. In addition, with their actions, the market-internal regulators will virtually always affect competition within the league or championship – regardless of whether they appear to be of

- *sporting nature* like the dimensions of a goal and a playing field or the number of participants including the conditions of their qualification (at the end of the day: the conditions of market entry), or
- commercial at heart like the marketing of the championship brand and the sale of media rights including the (re-)allocation of revenues.

In fact, many sports associations change sporting rules with a view to the television-marketability of the sports, i.e. to make the game more attractive for

7 Examples for (forced) mergers of rival leagues after a few years are NFL vs AFL (1960–1966) in US football, NBA vs. NBL (1937–1949) and NBA vs. ABA (1967–1976) in US basketball, as well as CART vs. Indy Racing League (1996–2008) in US open-wheel single-seater racing.
8 Ross (1989); Ross (2003).
9 Houben et al. (2022).
10 Decreasing prices for broadcasting rights directly benefit the media companies who buy these broadcasting rights but indirectly also benefit consumers/fans through lower subscription prices and through more investment in alternative programs by the media companies.
11 European Commission (2007a); European Commission (2007b).

a television audience, so that sporting and commercial nature are inextricably interwoven. Thus, the market-internal regulator usually combines championship management with government-like regulation in its daily business. In doing so, the market power that the market-internal regulator derives from its monopoly-like position may be abused at the detriment of consumers/fans (e.g., high prices, reduced quantities, lower quality, less innovation) but also at the detriment of participants (e.g., player wages, market entry, allocation of centralised revenues, cheerleader compensation and manipulating the competitive order)[12] – and, of course, at the detriment of possible competitors challenging their monopoly.[13]

While we so far have reasoned the existence of scope for market power and its abuse, the question remains: why should sports associations and their officials as acting market-internal regulators do such things, i.e. act anticompetitively? In other words, what are the incentives to abuse the existing power in an anticompetitive way? Looking at mission statements of sports associations and respective interviews and speeches by their leading officials, the emphasis is usually on the social contribution of sports and its cultural value. However, in economics, theoretical and empirical analysis has long shown that most individuals do not exclusively follow goals of the common good but also act according to self-interest, depending on the incentive schemes they find themselves in. According to political economics, this is not only true for individuals on markets or in companies but also for officials in politics, governments, administrations, regulators, etc. (political system,[14] bureaucracy and administration).[15,16] Thus, in order to discuss possible incentives for market-internal regulators in sports, we need to take a look at the possible elements of the utility function of a monopoly sports association and its officials and managers:

- Social goals: conceptualising officials in sports associations as self-interested and utility-maximising individuals does not imply that they are not driven by desires to do good things for society. Socially valuable goals (like promoting social values, public health, identification, social inclusion, anti-racism,

12 See for a case of market power abuse where the governing body colludes with selected teams against some of the other competitors in Formula One motor racing Budzinski & Müller-Kock (2018).

13 In their legal analysis, Houben et al. (2022) report insightful provisions and actions of UEFA as well as from the International Skating Union (ISU) which follow the objective of blocking all challenges to their monopoly position and are also in effect achieving this goal. There are similar provisions and arrangements in motor racing (Budzinski 2012; Budzinski & Müller-Kock 2019).

14 Downs (1957).

15 Niskanen (1968).

16 Unfortunately, a modern political economy of sports associations and officials is underdeveloped. It would serve to explain numerous relevant phenomena in commercial and professional sports as well as in more amateur and grassroots areas.

peace, etc.) certainly play a relevant role among the targets that most officials in sports pursue.

- Prestige of their sports: sports officials in disciplinary sports associations (like a football association) will usually have a special relation to 'their' sports and strive to enhance the prestige and popularity as well as to improve the reputation of 'their' sports.
- Profit, revenue or budget maximisation of the respective sports association: furthermore, the welfare of the sports association for which the individual officials act matters. In sports economics, there is a long-standing and controversial discussion on whether organisations in sports act as profit-maximisers.[17] Among the sports associations acting as a market-internal regulator, only some will be profit-oriented entities and their officials will have incentives to try to maximise profits. However, many sports associations are not-for-profit organisations. Here, maximising profits is not the agenda. Notwithstanding, their officials may still seek to maximise revenues of the association because being able to distribute more money to their stakeholders gives them more power and more prestige. Furthermore, not-for-profit organisations are likely to resemble administrations and, thus, be subject to the incentive schemes of bureaucracies.[18] Within bureaucracies, maximising budgets becomes an important goal for the acting officials, again because it is associated to increasing power, influence, prestige and career options – as well as the relevance of the organisation as a whole.
- Personal prestige and career including empire building: from the literature on organisations, it is well-known that managers and officials may pursue their own goals in addition to (or instead of) the goals of the organisation.[19] The personal prestige and/or power can be a value of its own for officials, which may lead to so-called empire building,[20] i.e., tasks and size of organisations get overblown at the expense of the original goals and functions of the organisation. Together with the incentive for budget-maximisation, empire building may lead to diseconomies of scale like x-inefficiencies and power abuse.[21] Furthermore, personal prestige and power may also serve as instruments to improve career options within the organisational hierarchy and beyond the organisation.
- Personal income: Increasing your own income motivates individuals everywhere in society and sports officials are certainly no exception.

17 See, *inter alia*, Sloane (1971), Garcia-del-Barrio & Szymanski (2009), Fort (2015), and Terrien et al. (2017).
18 Niskanen (1968).
19 *Inter alia*, Jensen (1986).
20 Roll (1986); Shleifer & Vishny (1988); Trautwein (1990).
21 Leibenstein (1966).

All these factors are present in the utility functions of sports officials but, from individual to individual, their weights differ significantly: some officials will be driven much more by social goals than anything else – and some others will be driven much more by prestige and income categories.[22] In any case, together with market power (i.e. the lack of competitive restrictions, see above), principal-agent problems (i) between associations and clubs as well as (ii) between association and officials/managers create scope for abuse and (at least partly) self-interested officials experience incentives for (ab-)use this scope in order to maximise their individual utility functions. The second dimension of principal-agent problems resembles classic agency theory:[23] organisations (as principals) are not perfectly able to control their managers/officials (as agents), so that the officials only imperfectly pursue the goals of the organisation and may use varying scope for following personal goals that deviate from the welfare of the sports association. However, in the context of a powerful market-internal regulator, the first dimension of principal-agent problems becomes particularly relevant. Many market-internal regulators are sports association in the guise of a membership association where the participants of the leagues and championships are the members ('owner') of the association.[24] This is typical in European football, where national football associations are formed by the clubs and international associations are formed by national associations. Through the chain of regional, national and supranational associations, the competitors (e.g., the football clubs) 'own' the market-internal regulator (e.g., the UEFA), so that the market-internal regulator as the agent should act in the interest of the competing teams (as the principals). However, control mechanisms through the chain of associations are rather weak and especially higher-level associations and their officials can act highly independent from the clubs – offering relevant scope for pursuing self-interests and (ab-)using their power to these ends.[25] Actually, single relevant big teams may have a more effective influence on the association through direct lobbyism than the group of teams through the hierarchy of association memberships.[26]

Most recent economic theory on digital ecosystems demonstrates that incentives to abuse market-internal regulatory power increase with so-called dual role situations, e.g., the same associations and officials acting in different parts,

22 An interesting avenue of research that we cannot pursue here would be to analyse whether the structures, power hierarchies, and typical career paths within sports associations favours officials who have an emphasis on social goals or those who have an emphasis on prestige and empire building.

23 *Inter alia*, Jensen (1986).

24 Note that this is not always the case. Instead of this bottom-up approach, the Olympic Committees, for instance, are organised top down with the International Olympic Committee forming national subsidiaries. Another case is motor racing: while the Fédération Internationale l'Automobiles (FIA) does consist of national motor racing associations, these are not built from the competing teams. See for more details on the competitive implications of different organisational models Budzinski & Szymanski (2015).

25 Budzinski & Szymanski (2015).

26 Budzinski (2014).

segments and stages of the sports market in question. Through self-preferencing strategies, these dual role agents can anticompetitively increase their own utility, manipulate consumers and stakeholders within the system and exploit co-producers of the ecosystem good.[27] In this analogue, the market-internal regulator acts as a gatekeeper and enjoys both the scope and the incentives for abusing its gatekeeping power.[28] The similarities are interesting: both ecosystem providers and sports associations define the rules of the game within their systems and pursue their own commercial interests within the system. Just like sports associations define the conditions for participating in a league, a marketplace service provider (like Amazon, like an app store provider, like a streaming service provider, etc.) defines the conditions for access to the marketplace and for the commercial conditions of doing business. And although the dual role situations may differ in detail (i.e., the sports association does not run its own team), the own commercial interest of the 'regulator' only partly overlaps with those of the participants.

Altogether, the absence of competition among market-internal regulators implies that there is scope and incentives for sports associations as market-internal regulators to abuse their power. Therefore, the fact that cooperation among the participants is elementary for the common product to be produced is both constitutive for establishing sports market competition and, at the same time, restricts competition. The derived reasoning that a monopoly championship on the premier level is superior to competing championships is sound. However, it does not imply that the resulting market power problem is of no concern. Here, standard economics wisdom is applicable to sports markets. Also, in cases where monopolies are potentially efficient (e.g., natural monopolies) or virtually unavoidable (e.g., in special cases of strong network effects), the theoretical superiority of the monopoly usually does not transform into superior empirical performance. Because of the lack of incentives to exploit the hypothetical efficiencies in the mid- and long-run as well as because of the incentive to invest in rent-seeking rather than in market performance,[29] even theoretically superior/efficient monopolies often turn out to harm social welfare. Consequently, such monopolies are usually put under strict abuse control regulation (like certain online platforms in the EU with the new Digital Markets Act), sector-specific or gatekeeper regulation (like often energy or railway nets) or are organised as a public utility (like the water network in many countries). In other words, even if one accepts the monopoly structure, the resulting market power still remains a problem that requires control.

27 In digital ecosystems, such dual role situations refer, for instance, to companies offering a marketplace service while at the same time acting as a shop owner on this marketplace or to companies providing a streaming service and, at the same time, competing on the content stage of the market. See, inter alia, de Cornière & Taylor (2019), Marty (2021), Bougette et al. (2022), Bourreau & Gaudin (2022), Hagiu et al. (2022).

28 Budzinski (2021).

29 Tullock (1967); Tollison (1982); Tollison (2012).

Looking into the existing regulation of hard-to-avoid monopolies, two important elements catch the eye:

(i) deconstruction of the market in order to identify the monopoly bottleneck that cannot be avoided – and allow monopolies only there.
(ii) implementation of checks and balances by the public government (i.e., a market-external regulator) in order to limit the abuse of market power by the remaining monopoly area.

In the next section, we apply these two principles to the problem of market-internal governance of European football. In doing so, we unbundle the monopoly governance by identifying specific tasks that require a single supplier/organiser and those that can be subject to market competition.

6.3 How much monopoly do we need in European football?

It has been established in EU antitrust practice that anticompetitive restrictions set by professional sports governing bodies could be justified (e.g., exempted from Article 101 and 102 TFEU) if these restrictions are inherent in the pursuit of legitimate objectives and are proportionate to these. The European Commission clarified in the International Skating Union (ISU) case that legitimate objectives might be (a) the integrity of sport, (b) the protection of health and safety, (c) the organisation and proper conduct of competitive sport (including the protection of the proper functioning of the sports calendar and the protection of uniform rules of sport), (d) solidarity between participants, and (e) the protection of the volunteer model of the sport.[30] Additionally, another objective that is not included in this list but that is brought forward by sports governing bodies regularly is the preservation of competitive balance.

In the following, we will identify the key tasks associated with the organisation of a sporting championships and, especially, assess if these constitute legitimate objectives as outlined above. The key tasks are:

- championship design (selection of participants, tournament mode, scheduling, etc.),
- rule setting,
- rule enforcement,
- revenue sharing agreements including the sale of commercial (media) rights, and
- licensing.

30 Houben et al. (2022), p. 6.

Additionally, we want to put a strong emphasise on the question whether granting monopoly governance over individual tasks are proportionate – an aspect that is often overlooked and taken for granted in the public debate once a legitimate objective has been established. Finally, we will use the clarifications for legitimate objectives as stated by the European Commission in the ISU case as a guiding principle for analysing and deconstructing the key tasks even further in order to clearly identify the monopoly bottleneck(s), which cannot be avoided.

Defining what constitutes the integrity of the sport is a complex question and a variety of rationales can be brought forward. For example, there is convincing anecdotical evidence that consumers' preferences for crowning an unambiguous champion are so strong that rival leagues do not seem to be able to survive for more than a couple of seasons and that the rival situation will end, after a short period of co-existence, in either the bankruptcy of one of the leagues or in a merger of the two leagues. Thus, it can be derived that, compared to a situation with two or more rival leagues at the premier level, consumers receive strong utility from just one single championship or league at the premier-level, which guarantees the unambiguously crowning of a sporting champion in a given sport, a given time-period (e.g., year, season), at a given level, and a given geographical dimension (e.g., country, region/continent, world).

Thus, if consumers prefer an unambiguous premier level championship, it can be assumed that the 'championship design' is a central element of the integrity of the sport and, hence, this task should generally reside with the market-internal regulator. However, we would argue that one could go even more in-depth and further deconstruct the task 'championship design' into sub-elements like selection of participants, tournament mode, scheduling and – at its core – maybe merely the sanctioning of the championship itself. If the governance monopoly would only be granted for the sanctioning of a championship as the premier-level championship but the business side of the championship (including the selection of participants, tournament mode, scheduling) would be outsourced to a different, legally independent organisation or company, the integrity of the sporting championship would still be preserved.

Furthermore, the lack of competition *in* the market may be partly compensated by a periodical competition *for* the market: If a licence to organise this championship would be exposed to regular competition – e.g., in form of a tender every few years/seasons offered and monitored by the market-internal regulator – negative effects of the general restriction of competition would be limited while significant benefits for consumers would be provided. Additionally, opening the tasks 'championship design' – except of the sanctioning of the championship itself – to competition periodically, will provide options for innovations in areas like tournament modes, scheduling etc., which is likely to benefit consumers too. Without competition – neither in the market, nor periodically for the market – the incentives to consider fans' interests (beyond sheer viewing and attendance figures) are comparatively weak. Finally, whether the championship design in a broader sense including all sub-elements will be located with the market-internal regulator or whether it is only the sanctioning of the competition, there is no reason that the sporting championship should be organised by the market-internal regulator itself. Here, it is important to highlight that separating the role of the market-internal regulator as sanctioning body from the role as supplier on the market will not interfere with the integrity of the sport (e.g., the pyramidal model).

However, a strong case can be made that the sanctioning of the competition and, thus, enforcing that only one unambiguous championship at the premier level exists during the period determined in the tender, should reside with the market-internal regulator. Here, it might be easily justifiable that the market-internal regulator can set the rules for the tender procedure and select the winner based on clear and transparent criteria in order to protect the integrity of the sport by, for example, preserving the pyramidal model. However, it needs to be made sure that the tender procedure only contains requirements that address those aspect that are necessary to protect the integrity of the championship from the perspective of the consumers while allowing for the greatest degree of competition for the right to organise the championship and, thus, innovations through the bids.

Following Houben, *et al.*,[31] preserving uniform rules of the sport – the tasks 'rule setting' and 'rule enforcement' – might fall under the second possible legitimate objective ('the organisation and proper conduct of competitive sport'). Since, at least in the European sports tradition, any premier-level championship will be part of the pyramidal model of open competitions, (relatively) consistent rules and rule enforcement throughout the pyramid will be strongly preferred by the consumers. However, it is not clear that both tasks (rule setting and rule enforcement) necessarily need to be located with the (same) market-internal regulator. One could easily argue in favour of separating these two tasks. This is, anyway, presently practice within the (European) football system, where the rules are set by the International Football Association Board (IFAB) – a board consisting of representatives of the four football associations from the United Kingdom as well as from the Fédération Internationale de Football Association (FIFA) – while the rule enforcement lies with the association organising the respective championship (i.e., UEFA). Thus, it seems to be reasonable to, first, separate the two tasks and, second, entrust the market-internal regulator with the task of enforcing the rules. Such a separation of powers for setting and executing rules would also fit to social models that are generally deemed to be advantageous incentive-wise.

Revenue sharing agreements (including the central sale of broadcasting rights), which are normally set and enforced by the market-internal regulator, are intended to generate funds for solidarity payments which benefit many participants

31 Houben et al. (2022), p. 7.

and levels of the sports pyramidal system.[32] While the aim of solidarity payments in order to improve competitive balance in directly affected championships, to fund development projects in non-premier-level professional leagues, or to fund grassroots sports projects, can be seen as a legitimate objective, it seems obvious that this can also be achieved if the organisation of a championship does not reside with the market-intern regulator but with a third-party organisation/ company. Here, a tender procedure for organising a premier-level championship that includes clear rules for a solidarity fee, which the third-party organisation/ company must pay to the market-internal regulator who will then redistribute the money in the form of solidarity payments, will satisfy the (legitimate) objective of solidarity in the sports system without generating too much negative effects through the restriction of competition.

Furthermore, another reason to establish revenue sharing agreements is maintenance of competitive balance – a concept that refers to the preferences of consumers for the uncertainty of outcome and balanced financial and sporting competition: a notion that dates to the seminal sports economics articles from Rottenberg[33] and Neale,[34] respectively. However, empirical evidence does not sufficiently support the claim that consumers show a strong preference for competitive balance.[35] If consumers do not perceive improvements in competitive balance as beneficial and, thus, no significant benefits can be brought forward in order to outweigh the negative effects of the (strong) competitive restrictions, it is clear that market interventions implemented by the market-internal regulator to alter competitive balance (e.g., the central sale of commercial rights or revenue sharing agreements), do not justify granting monopoly power. Even if the claim of positive effects of revenue sharing agreements on competitive balance is theoretically accepted,[36] it seems to be reasonable to generate the revenues in a competitive environment and redistribute a share of these revenues among the (participating) clubs and/or the sports system afterwards.

By contrast, however, the goal of maximising common revenues by bundling broadcasting rights and selling them in a cartel- or monopoly-style fashion does not constitute a legitimate objective – and is very likely to harm consumer/fan welfare.[37] Since the illegitimate objective of pocketing monopoly rents may be

32 However, see Budzinski & Müller-Kock (2019) for an overview of the revenue redistribution schemes of several premier-level professional championships. Often these redistribution schemes seem to follow more sports political reasons than true solidarity.

33 Rottenberg (1956).

34 Neale (1964).

35 For a comprehensive overview of the empirical literature, see Coates, Humphreys & Zhou (2014) as well as Pawlowski & Nalbantis (2019). Furthermore, they show theoretically and empirically that even the opposite can be found as they find evidence that consumers show reference-dependent preferences and loss-aversion.

36 Under specific conditions, this can at least be shown in theoretical models, see Fort & Quirk (1995); Késenne (2000).

37 Késenne (2000); Késenne (2009); Falconieri et al. (2004); Gürtler (2007); Peeters (2011); Peeters (2012).

hidden in the shadows of the legitimate objective of solidarity payments, the specific design of re-allocation mechanisms is crucial for identifying the true objectives or the ones effectively pursued by the revenue sharing agreement.[38] Similar considerations need to be considered when it comes to ostensible competitive balance objectives.

Finally, licensing systems are implemented by sports associations to make sure that teams are not going bankrupt during a running season. Since this would reduce the utilities of consumers strongly and, especially in the long-run, undermine the trust of consumers in the product, strict rules to guarantee that no mid-season bankruptcies occur can be seen as important to protect the integrity of the sport. Thus, a legitimate objective can be assumed here. Furthermore, in contrast to more sever market interventions that are intended to, inter alia, prevent intra-season bankruptcies (e.g., salary caps, luxury tax systems), licensing systems seem to be proportionate.

As we initially emphasise in this section, the question of proportionality is crucial to the (anti-) competitive effects of the actions by the market-internal regulator. Striking examples include the championship design as well as the sale of commercial media rights. Championship design includes, inter alia, the selection of the participants in the sporting competition as well as the total number of contestants on the premier level. Both decisions – selection and limitation of contestants – must be made; a design without setting such decisions is hardly conceivable. However, the criteria that determine these decisions can be pro- and anticompetitive:

- The total number of contestants (e.g., the number of teams in the premier-level league) can be chosen according to capacity and feasible scheduling – or it can be chosen according to revenue maximisation. The latter criterion would involve an artificial reduction of the quantity of top-level sporting competitions (so that revenues are allocated among fewer teams), which would be both anticompetitive (foreclosure; deterrence of competitors) and fan welfare-reducing (less games to watch/attend).
- Entry into the premier-level championship can be decided on sporting performance criteria (i.e. promotion/relegation) – or it can be decided on financial and political considerations (e.g., in closed leagues where newcomers are required to buy out an existing team or are only admitted if they fill a geographic void). The question whether (i) all European states/regions should be represented in premier-level football competition, (ii) performance-based the best clubs should compete there even if this means a geographic concentration on the big five football countries, or (iii) teams should be selected according to their reputation and market value constitutes one of the dividing lines between the UEFA and Superleague proposal for championship design.

38 Budzinski (2018).

Unfortunately, sports economic research has rarely ever addressed the important questions when contestant selection and quantity rules are procompetitive and when they constitute an abuse of market power.[39] Such research is an important desiderate.[40] This is particularly true since the separation of powers and the limitation of the governance monopoly reduce but not perfectly erode the scope and incentives for abusive/anticompetitive rules. Yet, only deconstructing the monopoly scope offers the option to include a criterion like proportionality for the selection of championship designs, i.e. providing incentives to suggest and select procompetitive solutions through the tender procedure. As long as the market-internal regulator does it all by itself, anticompetitive incentives are likely to prevail.

6.4 Results and their relevance for sports competition policy

As we explain, the dual role of sports associations of commercially exploiting a sporting championship and, at the same time, performing a regulatory function should be broken up as this would benefit, at least, consumers/fans and competitors. It seems necessary to analyse and deconstruct the market to identify the monopoly bottleneck(s), which cannot be avoided, like the sanctioning of unambiguous premier-level championships, and allow monopoly governance only there. Granting monopoly governance and exemptions from EU competition law to a market-internal regulator might be justifiable for tasks like rule enforcement, licensing and championship design. With respect to the task championship design, it can be further shown that, after deconstructing it into sub-tasks, not the organisation of the sporting championship constitutes the unavoidable monopoly but merely the sanctioning of the championship. One solution that would allow for (a) protecting the integrity of the pyramidal organisation model of sports championships and (b) competition for the right to organise the sporting championship by independent organisations/companies, would be a tender procedure controlled and monitored by the monopolistic sports organisation. Periodical competition for the market can be an imperfect proxy for competition in the market and may serve here to avoid a relevant portion of the problematic incentives to abuse market power.

The analysis in this chapter can only present a starting point for an important research programme: what separation of powers in internal governance would be optimal for different types of sports, leagues and championships as well as which rules do actually serve fan welfare and which rules rather secure

39 For an overview on the literature on competition policy in sports markets, see Budzinski (2019) and for an overview on the conditions for anticompetitive effects from market-internal financial regulations Budzinski (2018).

40 See, for instance, for an analysis whether fans from smaller countries prefer superstar club duels over the representation of local clubs in the Champions League, Budzinski, Feddersen & Kunz-Kaltenhäuser (2022).

overcompetitive rents and protect the market position of insiders of commercial sports markets? Both due to a lack of research and also a lack of enforcement activity, the potential of abuse control (as part of competition policy) for preventing welfare-reducing arrangements in commercial sports markets has not yet been exploited. More far-reaching interventions like specific gatekeeper regulation for market-internal regulators in sports or public utility regulation (i.e., externalising (parts of) the regulation to public authorities) should only come onto the agenda after the potential of competition policy has been fully employed. Still, given relevant cases like the fight between UCL and Superleague are happening now, the topic deserves and requires more treatment.

Bibliography

Bougette, P., Budzinski, O. & Marty, F. (2022) Self-Preferencing and Competitive Damages: A Focus on Exploitative Abuses. *The Antitrust Bulletin*, 67:2, 190–207.

Bourreau, M. & Gaudin, G. (2022) Streaming Platform and Strategic Recommendation Bias. *Journal of Economics and Management Strategy*, 31:1, 25–47.

Budzinski, O. (2004) *An Evolutionary Theory of Competition*, http://dx.doi.org/10.2139/ssrn.534862

Budzinski, O. (2012) The Institutional Framework for Doing Sports Business: Principles of EU Competition Policy in Sports Markets. *International Journal of Sport Management and Marketing*, 11:1–2, 44–72.

Budzinski, O. (2014) The Competition Economics of Financial Fair Play. In: Budzinski, O. & Feddersen, A. (eds) *Contemporary Research in Sports Economics: Proceedings of the 5th ESEA Conference*. Frankfurt a.M.: Lang, 77–98

Budzinski, O. (2018) Financial Regulation as an Anticompetitive Institution. In: Breuer, M. & Forrest, D. (eds) *The Palgrave Handbook on the Economics of Manipulation in Professional Sports*. Basingstoke: Palgrave, 159–179.

Budzinski, O. (2019) Competition Policy in Sports Markets. In: Downward, P., et al. (eds) *The SAGE Handbook of Sports Economics*. Los Angeles: Sage, 144–153.

Budzinski, O. (2021) Gatekeeping in the Audiovisual Sector: Economic Background, Competition, and Regulation. In: Cappello, M. (ed.) *Unravelling the Digital Services Act Package*, IRIS Special 2021-01. Strasbourg: European Audiovisual Observatory, 94–109.

Budzinski, O., Feddersen, A. & Kunz-Kaltenhäuser, P. (2022) Demand for TV Broadcasts of UEFA Champions League Games in Danish Television – The Impact of Uncertainty of Outcome, Team Reputation, and Superstars, Conference Paper, Ilmenau Economics Discussion Paper, 27:165, 1–19.

Budzinski, O. & Müller-Kock, A. (2018) Is the Revenue Allocation Scheme of Formula One Motor Racing a Case for European Competition Policy? *Contemporary Economic Policy*, 36:1, 215–233.

Budzinski, O. & Szymanski, S. (2015) Are Restrictions of Competition by Sports Associations Horizontal or Vertical in Nature? *Journal of Competition Law & Economics*, 11:2, 409–429.

Coates, D., Humphreys, B. R., & Zhou, L. (2014) Reference-dependent Preferences, Loss Aversion, and Live Game Attendance. *Economic Inquiry*, 52:3, 959–973.

De Cornière, A. & Taylor, G. (2019) A Model of Biased Intermediation. *Rand Journal of Economics*, 50:4, 854–882.

Downs, A. F. (1957) *An Economic Theory of Democracy*. New York: Harper & Row.

European Commission (2007a) White Paper on Sport, COM (2007) 391 final, Brussels.

European Commission (2007b) The EU and Sport: Background and Context, Commission Staff Working Paper, SEC(2007)935, Brussels.

Falconieri, S., Palomino, F. & Sákovics, J. (2004) Collective versus Individual Sale of Television Rights in League Sports. *Journal of the European Economic Association*, 2:5, 833–862.

Fort, R. (2015) Managerial Objectives: a Retrospective on Utility Maximization in Pro Team Sports. *Scottish Journal of Political Economy*, 62:1, 75–89.

Fort, R. & Quirk, J. (1995) Cross-Subsidization, Incentives, and Outcomes in Professional Team Sports Leagues. *Journal of Economic Literature*, 33:3, 1265–1299.

Garcia-del-Barrio, P. & Szymanski, S. (2009) Goal! Profit Maximization Versus Win Maximization in Soccer. *Review of Industrial Organization*, 34:1, 45–68.

Gürtler, O. (2007) A Rationale for the Coexistence of Central and Decentral Marketing in Team Sports. *German Economic Review*, 8:1, 89–106.

Hagiu, A., Teh, T.-H. & Wright, J. (2022) Should Platforms Be Allowed to Sell on their own Marketplaces? *Rand Journal of Economics*, 53:2, 297–327.

Hayek, F. A. von (1948) The Meaning of Competition. In: Hayek, F. A. von (ed) *Individualism and Economic Order*. Chicago: University of Chicago Press, 92–106.

Hayek, F. A. von (1978) *Competition as a Discovery Procedure*. In: Hayek, F. A. von (ed) *New Studies in Philosophy, Politics, Economics and the History of Ideas*. Chicago: Chicago University Press, 179–190.

Houben, R., Blockx, J. & Nuyts, S. (2022) UEFA and the Super League: Who Is Calling Who a Cartel? *The International Sports Law Journal*, https://doi.org/10.1007/s40318-021-00201-2, 1–12.

Jensen, M. C. (1986) Agency Cost of Free Cash Flow, Corporate Finance, and Takeovers. *The American Economic Review*, 76:2, 323–329.

Kerber, W. (2006) Competition, Knowledge, and Institutions. *Journal of Economic Issues*, XL:2, 457–463.

Kerber, W. (2011) Competition, Innovation, and Maintaining Diversity through Competition Law. In: Drexl, J., Kerber, W. & Podszun, R. (eds) *Economic Approaches to Competition Law: Foundations and Limitations*. Cheltenham: Edward Elgar, 173–201.

Késenne, S. (2000) Revenue Sharing and Competitive Balance in Professional Team Sports. *Journal of Sports Economics*, 1:1, 56–65.

Késenne, S. (2009) The Impact of Pooling and Sharing of Broadcasting Rights in Professional Team Sports. *International Journal of Sport Finance*, 4:3, 211–218.

Leibenstein, H. (1966) Allocative Efficiency vs. X-Efficiency. *The American Economic Review*, 56:3, 392–415.

Marty, F. (2021) *Competition and Regulatory Challenges in Digital Markets: How to Tackle the Issue of Self-Preferencing*, http://www.gredeg.cnrs.fr/working-papers/GREDEG-WP-2021-20.pdf

Neale, W. C. (1964) The Peculiar Economics of Professional Sports: a Contribution to the Theory of the Firm in Sporting Competition and in Market Competition. *Quarterly Journal of Economics*, 78:1, 1–14.

Niskanen, W. A. (1968) Nonmarket Decision Making: The Peculiar Economics of Bureaucracy. *The American Economic Review*, 58:2, 293–305.

Pawlowski, T. & Nalbantis, G. (2019) Competitive Balance: Measurement and Relevance. In: Downward, P. et al. (eds) *Handbook of Sports Economics*. London: Sage, 154–162.

Peeters, T. (2011) Broadcasting Rights and Competitive Balance in European Soccer. *International Journal of Sport Finance*, 6:1, 23–39.

Peeters, T. (2012) Media Revenue Sharing as a Coordination Device in Sports Leagues. *International Journal of Industrial Organization*, 30:2, 153–163.

Roll, R. (1986) The Hubris Hypothesis of Corporate Takeovers. *Journal of Business*, 59:2, 197–216.

Ross, S. F. (1989) Monopoly Sports Leagues. *Minnesota Law Review*, 73:3, 643–761.

Ross, S. F. (2003) Competition Law as a Constraint of Monopolistic Exploitation by Sports Leagues and Clubs. *Oxford Review of Economic Policy*, 19:4, 569–584.

Rottenberg, S. (1956) The Baseball Player's Labour Market. *Journal of Political Economy*, 64:3, 242–258.

Shleifer, A. & Vishny, R. W. (1988) Value Maximization and the Acquisition Process. *Journal of Economic Perspectives*, 2:1, 7–20.

Sloane, P. J. (1971) The Economics of Professional Football: the Football Club as a Utility Maximizer. *Scottish Journal of Political Economy*, 18:2, 121–146.

Smith, A. (1776) *The Wealth of Nations*. Glasgow: University of Glasgow Press.

Stigler, G. J. & Becker, G. S. (1977) De Gustibus Non Est Disputandum. *The American Economic Review*, 67:2, 76–90.

Terrien, M., Scelles, N., Morrow, S., Maltese, L. & Durand, C. (2017) The Win/Profit Maximization Debate: Strategic Adaptation as the Answer? *Sport, Business and Management: An International Journal*, 7:2, 121–140.

Tollison, R. (1982) Rent-Seeking: A Survey. *Kyklos*, 35:4, 575–602.

Tollison, R. (2012) The Economic Theory of Rent-Seeking. *Public Choice*, 152:1–2, 73–82.

Trautwein, F. (1990) Merger Motives and Merger Prescriptions. *Strategic Management Journal*, 11:2, 283–295.

Tullock, G. (1967) The Welfare Costs of Tariffs, Monopolies and Theft. *Western Economic Journal*, 5:2, 224–232.

7

ON THE ECONOMIC AND LEGAL STAKES OF INDEPENDENT SPORT LEAGUES

The case of football

Mickaël Terrien and Jean-Loup Chappelet

7.1 Introduction

> The Champions' League has already evolved into a sort of Superleague by including more round-robin matches and fewer knock-out games and, especially, by allowing more than one team per country to qualify. The only question is whether we're moving toward a Superleague within a framework set by UEFA, or whether the clubs will decide to set up their own structure. This is an economic and political issue. That being said, a move toward a more concentrated continental competition is inevitable, where big clubs will play more European games and less domestic matches.

No, this statement by Stephan Szymanski, the well-known sports economist, is not from April 2021, when 12 football clubs[1] announced the creation of a European Superleague (ESL). In fact, it comes from an interview he gave to Le Monde 15 years earlier[2] and shows that the spectre of a Superleague has haunted European football for many years. This spectre appeared to be looming once again at the time of writing.[3]

1 Six English clubs (Arsenal FC, Chelsea FC, Tottenham Hotspur FC, Liverpool FC, Manchester City FC, Manchester United FC), three Spanish clubs (Real Madrid FC, FC Barcelona, Atletico Madrid), and three Italian clubs (Juventus FC, Internazionale Milan, AC Milan).

2 d'Armagnac, B. (2006). Nous passons à une logique continentale. Le Monde. https://www.lemonde.fr/sport/article/2006/03/06/nous-passons-a-une-logique-continentale_747953_3242.html.

3 Cooper, A. (2022) Football's European Super League 'will be Relaunched Next Week,' with Juventus, Barcelona and Real Madrid 'to Reveal New Proposals Including Ditching permanent Members' After The Plan's Collapse Last Year, *Mail Online*, February 26 https://www.

DOI: 10.4324/9781003305989-7

The idea of creating a Superleague first arose in 1998, when a Milan-based company, Media Partners, attempted to launch a competition comprising 16 permanent teams and 16 invited teams.[4] A few months later, the Union of European Football Associations (UEFA) overhauled the formats of its European competitions, most notably by expanding the UEFA Champions League (UCL) to include third and fourth place clubs from Europe's leading championships and introducing two round-robin stages. These reforms put an end to Media Partners' project, but other plans for Superleagues would soon emerge.[5]

Europe's biggest clubs are well-aware of the pressure they can put on UEFA by threatening to create an independent league and on several occasions such threats have been followed by reforms to the UCL. As Macedo et al.'s bibliometric analysis[6] shows, the recurring spectre of a European football Superleague, in response to 'institutional and environmental factors,' has been accompanied by peaks in the number of publications on this issue. The first peak occurred in 2000, just after Media Partner's proposal. The second peak was in 2007, the year that UEFA increased the number of qualifying teams for the UCL to include the third-placed teams in Europe's top three domestic championships (according to UEFA rankings). The third peak occurred in 2012, just before significant changes to the draw for the UCL's round-robin stage[7] and to the UCL revenue distribution system.[8] Macedo et al. also predicted 'an increase in the number of the publications about the ESL in the near future,'[9] following the reemergence of the idea of creating a Superleague in April 2021.

However, this new proposal for a Superleague involving 15 permanent clubs (including the 12 'founding members') and 5 clubs that would qualify on the basis of their domestic performances) differed from previous proposals and was launched despite UEFA's most recent reforms to the UCL.[10] So, why did the 12 breakaway clubs come forward after these reforms? Why did Europe's top clubs follow through with their threat of creating a Superleague? Why are they so keen to overturn the status quo? The answers to these questions are undoubtedly related to recent evolutions in football's financial and legal landscape.

---

dailymail.co.uk/sport/sportsnews/article-10554423/European-Super-League-relaunched-WEEK-Juventus-Barcelona-Real-Madrid-involved.html (consulted on March 23, 2022).

4 Hoehn & Szymanski (1999).

5 Donzé, F. (1999) Media Partners relance son projet de Superligue européenne, Le Temps, 10th April, https://www.letemps.ch/sport/media-partners-relance-projet-superligue-europeenne (consulted on March 23, 2022).

6 Macedo et al.'s (2022), p. 7.

7 Dagaev & Rudyak (2019).

8 Feuillet et al. (2018).

9 Macedo et al. (2022), p.7.

10 The main changes involved increasing the number of qualifying teams from 32 to 36, increasing the number of matches from 96 to 180, and changing the qualification criteria for clubs.

7.2 Financial opportunities

According to Brannagan et al.,[11] four factors underlie the decision by 12 of Europe's top clubs to launch the ESL. The first factor was cultural and in line with the Americanization of European football,[12] as the ESL's strongest proponents include several American investors, who are culturally attuned to the idea of a closed league (which the ESL was due to be). The second factor is the reduced uncertainty of domestic[13] and European[14] competitions: An ESL would put an end to the sub-optimal competition of the domestic championships, whose competitive balance has been tilted by a highly unequal distribution of national broadcasting revenues aimed at increasing elite clubs' European competitiveness.[15] The desire to make elite football more attractive also underlies Brannagan et al.'s third factor, that is, financial gain, as the breakaway clubs' objective was to increase their revenues by increasing the sporting uncertainty of competitions. The fourth factor was guaranteeing the clubs' income, as, despite the reforms introduced by UEFA, qualification for the UCL, on which many clubs rely for a large proportion of their income, remains uncertain even for the biggest clubs.[16]

Although this analysis is interesting, it only brushes the surface of the ESL's two main goals: increasing its clubs' profitability and ensuring their place on the chessboard of European football by protecting them from the rise of England's Premier League.

7.3 Turnover, sporting success or profit?

An analysis of European clubs' revenues in 2006 led Soldberg and Gratton to conclude that joining a Superleague would be advantageous only for major clubs outside the dominant European championships.[17] In contrast, there was no financial incentive for clubs in the Big Five leagues[18] to join this type of competition. Nevertheless, all the breakaway clubs in 2021 were members of UEFA's three top-ranked championships (England, Spain and Italy). There are three possible reasons for this apparent paradox. First, the consequences of the 2020–2021 COVID-19 pandemic, both direct (e.g., playing matches behind closed doors) and indirect (economic crisis affecting clubs' consumers and partners), had a severe negative impact on European football clubs' finances.[19] Second, the

11 Brannagan et al. (2022).
12 Hoehn & Szymanski (1999).
13 Scelles et al. (2022).
14 CIES (2019).
15 Rocaboy (2017); Terrien et al. (2016).
16 Brannagan et al. (2022).
17 Solberg & Gratton (2006).
18 The Big Five is the name given to Europe's five leading championships: England, France, Germany, Italy, and Spain.
19 Drewes et al. (2021).

financialization of football[20] has brought in new stakeholders who are prepared to invest massively in football (e.g., the bank JP Morgan was ready to invest several million US dollars in the ESL). According to Brannagan and colleagues,[21] this would have resulted in the ESL's founders receiving €310 million for joining the competition and allowed them to earn up to €213 million per season, which is more than AC Milan earned before the COVID-19 pandemic.[22] Third, increasing/securing their revenues was not the clubs' only objective for launching the ESL.

Hence, in contrast to Solberg and Gratton's[23] and Brannagan et al.'s[24] analyses, the decisive factor underlying the launch of the ESL does not appear to be increasing the clubs' turnover. It has long been established that professional football is, overall, a loss-making business (Sloane, 1971), because clubs' top priority is not to make a profit but to win matches (Terrien et al., 2017). This focus on sporting success has resulted in an 'arms race' to recruit the most talented players and, as long as this arms race continues, 'enormous revenues (will not be) enough'[25] to guarantee clubs' profitability. Consequently, the primary reason for creating the ESL cannot be to maximize revenues.

In fact, its main objective is to introduce regulatory mechanisms that will change its member clubs' behaviours in such a way as to allow them to maximize their profits and, eventually, make them non-loss-making. This requires the clubs to move from a competition-based system (Nash equilibrium) to a collaborative system aimed at maximizing its members joint profits, in other words, to form a cartel (Walrasian equilibrium[26]). In addition to guaranteeing members a place in the competition, the ESL's members are actively discussing several other measures to modify clubs' behaviours, including introducing a draft, revenue sharing, a salary cap, and a luxury tax. However, there is no guarantee these measures will be successful.[27]

Nevertheless, the ESL must lead clubs to change their behaviour if it is to improve their profitability. Indeed, the competition's success depends on its ability to achieve a monopsonistic position[28] on the talent market by preventing the emergence of a rival league. To this end, the ESL must ensure it does not exclude too many major clubs,[29] and the only way to do this without increasing the cartel's size (which would reduce its stability due to unilateral incentives to deviate

20 Bastien (2021).
21 Brannagan et al. (2022).
22 Deloitte (2020).
23 Solberg & Gratton (2006).
24 Brannagan et al. (2022).
25 Solberg & Haugen (2010).
26 Szymanski & Késenne (2004).
27 On financial fair-play, see Ahtiainen & Jarva (2022).
28 A monopsonistic market is a market with just one buyer and several sellers.
29 Quirk & Fort (1997).

from the cooperative balance[30]) is to restrict itself to a specific geographical area. Consequently, the ESL's success appears to depend on two contradictory factors: restricting the number of members in order to ensure the cartel's stability and increasing its membership in order to avoid rivalry from another league.

7.4 Reduced dominance of the European elite

For Brannagan et al., one of the most important considerations motivating clubs to join the ESL was to guarantee their income,[31] as even top clubs cannot be certain of qualifying for every season's UCL, the competition on which they rely for a large proportion of their income. In fact, it is almost impossible for all six English clubs involved in the ESL to qualify for the same edition of the UCL, as only the top four clubs in the Premier League qualify directly for the competition. For all six clubs to qualify, the two clubs that finished outside the top four would have had to have won the previous season's UCL and Europa League—a highly unlikely combination of events.

Although ensuring income was undoubtedly a major motivating factor, it does not explain why Real Madrid FC, FC Barcelona, and Juventus FC are the only three clubs to continue backing the ESL, as none of these clubs are English and none of them have failed to qualify for the UCL in recent years. The last time Juventus failed to qualify was in 2010/2011, and Barcelona and Real Madrid have qualified for every edition of the UCL since 2003/2004 and 1993/1994, respectively. So why is the ESL so important to these clubs?

One reason may be the fact that they are no longer as dominant within Europe as they once were. A comparison of mean UEFA ranking coefficients[32] for the 12 breakaway clubs and the 12 most highly ranked clubs not involved in the ESL shows that the gap between these two groups has decreased greatly over recent seasons, from 4.82 points (21.63 vs. 16.81) for the 2017/2018 and 2018/2019 seasons to 0.67 points (19.92 vs. 19.25) for the 2019/2020 and 2020/2021 seasons. And it is the three clubs that continue to back the ESL that have seen the largest drop in their UEFA coefficients, which fell by 6 points in just six seasons, from 27.67 for 2015/2016 and 2016/2017 to 21.67 for 2019/2020 and 2020/2021. This reduced domination is also reflected in the slightly more even spread of talent[33] across Europe's elite clubs, as the percentage of playing talent in the Big Five leagues (which contain a total of 98 clubs) held by the 12 breakaway clubs fell from 37.33% in 2017/2018 to 'just' 32.17% in 2020/2021.

This reduced domination is the result of another marked trend in European football: the rise of the English Premier League. Given that the

30 Stigler (1968).

31 Brannagan et al. (2021).

32 Data available at: https://www.uefa.com/nationalassociations/uefarankings/club/#/yr/2022

33 As a measure of talent, we used the market values of players as listed on https://www.transfermarkt.com. This is a commonly used proxy in sport economics (e.g., Terrien & Andreff, 2020).

English championship accounted for 32% of the talent in the Big Five leagues in 2020/2021, compared with between 14% and 19% in the other four Big Five leagues, one might ask whether one can still talk about a Big Five. Moreover, the huge sums in broadcasting rights that the English clubs receive every year (€3.5 billion[34]) have few equivalents in the world of sport. Given the Premier League's earning power and attractiveness, especially internationally, it is rapidly becoming football's biggest club competition. For example, the Premier League earned €1.6 billion in international broadcasting rights for the 2019/2020 season, whereas as UEFA received just €2 billion in television rights[35] for the UCL.

This bonanza, which is distributed relatively equally between the Premier League's clubs, has helped 11 English clubs[36] enter the ranks of the 30 richest clubs in Europe.[37] This explains why the six English clubs—which were worried about stiffer competition in their domestic championship[38]—and the other six European clubs—which were concerned about new competitors on the talent market—wanted to join the ESL. From here to considering the English Premier League a Superleague is but a small step; a step that has been facilitated by its parachute payment system, under which teams that are relegated to the second division continue receiving a substantial proportion of Premier League broadcasting rights for three years. These payments double a relegated club's chances of winning promotion back to the Premier League, [39] thereby making it an almost closed 'English Superleague.'

7.5 Legal issues

In addition to these financial considerations, the recently proposed ESL raised three important questions[40] concerning competition law and UEFA's right to sanction the clubs involved, which it threatened to exclude from the UCL. UEFA also said it would ban these clubs' players from UEFA and FIFA competitions, notably the Euro and Football World Cup.

The first question is whether the ESL would be considered a cartel and therefore contravene European competition law. In 2020, the General Court of the European Union (EU) ruled that the International Skating Union (ISU) had

34 https://theathletic.com/news/premier-league-to-roll-over-domestic-tv-rights-deal-after-government-approval/JdSHeIFxULbW/+https://media.sportbusiness.com/news/premier-league-rights-value-up-8-to-9-2bn-on-overseas-income.

35 https://editorial.uefa.com/resources/0268-1215a6daaf78-a6ca16cd1df1-1000/04_uefa_financial_report_2019-20_en.pdf.

36 The six breakaway clubs plus West Ham United, Everton, Leicester City, Wolverhampton Wanderers, and Crystal Palace. All the clubs involved in the ESL were in this top 30. This is not (yet) the case for Newcastle United FC, which is starting to benefit from the financial backing of its new owners, a Saudi sovereign wealth fund.

37 Deloitte (2020).

38 Brannagan et al. (2022).

39 Wilson et al. (2018).

40 Darcis & Omnes (2021).

broken this law when it imposed lifetime bans from Olympic competitions on speedskaters who took part in non-ISU approved competitions, most notably those planned by the company Ice Derby.[41] The court not only found this punishment to be excessive but also highlighted the ISU's conflict of interest as both the regulator of (speed) skating and a commercial organization that sold broadcasting and marketing rights to its own competitions. In 2001, an EU investigation into a similar conflict of interest at the International Motorsport Federation (FIA) resulted in the FIA withdrawing from organizing motor racing competitions (including the F1 circuit) in order to focus on its regulatory role (rules, calendar, sanctions etc.).

The ISU, which does not have at all the same financial dimension as the FIA, has appealed against the General Court's decision on the grounds that it did not take account of 'the specific nature of sport,' as set out in Article 165 of the 2009 Treaty on the Functioning of the European Union. This article, which was not in force when the decision concerning the FIA was taken, may allow sport federations to keep their double role, as long as they follow the principles of good governance, integrity, and proportionality, and ensure their sporting rules are 'reasonably justifiable.' At the time of writing (mid-2022), the European Court of Justice had not yet handed down its ruling.

In the case of the ESL, Real Madrid FC—one of the three clubs remaining within the project—took its case against the sanctions imposed by UEFA to a Spanish court, which has asked the European Court of Justice to make a preliminary ruling so it can ensure that its final ruling is in line with European jurisprudence. At the time of writing, the Spanish court had still not received an answer to its request. If the General Court of the EU rules that UEFA's sanctions do not infringe EU competition law, there is little chance of the ESL, or any similar project, coming about. Conversely, if the court finds in favour of Real Madrid, this jurisprudence could lead to a separation between regulatory and commercial functions throughout European and, undoubtedly, world football (and, potentially, across all sports).

The second legal question is whether a national federation with the power to license clubs can punish its clubs for joining the ESL by withdrawing their license to compete in their domestic championship. The answer to this question probably varies from country to country, according to national legislation governing sport federations.

The third legal issue concerns the two Spanish clubs still involved in the ESL—FC Barcelona and Real Madrid FC. In contrast to most of Spain's professional clubs,[42] which are limited companies, FC Barcelona and Real Madrid FC are not-for-profit associations under Spanish law and must therefore comply with the statutes of the Royal Spanish Football Federation. Because the federation

41 General Court of the European Union (2020) Judgment T-92-18, International Skating Union vs. Commission, Press Release *159/20*, December 16.

42 The exceptions are Athletic Bilbao and Atletico Osasuna.

recognizes only UEFA's and FIFA's international competitions, FC Barcelona and Real Madrid FC cannot legally take part in other competitions, such as the ESL.

7.6 Conclusion

The creation of an ESL, as proposed by 12 of Europe's biggest football clubs in 2021, would have far-reaching financial implications for the clubs involved and for European football in general. Although it was unprecedented pressure from fans and the subsequent withdrawal of the six English clubs involved that led to the project quickly being suspended, the ESL also faced a number of legal challenges at both the national and European levels. Nevertheless, the project raises interesting questions about the governance of football and of sport in Europe and throughout the world. As has already been noted, the financial benefits to the ESL's member clubs will depend on ensuring the league is governed in such a way as to maintain the cartel's stability.

The ESL also raises questions about the compatibility between the soft law formed by sporting regulations (e.g. UEFA's and FIFA's rules) and domestic and European hard law. This issue has plagued European and world sport since the 1970s (*Walrave* and *Dona* rulings) and especially since the 1995 Bosman ruling in football,[43] which led sport organizations to lobby the EU to recognize the 'specific nature of sport' (which it did in 2009 in the TFEU) and to defend a 'European model of sport.' Notwithstanding the huge financial interests associated with football and other sports in Europe, is there such a thing as a European model of sport that would justify relaxing—as long as sport organizations meet certain conditions—European competition law and enable sport federations to conserve their dual regulatory and commercial roles? In fact, it is surprising that that this duality has not been challenged more vigorously in Europe's courts. Nevertheless, the dual role played by many sport federations has not prevented private enterprises creating commercial (and potentially competing) leagues in sports such as swimming (International Swimming League, created in 2019), basketball (Euroleague), and show jumping (Global Champions Tour).

Significantly, the launch of the ESL coincided with the adoption of three documents supporting a European model of sport, drawn up by the European Parliament (of the EU), the European Council (of the EU), and the Council of Europe (which has almost twice as many member countries as the EU). These documents not only reiterated the primacy of sporting performance (and therefore of promotion/relegation systems) over the search to maximize financial returns, they highlighted the need for sport organizations to involve fans in their decisions. Indeed, it was a 'revolt' by fans that led the six English clubs to withdraw from the ESL. UEFA 'welcomed' the Council of Europe's resolution on

43 Chappelet (2018).

European football, even though fans are not represented on any of UEFA's committees, in contrast to clubs (represented by the ECA), players (represented by FIFPRO) and the leagues (represented by EPFL).[44] The European Court of Justice will undoubtedly refer to these documents when drawing up future rulings.

Bibliography

Ahtiainen, S. & Jarva, H. (2022) Has UEFA's Financial Fair Play Regulation Increased Football Clubs' Profitability? *European Sport Management Quarterly*, 22:4, 569–587.

Bastien, J. (2021) Effets mésoéconomiques de la crise de la covid-19. Vers une accentuation de la financiarisation du football professionnel européen. *Revue de la régulation. Capitalisme, institutions, pouvoirs*, (29). https://journals.openedition.org/regulation/18504 https://journals.openedition.org/regulation/18504

Brannagan, P. M., Scelles, N., Valenti, M., Inoue, Y., Grix, J. & Perkin, S. J. (2022) The 2021 European Super League Attempt: Motivation, Outcome, and the Future of Football. *International Journal of Sport Policy and Politics*, 14:1, 169–176.

Chappelet, J.-L. (2018) The Autonomy of Sport and the European Union. In Anderson, J., Parrish, R. & Garcia, B. (eds.) *Research Handbook on EU Sports Law and Policy*. Cheltenham: Edward Elgar, 157–172.

CIES (2019) *Evolution de l'équilibre compétitif en Ligue des champions (2003–2018)*. https://www.cies.ch/fr/cies/actualites/actualites/article/evolution-of-competitive-balance-in-the-champions-league-2003-2018

Dagaev, D. & Rudyak, V. Y. (2019) Seeding the UEFA Champions League Participants: Evaluation of the Reforms. *Journal of Quantitative Analysis in Sports*, 15:2, 129–140.

Darcis, L. & Omnes, V. (2021) Les barrières juridiques au projet de super league. *Jurisport*, 222, September.

Deloitte (2020) *Football Money League. Eye on the Prize*. https://www2.deloitte.com/content/dam/Deloitte/uk/Documents/sports-business-group/deloitte-uk-deloitte-football-money-league-2020.pdf

Drewes, M., Daumann, F. & Follert, F. (2021) Exploring the Sports Economic Impact of COVID-19 on Professional Soccer. *Soccer & Society*, 22:1–2, 125–137.

Feuillet, A., Durand, C. & Scelles, N. (2018) Revenus TV du football européen : Le rôle politique clé de la ligue professionnelle. *Jurisport*, 183:2018, 39–44.

Hoehn, T. & Szymanski, S. (1999) The Americanization of European Football. *Economic Policy*, 14(28), 204–240.

Macedo, A., Ferreira Dias, M. & Mourão, P. R. (2022) A Bibliometric Study of the European Super League of Football–A New Plan or an Old Threat? *Soccer & Society*, 1–21. https://doi.org/10.1080/14660970.2022.2038574

Quirk, J. & Fort, R. D. (1997) *Pay Dirt: The Business of Professional Team Sports*. Princeton University Press.

Rocaboy, Y. (2017) Competition among National Football Leagues. Does it Exist? Should we Regulate? *Scottish Journal of Political Economy*, 64:1, 88–114.

44 UEFA Press Release (2022), *UEFA Welcomes Council of Europe Backing for European Football Model*, January 26, https://www.uefa.com/insideuefa/mediaservices/mediareleases/news/0271-144b7e36cfdb-8acc197231c6-1000--council-of-europe-backing-for-european-football-model/

Scelles, N., Dermit-Richard, N. & Haynes, R. (2020) What Drives Sports TV rights? A Comparative Analysis of their Evolution in English and French Men's Football First Divisions, 1980–2020. *Soccer & Society*, 21:5, 491–509.

Scelles, N., François, A. & Dermit-Richard, N. (2022) Determinants of Competitive Balance Across Countries: Insights from European Men's Football First Tiers, 2006–2018. *Managing Sport and Leisure*, 27:3, 267–284.

Sloane, P. J. (1971) Scottish journal of political economy: the economics of professional football: the football club as a utility maximiser. *Scottish Journal of Political Economy*, 18:2, 121–146.

Solberg, H. A. & Gratton, C. (2006) Would European Soccer Clubs Benefit from Playing in a Super League? *Soccer & Society*, 5:1, 61–81.

Solberg, H. A. & Haugen, K. K. (2010) European Club Football: Why Enormous Revenues Are Not Enough? *Sport in Society*, 13:2, 329–343.

Stigler, G. J. (1968) Price and Non-Price Competition. *Journal of Political Economy*, 76:1, 149–154.

Szymanski, S. & Késenne, S. (2004) Competitive Balance and Gate Revenue Sharing in Team Sports. *The Journal of Industrial Economics*, 52, 165–177.

Terrien, M., Scelles, N. & Durand, C. (2016) French 75% Tax Rate: An Opportunity to Optimize the Attractiveness of the French Soccer League. *International Journal of Sport Finance*, 11:3, 183–203. https://fitpublishing.com/journals/international-journal-sport-finance-ijsf-113

Terrien, M., Scelles, N., Morrow, S., Maltese, L. & Durand, C. (2017) The win/profit maximization debate: strategic adaptation as the answer?. *Sport, Business and Management: An International Journal*, 7:2, 121–140.

Terrien, M. & Andreff, W. (2020) Organisational Efficiency of National Football Leagues in Europe. *European Sport Management Quarterly*, 20:2, 205–224.

Wilson, R., Ramchandani, G. & Plumley, D. (2018) Parachute Payments in English Football: Softening the Landing or Distorting the Balance? *Journal of Global Sport Management*, 3:4, 351–368.

8

ANTITRUST LAW, SPORT AND THE EUROPEAN SOCIAL MODEL

An Olympic choice

Walter S. Palmer

8.1 Introduction

The International Olympic Committee (IOC) owns the Olympic Games and regulates the entire Olympic Movement with rules and standards cascading down through the governance of international federations and National Olympic Committees (NOCs) to national federations, associations, leagues, clubs and individual athletes.[1] Sport organisations with a regulatory or sanctioning function are known as sport governing bodies (SGBs). SGBs are often the only buyer of high-performance athlete labour and intellectual property in specific markets. This creates an imbalance in bargaining power between SGBs and athletes and is what economists call monopsony power.[2] As is common in concentrated markets, this imbalance in the labour market for high-performance athletes allows SGBs to retain control over how revenue from competitions, and especially the Olympic Games, is distributed. The IOC's preferred model of revenue distribution, the so-called 'solidarity' model, prioritises administration and management expenses over labour. Olympic athletes are denied worker status by the IOC at the Olympics and receive approximately 5% of Olympic revenue in direct compensation.[3] To maintain its bargaining power, the Olympic Movement pursues a global campaign to assert what it calls the 'autonomy of sport' that, not coincidentally, undermines high-performance athletes' rights to freedom of association and collective bargaining. The enforcement of antitrust laws has the

1 What Is the Olympic Movement? https://olympics.com/ioc/faq/olympism-and-the-olympic-movement/what-is-the-olympic-movement.

2 Farzin (2015).

3 Bradish, C., Koehler, R., & Bailey, A. (2019). Olympic Commercialization and Player Compensation: A Review of Olympic Financial Reports. Global Athlete and Ryerson University.

DOI: 10.4324/9781003305989-8

potential to pierce this attempt to 'encase'[4] sporting rules from the influence of national, European laws and bring the IOC into alignment with core elements of the European Social Model, decent work and basic social protections. Antitrust enforcement has the potential to bring SGBs to the table for European-level discussions and negotiations under the auspices of a European Sectoral Social Dialogue Committee. Decent work will remain an aspirational concept for Olympic athletes as long as the bargaining power of SGBs remains unchallenged. Athlete trade unionism has an important role to play in reconciling the future challenges facing European sport.

This chapter will start by exploring the negative impact monopsony in sport has on athletes. It will then outline the rising antitrust risks and describe how SGBs have attempted to hold on to their bargaining power and undermine the growing movement for athlete labour unions through campaigns for a legislative exemption from antitrust laws using the catchphrases 'autonomy,' the 'specificity of sport' and the 'European Sport Model.' The chapter concludes by arguing that a sport governance system based upon social dialogue or collective bargaining for high-performance athletes, rather than a legislative antitrust exemption, would be the best way to balance Europe's social policy goals in sport and labour relations.

8.2 SGBs are monopsonies

It is now settled law that European competition law applies to SGBs and that sporting rules are not exempt from antitrust analysis. SGBs are economic undertakings and hold dominant positions in the market for organising and marketing sport competitions.

One of the most significant cases that supports this statement is the *Meca-Medina* case. Two swimmers, David Meca-Medina and Igor Macjen, were banned under the world anti-doping rules and filed a complaint with the European Commission challenging their suspension. On July 18, 2006, the European Court of Justice did not rule in favour of the swimmers but its method of analysis through which it reached its conclusion overturned the previous approach that had excluded 'sporting rules' from assessment under competition law. The European Commission accepted that 'the IOC was to be treated as an undertaking and, within the Olympic Movement, as an association of international and national associations of undertakings.'[5] And, further, the court stated:

> It is apparent that the mere fact that a rule is purely sporting in nature does not have the effect of removing from the scope of the Treaty the person

4 Slobodian (2020).
5 Meca-Medina v. Commission [2006] ECR I-6991.

> engaging in the activity governed by that rule or the body which has laid it down.[6]

The decision in this case increased the risk that other sporting rules imposed by SGBs would no longer be excluded from antitrust analysis and set an important precedent for the rest of Europe.

In 2018, at the national level, the *Bundeskartellamt* (German Competition Authority) investigated the anticompetitive nature of Rule 40 of the Olympic Charter, which limits athletes' ability to market themselves, and found, in its preliminary antitrust assessment, that the Olympic Movement has

> a dominant position on the market for the organisation and marketing of the Olympic Games, which the German Olympic Sports Confederation (DOSB) and the IOC as members of the Olympic Movement abused to unfairly impede German athletes and their (potential) sponsors.[7]

The German Competition Authority considered the Olympic Movement 'as a collective or competitive entity'[8] and stated that the IOC had violated Article 102 TFEU and that a violation of the ban on cartels pursuant to Article 101 TFEU could have been considered as well.[9]

Whereas the analysis by the *Bundeskartellamt* was focused on the anticompetitive effect of Rule 40, it positioned athletes as 'customers of the organisation and marketing of sports events.'[10] But the legal ground is shifting, and we may already have entered a world where the anticompetitive practices of the Olympic Movement as the sole buyer in the market for athlete labour will take centre stage. This is because antitrust authorities are beginning to pay more attention to price fixing in labour markets in both the United States and Europe.

In 2016, the United States Justice Department Antitrust Division and the Federal Trade Commission issued guidance that was 'intended to alert human resource (HR) professionals and others involved in hiring and compensation decisions to potential violations of the antitrust laws.'[11] The guidance states that US antitrust laws 'apply to competition among firms to hire employees.' and that

6 *Ibid.*, at 27.

7 Bundeskartellamt, Decision B2-2617. Deutscher Olympischer Sportbund (DOSB), et al. Decision pursuant to Section 32b GWB. Public version. https://www.bundeskartellamt.de/SharedDocs/Entscheidung/EN/Entscheidungen/Missbrauchsaufsicht/2019/B2–26-17.pdf?__blob=publicationFile&v=2, at 42.

8 *Ibid.*, at 63.

9 *Ibid.*, at 41.

10 *Ibid.*, at 53.

11 US Department of Justice & Federal Trade Commission (2016) Antitrust Guidance for Human Resource Professionals. Accessed at https://www.ftc.gov/legal-library/browse/antitrust-guidance-human-resource-professionals-department-justice-antitrust-division-federal-trade.

> an agreement among competing employers to limit or fix the terms of employment for potential hires may violate the antitrust laws if the agreement constrains individual firm decision-making regarding wages, salaries, or benefits; terms of employment; or even job opportunities.

In Europe, the plight of platform workers, such as Uber drivers, who were classified as self-employed and were thus prevented by competition law from collectively bargaining their working conditions, has led to a proposed Directive and additional guidance from the European Commission. Consequently, platform workers are increasingly being classified as employees.[12] Recent cases at the national level focused on sport indicate that sport may be a sector that could lead the way. In 2021, the Competition Authority in Portugal sent a statement of objections to the Portuguese Professional Football League for their use of no-poach agreements and Poland opened an investigation into potential collusion between basketball clubs to terminate contracts and withhold player salaries. In Lithuania, the national competition authority fined the top basketball league for colluding to restrict player salaries after cancelling the season due to Covid-19.[13] EU competition commissioner, Margrethe Vestager, stated in a speech on 22 October 2021 that the European Commission would be looking to investigate suspected anti-competitive behaviour in the human resources area very soon, including wage-fixing and no-poach agreements.[14] She might have been speaking directly to sport when she said,

> Some buyer cartels do have a very direct effect on individuals, as well as on competition, when companies collude to fix the wages they pay; or when they use so-called 'no-poach agreements' as an indirect way to keep wages down, restricting talent from moving where it serves the economy best.[15]

12 Colin-Dubuisson, C. & Eichlin, J. (2021) Employing Old Antitrust Theories in New Markets: A Look at Antitrust Enforcement in Labor Markets in the US, EU and Beyond. *Linklaters LLP*, 17 June, https://www.linklaters.com/en-us/insights/blogs/linkingcompetition/2021/june/employing-old-antitrust-theories-in-new-markets-a-look-at-antitrust-enforcement-in-labor-markets.

13 Masson, J. (2021) Lithuania Calls Foul on Basketball League Conspiracy. *Global Competition Review*, 22 November, https://globalcompetitionreview.com/lithuania-calls-foul-basketball-league-conspiracy.

14 Kuhn, T., Sakellariou-Witt, S., Gidley, M., Mims, K., Paul, M., Powell, M., Caroppo, C., & Citron, P., (2021) No-poach Agreements on the European Commission Dawn Raid Radar. *White & Case LLP*, 8 November, https://www.whitecase.com/publications/alert/no-poach-agreements-european-commission-dawn-raid-radar.

15 22 October 2021. Speech by EVP M. Vestager at the Italian Antitrust Association Annual Conference: 'A New Era of Cartel Enforcement'. https://ec.europa.eu/commission/commissioners/2019–2024/vestager/announcements/speech-evp-m-vestager-italian-antitrust-association-annual-conference-new-era-cartel-enforcement_en.

In the United States, this approach is also influencing sport. An antitrust case brought by an American football player from the University of Nebraska, David Alston, wound its way through the court system to finally reach the US Supreme Court in 2020. The case was decided unanimously, 9-0, in favour of the player. The decision and concurring opinion essentially wiped away the legal argument of the National Collegiate Athletic Association (NCAA) for amateurism in the United States. In a key paragraph, the Supreme Court agreed with the analysis of the lower court, 'in applying the rule of reason, the district court began by observing that the NCAA enjoys 'near complete dominance of, and exercise[s] **monopsony** power in, the relevant market' – which it defined as the market for 'athletic services in men's and women's Division I basketball and FBS football, wherein each class member participates in his or her sport-specific market.' There are no 'viable substitutes,' as the 'NCAA's Division I essentially is the relevant market for elite college football and basketball.' In short, the NCAA and its member schools have the 'power to restrain student-athlete compensation in any way and at any time they wish, without any meaningful risk of diminishing their market dominance.'[16]

In his concurring opinion, Justice Brett Kavanaugh laid down a line that the court would almost certainly take in future decisions related to antitrust issues in college sport:

> The NCAA and its member colleges maintain important traditions that have become part of the fabric of America, but those traditions alone cannot justify the NCAA's decision to build a massive money-raising enterprise on the backs of athletes who are not fairly compensated. The NCAA's business model would be flatly illegal in almost any other industry in America. All of the restaurants in a region cannot come together to cut cooks' wages on the theory that 'customers prefer' to eat food from low-paid cooks. Law firms cannot conspire to cap lawyers' salaries in the name of providing legal services out of a 'love of the law.' Hospitals cannot agree to cap nurses' income in order to create a 'purer' form of helping the sick. News organisations cannot join forces to curtail pay to reporters to preserve a 'tradition' of public-minded journalism. Movie studios cannot collude to slash benefits to camera crews to kindle a 'spirit of amateurism' in Hollywood. Nowhere else in America can businesses get away with agreeing not to pay their workers a fair market rate on the theory that their product is defined by not paying their workers a fair market rate. The NCAA is not above the law.[17]

16 National Collegiate Athletic Association v. Alston. American Athletic Conference v. Alston. Argued March 31, 2021. Decided June 21, 2021. https://www.supremecourt.gov/opinions/20pdf/20–512_gfbh.pdf.

17 *Ibid.*, Justice Kavanaugh (concurring), p. 3.

One might say the same thing about the IOC and the Olympic Movement. We will see later in the chapter how the IOC and the Olympic Movement, like the NCAA, assert a type of parallel sovereignty mixed with a well-branded social mission that, it contends, should exempt its multi-billion-dollar business model from the application of the law. But first, let's examine the negative effects of monopsony power on high-performance athletes.

8.3 The negative impact of monopsony power on athletes

8.3.1 General remarks

In an online forum hosted by the Federal Trade Commission in the United States, Lisa Frank, an Executive Vice President for the Service Employees International Union (SEIU), described the effects of monopsony on workers. She said,

> In functional, competitive markets workers have the option to leave, what economists call 'exit.' The threat of exit, we are told, is what pushes employers to improve wages, benefits and other working conditions. But in dysfunctional or monopsonistic markets, exit for workers is impossible or impossibly costly and the risk of workers exiting isn't sufficient for employers to offer competitive wages, benefits and working conditions.[18]

'So, monopsonistic markets demand another solution, what economists call "voice". Voice means empowering people who have few market options to make improvements directly on the job they already have. With voice on the job, workers can address compensation issues. But the harm from monopsonies goes much further than that. Through collective bargaining agreements workers in monopsonistic industries like coal, auto, or steel are able to level the playing field and make change over time.'[19] 'Voice,' in this context, means the right to organise a union and collectively bargain when faced with a monopsony.

As is the case with other monopsonistic employers, SGBs unilaterally make rules that limit high-performance athletes' ability to 'exit' and set financial priorities that embed their monopoly on bargaining power. Some examples from sport include restrictions on mobility such as one federation/one sport rules, nationality rules, economic exploitation, discrimination, high injury rates, co-opted voice, forced arbitration, workplace surveillance and controversial host cities.

18 Lisa Frank, Panel on Labor Perspective on Competition Issues, Federal Trade Commission, 6 December, 2021, https://www.ftc.gov/media/80858.

19 *Ibid.*

8.3.2 Restrictions on the mobility of Olympic athletes

As there are very few analyses of monopsony power in Olympic sport, we can draw general principles from studies that focus on other types of workers. In the case of worker mobility, a study on workers in the urban informal sector finds that 'monopsonistic exploitation is propelled by employers' expectations about the degree of (im)mobility of workers'[20] This is also the case for Olympic athletes. In Olympic sport, there are a variety of factors that create enormous friction for athletes who may want to use 'exit' as a form of individual leverage to improve their compensation or working conditions. Whereas the *Bosman* decision allowed club-level athletes to enjoy their freedom of movement rights in the European Union (EU) when playing for a professional club, national team athletes in Europe still face a variety of restrictions that limit competition for their labour.

First, the practice by the IOC of only recognising one federation per sport embeds the monolithic governance structure and creates a fundamental conflict of interest between the regulatory role and the economic interests of a federation.

Second, the incredible amount of training needed to develop the specific skills necessary to succeed in high-level sport makes it almost impossible for athletes to credibly threaten to change sports once they have reached a certain level. The IOC, through its 'solidarity mechanism' that distributes 90% of the revenues from the Olympic Games to the Olympic Movement, often takes credit for funding athlete training. However, it is normal that an employer should pay for training that makes an employee more valuable to the employer but less competitive in the open market. Employees are normally responsible for training that makes them more competitive in the labour market. In the case of sport, the more training an athlete receives in their sport, the more valuable they are to their club, league and/or federation but even less able to consider moving to play another sport.

Third, nationalism is the main product marketed by the Olympic Movement and the structure of national teams based on nationality limits labour mobility. As Jean-Loup Chappelet wrote in an Op-ed in the New York Times in 2012, Rule 6.1 of the Olympic Charter states:

> The Olympic Games are competitions between athletes [...] and not between countries. But to participate in the Olympics you must be entered by a National Olympic Committee (N.O.C.) and you must be a national of the country of your N.O.C.[21]

20 Gangopadhyay & Shankar (2016).

21 Chappelet, J. (2012) Make the Rules for Sports Teams and Olympic Teams Consistent. *New York Times*, The Opinion Pages, Updated July 27, 11:33 AM, https://www.nytimes.com/roomfordebate/2012/07/26/which-country-did-you-say-you-were-playing-for-in-the-olympics/make-the-rules-for-sports-teams-and-olympic-teams-consistent.

While nationality restrictions are taken for granted and may be considered to pursue a legitimate objective, they certainly have an anticompetitive effect on the market for high-performance athlete labour. There are cases where an athlete may be legally considered a national of a country but not be able to compete for the national team. For example, the International Federation of Basketball (FIBA) only allows only one naturalised player to play on each national team.[22] This affected the author's brother, Crawford Palmer, when he competed for France in the 2000 Sydney Olympics as a dual national (US/France). Nationality requirements might be seen as a form of 'no-poach' agreement between SGBs in different countries. While citizenship in a European country is enough to unlock the entire European market for club-based competitions (i.e., in football, basketball etc.) thanks to the *Bosman* decision, when a competition is based upon national selection, the bargaining power of an elite athlete is constrained, to the financial benefit of the SGB. While a complete opening of the market does not seem realistic due to longstanding tradition and cultural norms, a proportionate response might be legislation guaranteeing a minimum level of compensation and social protections, including unemployment and retirement for Olympic athletes.

Nationality affects mobility in other ways, as well. It has deep cultural and social roots. The conflation of national team participation with national pride creates another source of pressure for high-level athletes seeking to improve compensation or working conditions. There can be an intensely negative public relations dynamic when an athlete changes nationality or competes for one country over another.[23]

8.3.3 Economic exploitation

8.3.3.1 General remarks

Employers with a concentrated market position typically depress the wages and working conditions of their workers for their own financial benefit. A classic example is to be found in the film *How Green Was My Valley*, a film about a mining company that was the only employer in a town in Wales and, as such, imposed low wages and horrendous working conditions on the local population who had very little mobility or choice of where to work. In the case of global sport, the market concentration is so great that, in the absence of any countervailing labour organisation, sport organisations are able not only to depress wages but also to

22 FIBA Internal Regulations Book 3, Players and Officials, https://www.fiba.basketball/en/Module/c9dad82f-01af-45e0-bb85-ee4cf50235b4/b5395573-fcd7–44d6–9ae7–20b752b50554, Rule 20.a.

23 Wu, H. (2022) Eileen Gu and Zhu Yi, Both American-Born Athletes Competing for China in the Olympics, Polarize Chinese Social Media. *Associated Press*, 8 February 8,https://www.pbs.org/newshour/world/eileen-gu-and-zhu-yi-both-american-born-athletes-competing-for-china-in-the-olympics-polarize-chinese-social-media.

construct the market in such a way as to misclassify workers or deny worker status outright.

It is common for monopsonistic employers to pay lower wages than would be the case in a perfectly competitive market.[24] Research done by Global Athlete and the Ted Rogers School of Business at Ryerson University in Toronto, Canada, shows that Olympic athletes receive only a 4.1% share of revenue from the Olympic movement and only .5% directly from the IOC on revenues of $1.4 billion annually. 58% of the 500 Olympians that responded to the survey did not feel financially stable.[25] According to the same study, university athletes in the United States receive an even smaller share of overall revenue as their compensation is capped at the value of a scholarship with some minor adjustments allowable as a result of recent court decisions. In golf and tennis, sports with more competitive markets but without collective bargaining, athletes receive 22.6% and 17.5%, respectively. In sports with collective bargaining, athletes receive a much larger share of revenue, just as would be expected in a monopsonistic market where the workers had achieved 'voice.' Premier league players receive an estimated 61% of revenue, Bundesliga players receive 53%, the professional players in the United States in baseball, ice hockey, basketball and American football all receive between 47% and 50%, while the Australian Football League (AFL) receive 28%.

8.3.3.2 Disguised work

In the case of the Olympic Games, the market concentration is so great that, in the absence of any countervailing labour organisation, SGBs are able to construct the market in such a way as to misclassify workers or deny worker status outright. In 2020, Lana Hadad, the chief operating officer (COO) of the IOC, wrote in a response to the previously cited report by Global Athlete that 'athletes are not employed by the IOC and should not be considered workers' and that 'calls for direct payments to athletes are disturbing.'[26] Employment relations for Olympic athletes are structured in a variety of different ways across the EU. In many countries, some categories of high-performance athletes are employed by the police or military but not directly by SGBs. Some high-performance athletes may receive a stipend or scholarship which covers some of their expenses and provides a basic income.[27] As stated earlier, the European Commission recently proposed a Directive on improving working conditions in platform work those addresses

24 Naidu et al. (2018).

25 Associated Press (2020) Survey Finds Olympic, Elite Athletes Struggling Financially. *USA Today*, 24 February, https://www.usatoday.com/story/sports/olympics/2020/02/24/survey-finds-olympic-elite-athletes-struggling-financially/111365842/.

26 Haddad, L. (2020) The IOC Stands in Solidarity with All Athletes and All Sports. *International Olympic Committee*, 20 May, https://olympics.com/ioc/news/the-ioc-stands-in-solidarity-with-all-athletes-and-all-sports.

27 Norlander (2022).

many of the same issues that high-performance athletes face. Its text states that 'bogus self-employment occurs when a person is declared to be self-employed while fulfilling the conditions characteristic of an employment relationship, in order to avoid certain legal or fiscal responsibilities' and, 'the determination of the existence of an employment relationship should be guided by the facts relating to the actual performance of the work and not by the parties' description of the relationship.'[28] Looking at the standards laid out in the International Labour Organization's (ILO) Employment Relationship Recommendation,[29] it is quite clear that there are very few, if any, high-level athletes that would be excluded from worker status no matter how an SGBs defines the relationship. These standards include:

- A level of control
- Integration into activities
- Consideration for who the work benefits
- Definition of training and/or competition times and schedules
- Provision of equipment, uniforms and materials to participate
- Compensation or other benefits in kind including food, lodging, or transport

There are three important cases that have addressed the issue of the employment status of Olympic athletes in Europe. Although no longer in the EU, an Employment Tribunal in the UK found that the national team cyclist, Jess Varnish, who filed a claim of discrimination and wrongful termination, was not an employee. It found, instead, that she was receiving services from UK Cycling. Considering that her compensation came from the UK Lottery, not UK Cycling, and that she was free to choose her own coach, the tribunal did not grant her claim. In Austria, on the other hand, two athletes, Vanessa Sahinovic and Lukas Muller,[30] were injured while competing for their national teams and sued successfully to have the injuries considered to be work-related accidents. Sahinovic was 15 years old and a synchronised swimmer when she was hit by a bus during the European Olympic Games in Baku, Azerbaijan.[31] Muller was a skier who suffered a terrible crash during competition.[32] These two Austrian cases set an important precedent going forward that will be difficult for SGBs to deny.

28 Directive (EU) 2019/1152 of the European Parliament and of the Council of 20 June 2019 on transparent and predictable working conditions in the European Union. OJ L 186, 11.7.2019, pp. 105–121.

29 R198 – Employment Relationship Recommendation, 2006 (No. 198), https://ilo.org/dyn/normlex/en/f?p=NORMLEXPUB:12100:0::NO::P12100_INSTRUMENT_ID:312535.

30 Kamps, A. (2019) VwGH stuft Lukas Müllers Sturz als Arbeitsunfall ein, https://www.juve.de/verfahren/arbeitnehmer-am-start-vvgh-stuft-lukas-muellers-sturz-als-arbeitsunfall-ein/.

31 Neuman, F. (2017), Gericht: Sahinovic hatte einen Arbeitsunfall. *Der Standard*, https://www.derstandard.at/consent/tcf/story/2000057794007/gerichtvanessa-sahinovic-war-arbeitsunfall.

32 Austrian Press Association (2019). Lukas Müller nach VwGH-Urteil erfreut, https://www.spox.com/at/sport/mehrsport/wintersport/1905/Artikel/lukas-mueller-nach-vwgh-urteil-erfreut.html.

8.3.3.3 Abuse of transnational labour

In my early years as a labour organiser in professional basketball in Germany, I would visit teams around the country, meeting players in the locker rooms. On one of my first visits to the team in Berlin, a young player from Burkina Faso, Thomas Compaore, approached me with questions about his contract. Thomas was 18 years old and did not have an agent. He spoke very little, if any, German and wanted to transfer to the French league where he spoke the language and felt more at home. He had signed his contract shortly after his 18th birthday. It was a seven-year contract for €400 a month, increasing in increments after year four. It contained a buyout clause for the team if Thomas developed into a quality player and transferred teams. It was a valid contract, but the question was, how had Thomas been able to get a work permit. German law, at the time, required certification from the team that Thomas was making over €2,625 a month and a certification from the national federation that he was playing in the first division. Thomas was making €400 a month and was playing in the 3rd division.[33] We asked him to go to the immigration office to ask for his paperwork. When he arrived, they were very reluctant to give him copies and made him wait several hours. He finally received copies and we found that both the team and the federation had made what appeared to be false declarations. We asked the team to release him, or we would need to refer the case to the public prosecutor's office. In the end, the case was referred but the team made a deal with Thomas that he would be released if he dropped the union from the case to avoid further legal issues. Thomas went on to play in France but was diagnosed with a heart condition shortly afterwards. He died only a few years later of a heart attack.

There are innumerable cases of young athletes being trafficked for sport, especially in Europe.[34]

> Global sport requires transnational labour, often with tragic human externalities that include trafficked, exploited and abandoned human and child labour. For all the glory associated with known and valorised transnational athletes, there remain many unnoticed others: 'many of the world's football migrants, employed on the margins of the professional game – in semi-professional or even amateur leagues – and with precarious working contracts, fit categories which can be more easily located within general patterns of mass labour[35]

33 Rößner, J. (2006) Fall Compaoré: Alba Berlin prüft rechtliche Schritte gegen, 'Spin.' *Berliner Morgenpost*, 07 April 2006, https://www.morgenpost.de/printarchiv/sport/article104567221/Fall-Compaore-Alba-Berlin-prueft-rechtliche-Schritte-gegen-Spin.html.

34 Esson (2015).

35 *Ibid.*

8.3.4 Non-monetary issues regarding athletes' rights

8.3.4.1 Discrimination

One of the areas that has become accepted as part of the 'specificity of sport' is the division of sport between male and female categories. Unfortunately, in the economic sphere, the narrative that men's sports are more marketable has, in effect, become a self-fulfilling narrative. Women's sport often receives much less investment and media attention despite massive grassroots interest and participation. Discrimination in the form of underinvestment in women's sport is rampant and it is only where there is strong athlete collective representation where equal pay conditions are being enforced at levels appropriate to the market. It is common for firms with monopsony power to discriminate against vulnerable groups of workers.[36] Peter Norlander, an Associate Professor of management at Loyola University in Chicago, wrote:

> An employer with monopsony power can profit through exploiting the difference between the value of work and the lowest wage at which a worker is willing to work (this 'reservation price' is often set by a worker's best option in the external labour market, which is lower for groups facing discrimination in the labour market). When non-discrimination laws require a firm to pay equal wages to disadvantaged groups, a monopsonist has less profit from exploitation, but more workers who had faced discrimination may enter the labour market as wages go higher. In the study of the UK Equal Pay Act, both wages and employment of women increase, suggesting that non-discrimination and curtailing the use of monopsony power go hand in hand and can improve labour market outcomes.[37]

In the case of sport, if equal pay were enforced for women, we would see more women choosing more women to become high-performance athletes or stay in competitive sport longer, potentially creating a virtual cycle of investment.

In US college sports, we are already witnessing what can happen for women athletes when collusive and discriminatory practices are ended. It was assumed by some that when rules against athletes profiting from the marketing of their own name, image and likeness were lifted that it would be male athletes from the so-called 'revenue' sports of American football and basketball that would benefit the most. Instead, many of the top earners in the new NIL marketplace are women athletes in sports like basketball, gymnastics and figure skating.[38]

36 Norlander (2022).

37 *Ibid.*

38 Wegryn, R. (2021) The NCAA Rich List: The Athletes Cashing in Most on Their NIL. WegENT blog, https://wegrynenterprises.com/2021/09/30/the-ncaa-rich-list-the-athletes-cashing-in-most-on-their-nil/.

An organised athlete voice and collective bargaining has an important role to play in countering pay discrimination. There have been several recent cases where women athletes, through their player associations, have launched successful campaigns for equal pay. Most recently, the women's national team players in the United States settled an equal pay dispute for $24 million, most of which would go towards back pay for the players.[39]

In university sports in the United States, racial discrimination remains a serious issue. In the two main revenue producing sports of men's basketball and American football (played only by men), most players are black; however, graduation rates for black football and basketball players rank well below those of white athletes and other students.[40] In his seminal article on the NCAA in *The Atlantic* magazine in 2011, Pulitzer Prize–winning author, Taylor Branch, described the NCAA's college model as having 'a whiff of the plantation.'

8.3.4.2 High injury rates

Workplace injuries are common, even taken for granted, in the athletic workplace. Investment in health and safety is uneven and often inadequate, especially below the very highest and most visible levels. Athletes are often celebrated for their resilience and toughness for continuing to compete when injured. Without safeguards and high standards in collective bargaining agreements, the pressure to compete when injured from the coaches, administrators and even the athletes themselves, is often impossible to overcome.

8.3.4.3 Co-opted voice

The Olympic Movement recognises the power of the athlete voice. The first Athlete Commission was founded after the Olympic boycott in 1980 and it has been reformed and highlighted over the years in the wake of other scandals such as the 2002 Salt Lake City bribery scandal and the 2014 Sochi Games Russian doping scandal. It is important to recognise that Athlete Commissions are internal management structures that are susceptible to being co-opted. In the case of the IOC Athletes Commission, they are IOC members and swear an oath to uphold the interests of the IOC. There is potential that they could play a positive role in addressing issues of bargaining power if structured with intention and with active participants. They might fill the role of works councils to exercise certain rights of consultation around working time, time off and professional

39 Knutson, J. (2022) U.S. Soccer and Women's Players Settle Equal Pay Suit. *Axios,* 22 February, https://www.axios.com/uswnt-soccer-equal-pay-lawsuit-settlement-71ba835c-c9c0-4b17-b2cd-ffdf866bc20a.html.

40 Brenneman, R. (2018). Black Athletes' Graduation Rates Lag at U.S. Universities with Top Sports Teams, https://news.usc.edu/138228/leading-sports-schools-black-athletes-graduation-rates-lower/.

development (*Mitbestimmung*), but leave negotiations on issues related to compensation and working conditions to independent athlete organisations and unions.

8.3.4.4 Forced arbitration

High-performance athletes are confronted with the 'choice' of either accepting an arbitration clause in their participation licences and agreements that requires them to take all disputes to the Court of Arbitration for Sport (CAS) or leave their sport. The structure of the CAS is decidedly undemocratic and tips in the favour of SGBs. The CAS arbitrators are selected by the International Council of Arbitration for Sport (ICAS). Its current President is John Coates, a Vice President of the IOC; its Vice-President is Michael B. Lenard, a former executive with the United States Olympic Committee (USOC). Many of the current members of the ICAS were formerly executives or employees of SGBs. As Antoine Duval, a Senior Researcher at the T.M.C. Asser Institute, described the process in his assessment of the Claudia Pechstein judgment, that 'CAS arbitration is forced arbitration.'[41]

8.3.4.5 Workplace surveillance

While much has been made of the onerous requirements and workplace surveillance techniques in Amazon.com warehouses, high-level athletes undergo a much more invasive and personalised level of proactive surveillance related to their work. All Olympic athletes must agree to abide by the World Anti-Doping Code (WADC) which includes a whereabouts reporting requirement. Athletes, not under any form of indictment or suspicion, must fill out their whereabouts 24/7/365, three months in advance into WADA's ADAMS reporting system. Athletes are required to stay in place for one hour every day to be available to testers. If a tester arrives at their home, they are required to allow the tester to remain in their presence until they can urinate while the tester watches. The Article 29 Working Party on Data Protection, now the European Data Protection Board,[42] stated in its submission during the third stage of the revision of the WADC in 2013 that 'any form of proactive surveillance in order to detect potential violations goes against the principle of proportionality.'[43]

41 Duval (2016).

42 The European Data Protection Board (EDPB) is an independent European body, which contributes to the consistent application of data protection rules throughout the European Union and promotes cooperation between the EU's data protection authorities. The EDPB replaced the Article 29 Working Party on 25 May 2018.

43 Article 29 Working Party (2013) Contribution of the Article 29 Working Party to the 3rd Stage of WADA's Consultation in the Context of the Review of the World Anti-Doping Code and its International Standards, https://ec.europa.eu/justice/article-29/documentation/other-document/files/2013/20130305_letter-to-wada_annex_en.pdf.

8.3.5 Wider governance issues

8.3.5.1 Inappropriate enrichment

One common characteristic in sport organisations that limit or regulate payment of athletes like the Olympics and the NCAA[44] is that revenue is often channelled into facilities and compensation for coaches and/or administrators. In the NCAA, college basketball or football coaches were the highest-paid public employees in 40 states.[45] Olympic officials receive daily stipends of $450/$900 a day, travel business class and stay in the very best hotels. The University of Oklahoma recently spent $370 million to upgrade its (American) football facilities. And the IOC recently completed the construction of the 'Olympic House' with revenues from the Olympic Games that cost an estimated $190 million.[46]

8.3.5.2 Controversial host cities

Athletes have extremely limited voice when it comes to choosing the location of their work. The location of competitions like the Olympic Games is determined, in large part, for financial or political reasons that benefit the SGB. Over the past few years, cities like Baku, Minsk, Sochi and Beijing have hosted either the European or Olympic Games. Many other candidate cities have dropped out of the running due to popular referendums or public pressure.

8.3.6 Findings

With all these negative factors impacting athletes, one must wonder what would happen if there were competition in the market for high-performance athlete labour. If athletes had a choice of where to work, would we see improvements in any of these areas? Without competition, or 'exit,' and as athletes become sensitised to these negative impacts, they become more inclined to challenge the status quo. This creates a new challenge for SGBs when trying to maintain their current business model.

44 Gaio, M. (2014) Oklahoma Sooners Announce $370M Stadium Renovation? *Athletic Business*, 26 June, https://www.athleticbusiness.com/facilities/stadium-arena/article/15145875/oklahoma-sooners-announce-370m-stadium-renovation.

45 Gibson, C. (2019) Who Is the Highest Paid in Your State? http://www.espn.com/espn/feature/story?id=28261213&_slug_=dabo-swinney-ed-orgeron-highest-paid-state-employees&redirected=true.

46 Owen, D. (2019) Final Bill for New IOC Headquarters Set to be More than $190 Million, Latest Figures Reveal. *Inside the Games*, 25 June, https://www.insidethegames.biz/articles/1081196/final-bill-for-new-ioc-headquarters-set-to-be-more-than-190-million-latest-figures-reveal.

8.4 Growing antitrust risk

Globally, sport organisations are facing increased antitrust risk. This is due to several legal and social policy trends colliding with the monopoly structures (i.e., one sport, one federation) of sport governance and certain innate characteristics related to the organisation of competitions.

The first key trend is the dramatic rise in the commercialisation of global sport. The IOC owns the Olympic Games, operating them as a non-profit much like the National Football League did until 2015.[47] Revenues for the Olympic Games have increased to $5.7 billion during the Olympiad spanning from 2013–2016 that included the Winter Games in Sochi and the summer Olympic Games in Rio de Janeiro.[48] The global market for sport is expected to exceed $500 billion by 2022. Indeed, US Supreme Court justice, Neil Gorsuch, might as well have been referring to the global model of sport governance when he wrote in his ruling in *NCAA v. Alston*, 'at the centre of this thicket of associations and rules sits a massive business.'[49]

Second, the growth in commercialisation has coincided with the rapid increase in the number of countries with antitrust laws. Before the Single European Act of 1987, barely a half-dozen jurisdictions in the entire world could claim any significant antitrust enforcement record.[50] Today, following the collapse of the Soviet Union in 1991 and with encouragement from the EU, United States, International Monetary Fund (IMF) and World Bank,[51] more than 120 countries have some form of antitrust or competition laws.[52]

Third, there is an increased emphasis on private enforcement of antitrust laws in the EU. Public and private enforcement of antitrust laws play different, yet complementary roles.[53] State antitrust authorities protect the public from harms resulting from anticompetitive conduct. Private enforcers typically act on their own behalf or on behalf of an affected group of which they are a member, usually seeking damages for any antitrust harms.[54] In the EU, an emerging focus

47 Bryson Law Firm (2015) Touchdown: Pay up – NFL Is a Nonprofit No More. 6 May. https://www.brysonlawfirm.com/news/122-touchdown-pay-up-nfl-is-a-nonprofit-no-more.html#gref.

48 See Funding: How the IOC Finances a Better World Through Sport, https://olympics.com/ioc/funding

49 *NCAA v. Alston* (fn 16), Opinion of the Court, p. 7.

50 Lipsky (2009).

51 *Ibid.*

52 Morton, F. (2016) How Do You Enforce Antitrust Law in a Global Marketplace? *Yale Insights*, 16 June, https://insights.som.yale.edu/insights/how-do-you-enforce-antitrust-law-in-global-marketplace.

53 European Commission (2014) Antitrust: Commission Welcomes Council Adoption of Directive on Antitrust Damages Actions. IP/14/1580, 10 November, https://ec.europa.eu/commission/presscorner/detail/en/IP_14_1580.

54 OECD Working Party No. 3 on Co-operation and Enforcement (2015), Relationship Between Public and Private Antitrust Enforcement. Note by the Secretariat. DAF/COMP/WP3(2015)14,

on private enforcement culminated with the passage of the Antitrust Damages Directive in 2014.[55]

In the United States, the threat of private enforcement of antitrust claims is a common form of leverage for player associations when locked out by their leagues. Player associations have used the threat of decertifying their union to increase legal pressure on leagues to resolve the lockout. In March of 2011, the NFL Players Association decertified and became a trade association. The legal theory behind this strategy was that without a union to negotiate with, the NFL would no longer be eligible for the non-statutory antitrust exemption through collective bargaining and would be susceptible to antitrust challenges.

Because the EU is a transnational confederation of states that is relatively immune, in the aggregate, from the leverage that the IOC can bring against individual nation states, European laws and courts are somewhat insulated from pressure being brought to bear from the Olympic Movement. The European Commission has taken what it describes as a 'balanced approach' to sport, the 'activity of sport associations, leagues, teams and other organisers has not been significantly disturbed over the past few years by competition law scrutiny.'[56] However, with several recent decisions, this trend appears to be changing course. The most recent of real significance is the case of Dutch speed skaters, Mark Tuitert and Nils Kerstholt, who brought a complaint to the European Commission that the International Skating Union was in violation of Article 101 TFEU for rules restricting athletes from taking part in rival events. In 2017, the Commission found that the International Skating Union's (ISU) eligibility rules were incompatible with antitrust laws. In December 2020, the General Court affirmed this decision. The ISU has filed an appeal but until that is heard and decided, the decision of the General Court stands. As referred to earlier, the ISU's restrictions on the mobility of athletes to compete in other competitions was an assertion of their monopsonistic bargaining position. The decision against them is another indication of the direction the winds are blowing.

8.5 The transnational governance of sport and a campaign for 'autonomy'

In 2013, Thomas Bach, the current President of the IOC, addressed the General Assembly of the United Nations and declared: 'Sport [is] truly the only area of human existence which has achieved universal law, but to apply this universal

https://www.oecd.org/officialdocuments/publicdisplaydocumentpdf/?cote=DAF/COMP/WP3(2015)14&docLanguage=En.

55 Directive 2014/104/EU of the European Parliament and of the Council of 26 November 2014 on certain rules governing actions for damages under national law for infringements of the competition law provisions of the Member States and of the European Union. OJ L 349, 5.12.2014, pp. 1–19.

56 Kolasiński (2016).

law worldwide, sport has to enjoy responsible autonomy. Politics must respect this sporting autonomy.'[57] This assertion of autonomy tracks well with the constant tension between the IOC's supranational governance of international sport and national politics. Quinn Slobodian, a professor at Wellesley College in the United States, describes in his book *Globalists: The End of Empire and the Birth of Neoliberalism* the neoliberal ideal as a 'double government' with 'one world of the economy and ownership, coexisting with another world of nations.' The IOC with its assertion of 'supreme authority'[58] over the world of international sport and the market for athlete labour appears to be attempting to create a parallel sovereignty,[59] or a *lex sportiva*, to avoid accountability to democracy and national law and, thus, keep its Olympic profits out of reach of antitrust laws.

8.5.1 European campaign for 'specificity' or the 'European Model of Sport'

A key, but often overlooked component of the campaign in Europe, was a lobbying push for block exemptions from antitrust law. The UK Presidency of the EU in 2005 established an initiative to review the rules applicable to European football that morphed into a broader report called the 'Independent European Sport Review.' UEFA, the European football federation, commissioned and funded the report. One of the conclusions was to implement block exemptions from antitrust law for 'certain categories of agreements and concerted practices in sport' and that EU governments would commit to enforce the recommendations outlined in the 'Independent European Sport Review.'[60] The appeal for block exemptions was not adopted but the concept of 'specificity' was further developed in the White Paper on Sport that was published by the European Commission in 2007. In 2009, the Treaty of Lisbon entered into force and gave, for the first time, European institutions a competence for the 'promotion of European sporting issues' while 'taking into account the specific nature of sport.'[61] For SGBs and the Olympic Movement, this nod to sport being somehow different from other areas of economic activity provided renewed hope that the antitrust risks facing the 'European Model of Sport' might be overlooked by EU institutions in the future. This had the corresponding effect of reducing the motivation for any

57 IOC Press Release (2014) Historic Milestone: United Nations Recognises Autonomy of Sport, 3 November, https://www.olympic.org/news/historic-milestone-united-nations-recognises-autonomy-of-sport.

58 Olympic Charter, Charter in force as from 8 August 2021, https://stillmed.olympics.com/media/Document%20Library/OlympicOrg/General/EN-Olympic-Charter.pdf?_ga=2.77769236.1083376507.1654781249-528988693.1654781249.

59 Duval (2018).

60 Arnaut, J.L. (2006) Independent European Sport Review. [No place of publication; no publisher] [Original website, no longer functional: www.independentsportreview.com]. http://eose.org/ressource/independant-european-sports-review/.

61 Article 165 TFEU.

SGBs to participate in social dialogue or collective bargaining with their athletes. Concretely, this was seen by the almost complete lack of engagement with a pilot European Sectoral Social Dialogue Committee that ran approximately between 2009 and 2017. If there had been a real threat of antitrust enforcement during that time, the results of the pilot might have been different. Considering the recent trends outlined in this chapter, another opportunity for social dialogue at the European level may emerge again soon.

8.5.2 The IOC and the Olympic movement have a choice

SGBs in Europe, when faced with the risk of antitrust enforcement, have a choice to make between continuing to campaign for a political exemption or looking to collaborate with their athletes to take advantage of the autonomy provided in the collective bargaining process. *Albany International BV v Stichting Bedrijfspensioenfonds Textielindustrie,* a case decided by the European Court of Justice in 1999, resolved the issue of a collective bargaining agreement's status under competition law, as long as it seeks to improve conditions of work and employment.[62] So far, the choice made by the Olympic Movement was to campaign vigorously, but with limited success, for a 'statutory' exemption from European antitrust laws while undermining or ignoring athlete labour rights. This campaign has ebbed and flowed over the years, returning with renewed vigour in the wake of each of the *Bosman*, *Meca-Medina* and *ISU* decisions. Respect sport's 'autonomy,' the argument goes, and the legal certainty that follows will give sport the necessary stability to address the burning governance issues currently faced by sport. The campaign for 'specificity' and 'autonomy' is an anti-union campaign by a global business that wants to write its own rules. Seen from the perspective of the international federation and NOC, the primary threat to their current business model, where sport organisations keep 96% of the revenues, is countervailing athlete power. The question that must be asked by European institutions, however, is whether sport's business model is consistent with the European Social Model.

8.6 Conclusion

As antitrust risk increases for SGBs due to some of the trends outlined in this chapter, they must choose between continuing to lobby for an exemption from European law or begin a real dialogue with their athletes to bring their anticompetitive practices under the umbrella of an autonomous social dialogue

62 Judgment of the Court of 21 September 1999. Albany International BV v Stichting Bedrijfspensioenfonds Textielindustrie. – Reference for a preliminary ruling: Kantongerecht Arnhem – Netherlands. – Compulsory affiliation to a sectoral pension scheme – Compatibility with competition rules – Classification of a sectoral pension fund as an undertaking. – Case C-67/96. ECR 1999 Page I-05751.

process. The IOC and the Olympic Movement are surely aware of this choice. Therefore, the recent campaigns for the 'specificity of sport' and the 'European Model of Sport,' like the NCAA's 'college model,' must be seen fundamentally as anti-union campaigns designed to avoid sharing revenue with high performance athlete workers. The author of this chapter, as the Co-chair of the Committee, saw, in practice, how SGBs in Europe avoided participating in the test phase for the European Sectoral Social Dialogue Committee in the sport sector. The door was open. Invitations were sent. But very few SGBs answered the call, despite an active presence of the European Olympic Committee in Brussels and Strasbourg.

In the United States, one can discern three different approaches. First, the outright denial of any antitrust liability – the NCAA's 'college model' – resulting in decades of litigation and continued exploitation and damage to athletes. Second, the limited statutory exemption granted to the USOC and the Olympic federations through the Amateur Sports Act (ASA) that maintains the bargaining power and monolithic governance model of the federations, resulting in multiple athlete abuse scandals and continued economic exploitation. Finally, the collectively bargained sport governance model of the so-called professional leagues (i.e., NBA, NFL, NHL and MLB) where athletes have fought for 'voice' in a monopsonistic market to be represented by a democratic labour union, could negotiate wages and working conditions, have more balanced outcomes than European leagues[63] and both athletes and the business model have thrived.

In 2020, the ILO hosted a Global Dialogue Forum on Decent Work in the World of Sport. A key recommendation from the Forum was that 'governments, employers' and workers' organizations and other relevant stakeholders should promote all forms of effective social dialogue to advance decent work in sport, including through collective bargaining, at national, regional and global levels, as appropriate.' The IOC participated as an observer and its representative, the Chair of the Athletes Commission, made a statement in emphasising the IOC's preference for its own internal system of athlete representation and in support of the 'solidarity' system of revenue distribution.[64]

At the beginning of this chapter, I stated that antitrust law has the potential to bring the social policy objectives of sport and labour relations into balance in the EU. It might be better to say that the risk of antitrust enforcement has the potential to bring a monopsonist to the table to engage in social dialogue or collective bargaining. It is only in this context that high-performance athletes will have a chance to create more balance in the bargaining positions of the two sides. At the end of the day, it is not a zero-sum game. As we have seen from the experience in the United States, an improvement in conditions for athletes grows the market for both SGBs and athletes. Like the team owners in the United States, the IOC

63 Buzzacchi et al. (2003).

64 Points of Consensus (2020) *Global Dialogue Forum on Decent Work in the World of Sport*. International Labour Organization, https://www.ilo.org/wcmsp5/groups/public/---ed_dialogue/---sector/documents/meetingdocument/wcms_735388.pdf.

owns the Olympic Games. Unlike the US team owners and league commissioners, the IOC could prove that Olympic values are more than just a branding exercise, by bringing them into alignment with the European Social Model. It's straightforward, athletes performing in an environment free from discrimination, that is safe, where they are justly compensated, with social protections, and allowed to organise and collectively bargain will perform better, for longer. That outcome is in the interest of sport, athletes, spectators and society at large; but it hinges on the Olympic Movement making the right choice.

Bibliography

Buzzacchi, L., Szymanski, S. & Valletti, T.M. (2003) Equality of Opportunity and Equality of Outcome: Open Leagues, Closed Leagues and Competitive Balance. *Journal of Industry, Competition and Trade*, 3, 167–186.

Duval, A. (2016) The Pechstein case: Transnational Constitutionalism in Inaction at the Bundesgerichtshof? *Verfassungsblog*, 10 June, https://verfassungsblog.de/the-pechstein-case-transnational-constitutionalism-in-inaction-at-the-bundesgerichtshof/

Duval, A. (2018) The Olympic Charter: A Transnational Constitution Without a State? *Journal of Law and Society*, 45:S1, S245–S269.

Esson, J. (2015) Better Off at Home? Rethinking Responses to Trafficked West African Footballers in Europe. *Journal of Ethnic and Migration Studies*, 41:3, 512–530.

Farzin, L. (2015) On the Antitrust Exemption for Professional Sports in the United States and Europe. *Jeffrey S. Moorad Sports Law Journal*, 22:1, 75–108.

Gangopadhyay, P. & Shankar, S. (2016) Labour (im)mobility and Monopsonistic Exploitation of Workers in the Urban Informal Sector: Lessons from a Field Study. *Urban Studies*, 53:5, 1042–1060.

Kolasiński, M. (2016) Influence of the Private Enforcement of Competition Law on Sport in the European Union against the United States Law Background. *Harvard Journal of Sports and Entertainment Law*, 23 March, https://harvardjsel.com/2016/03/influence-of-the-private-enforcement-of-competition-law-on-sport-in-the-european-union-against-the-united-states-law-background/#_ftn1

Lipsky, A. (2009) Managing Antitrust Compliance through the Continuing Surge in Global Enforcement. *Antitrust Law Journal*, 75:3, 965–995.

Naidu, S., Posner, E. & Weyl, G. (2018) Antitrust Remedies for Labor Market Power. *Harvard Law Review*, 132, 537–601.

Norlander, P. (2022) Countering Employer Monopsony Power with Fundamental Labor Rights. *PROMARKET* (Stigler Center at the University of Chicago's Booth School of Business). https://www.promarket.org/2022/01/20/countering-employer-monopsony-power-with-fundamental-labor-rights/

Slobodian, Q. (2020) *Globalists: The End of Empire and the Birth of Neoliberalism*. Harvard University Press.

9

CONCLUSION

EU antitrust law and the future of the sports pyramid and the 'one federation' principle

Jacob Kornbeck

9.1 Introduction

9.1.1 Aims

The present book was designed to address currently topical issues related to the application of European Union (EU) antitrust law to sport, including in relation to sports governance. While the book was conceived in the context of the three test cases then pending before the Court of Justice of European Union (CJEU), it was designed to take stock of the development of EU sports antitrust law up until 2022. In so doing, it should identify its salient points and draw some lessons, not only from the perspective of compliance work (steering clear of trouble with regulators and courts) but also as an opportunity for reform and renewal within the sector. At this writing (Summer 2022), the outcome of the three test cases remained unknown, whereas it seemed reasonable – even warranted – to extrapolate as much as possible from the accumulated wisdom of administrative decisional practice and the case law of the judiciary. The purpose of this Conclusion, therefore, is to summarise the lessons learnt through the substantive chapters of this book, and to develop some thoughts regarding sports governance.

This book was conceived at the very moment when another edited book was going to press (*Sport & Brexit*[1]), which went a long way to demonstrate the impact and relevance of the EU's regulatory capacity, yet without a chapter on antitrust law, while state aid, that other third of EU competition policy (alongside merger control), was on board. One reason for editing the present book was probably an urge (of its editor) to compensate for the absence of antitrust in the previous one, yet another – even stronger – urge came from developments unfolding within

1 Kornbeck (2022).

DOI: 10.4324/9781003305989-9

the past few years. While recent, these developments actually hark back quite some decades and seem to confirm that something had been building up over quite some time. Drawing inspiration from a paper on state aid law and sport,[2] one might well ask the question: 'EU antitrust law and sport: why now?' For while timing is always somehow involved whenever social and legal issues are at stake, observers and analysts of the current discords, rifts and struggles will be grappling with questions such as those set out in the following section.

9.1.2 The sports pyramid and the 'one federation' principle

In drawing the main lessons from the substantive chapters of the book, the present Conclusion will address the question of what impact EU antitrust law may be expected to have, in 2022 and beyond, upon the future of the sports pyramid as we know it in the EU and worldwide. The pyramid is an evocative image of European and Olympic sports (but not of North American league sports), with all levels of organisation and practice being integrated vertically within the same structure. The pyramidal structure and the concomitant monopoly of one sports governing body (SGB) for each geographical catchment area (global, continental, national etc.) were recognised by the European Commission, in its 1999 'Helsinki Report' on the 'European sports model,' as constitutive of this model.[3] This empirical reality was acknowledged once more in the 2007 White Paper on Sport, defining these two elements as central to the 'specificity' of sport while also warning that their existence should not be taken as evidence of 'a general exemption from the application of EU law.'[4] While acknowledging the existence of debates referring to a 'European model' of sport, the Commission further found it 'unrealistic to try to define a unified model of organisation of sport in Europe.'[5]

For all practical purposes, and certainly as far as the application of antitrust law is concerned, the pyramidal structure must be interpreted in conjunction with the monopoly enjoyed by SGBs, sometimes explicitly recognised by public authorities and sometimes merely tolerated yet not challenged. The 'one federation' or 'one place' principle[6] is a concept derived from German, where it has been in common parlance (at least within the relevant professional and academic communities) for three to four decades. It has no direct English or French translation

2 Van Rompuy & van Maren (2016).
3 Report from the Commission to the European Council with a view to safeguarding current sports structures and maintaining the social function of sport within the Community framework – The Helsinki Report on Sport – Brussels, 10.12.1999. COM(1999) 644 final, p. 9, sec. 4.2.3.
4 White Paper on Sport. Brussels, 11.7.2007. COM(2007) 391 final, p. 13, sec. 4.1: 'In line with established case law, the specificity of sport will continue to be recognised, but it cannot be construed so as to justify a general exemption from the application of EU law.'
5 Ibid., p. 12, sec. 4.
6 Vieweg (1983); Gießelmann-Goetze (1987); Kornbeck (2020).

but remains a useful analytical tool.[7] Yet one thing is acknowledging the current relevance of the pyramid and the 'one federation' principle; quite another matter is whether public authorities can be expected to defer to them in perpetuity. As the Munich District Court (*Landgericht*) N° I (LG München I) noted in a judgment issued in 2018, the mere fact that the 'one federation' principle is applied worldwide 'does not justify the interest of the respondent in its preservation.'[8] If the pyramid and the 'one federation' principle are to be retained, adjustments may be needed, in which case EU antitrust law may provide precious guidance as to how they could be applied in the future.

9.2 Lessons learnt

9.2.1 Opportunistic litigation or ineluctable change?

As debates accompanying the Superleague initiative have shown,[9] challenges (whether legal or otherwise) to extant arrangements regarding the ownership and governance of sports have the potential to trigger emotionally strong responses. The emotional aspect is so outspoken that the matter has revealed a certain potential for populist responses, as in the threat by (then) British Prime Minister Boris Johnson that he might drop 'a legislative bomb.'[10] While populism is not new to the antitrust community,[11] Johnson's menace implies a further example of reaping the 'Brexit dividend' by profiting from regained British legislative autonomy to adopt measures which might have been unlawful for an EU Member State. The same might apply to state aid enforcement, across sectors,[12] as an apparent illustration of the sport sector being subjected to generic Brexit dynamics in the same way as other sectors. Alternatively, Johnson's statements could be interpreted as evidence that a sports regulation file holds particular potential for conflict with the EU, even if there may currently seem to be little potential for UK-EU confrontation in the field of sport (although this might change in the

7 At the CJEU hearings in *International Skating Union* (Case C-124/21 P) and *European Superleague Company* (Case C-333/21) on 11–12 July 2022, it was noteworthy how many interventions relied on the concept, sometimes even quoting the German term *Ein-Platz-Prinzip* while speaking English or French.

8 2018 LG München I, Urt. v. 25. 4. 2018, Az. 37 O 7111/17 (translation: J.K.).

9 No attempt will be made here to summarise debates in the media, on blogs etc. Suffice to say, an event cursory internet search will provide an indication of the arguments found, especially as regards the expectations of fans.

10 Walker, P., Gayle, D. & Elgot, J. (2021) Boris Johnson Threatens to Use 'legislative bomb' to Stop European Super League. *The Guardian*, Tue 20 Apr 2021 13.20 BST, https://www.theguardian.com/football/2021/apr/20/uk-government-may-legislate-to-stop-european-super-league-says-minister

11 For a discussion see e.g. Shapiro (2018).

12 On mergers e.g., see Rodger & Stephan (2022), p. 70. The same applies, *mutatis mutandis*, to State aid rules versus national industrial policy strategies.

future[13]). At any rate, Johnson's 'legislative bomb' may certainly serve as an illustration of the centrality of EU legislation to sensitive sports regulatory files such as the three text cases currently pending before the CJEU.

Yet even if contestation is based on values and objectives which may be deemed legitimate and even necessary, the question remains what triggered such developments as the – apparently universally (?) unpopular[14] – Superleague. Is the increasing commercialisation and professionalisation of sport to blame (caused by SGBs themselves, who wanted to make maximum profit out of an organisational model cast in times when sport was mainly a pastime, seldom remunerated and rarely capable of generating wider marketing activities, and certainly not on the scale seen today)? Or would the culprits rather be independent event organisers raising capital on financial markets (i.e. not SGBs themselves)? Has the recent increase in challenges to the regulatory authority of SGBs been caused by structural changes within the sport sector itself, or should it rather be attributed to factors located outside the traditional ecosystem of sport governance?

Investors like those backing the Superleague may be playing the familiar role of speculating investors, presumably in opposition to purportedly more responsible 'entrepreneurs,'[15] pursuing strategies based on identifying gaps and loopholes, inconsistencies and contradictions, to profit from them for short-term gain. Annoying as they may be, they point to shortcomings in extant policies and regulatory frameworks, thereby implicitly (and unwittingly) providing suggestions for regulatory adjustments which may be long overdue. In democratic societies, guaranteeing economic freedom within limits set by the law, with legislation enacted democratically and applied in accordance with the rule of law, their self-interested activities are perfectly legitimate, while they may also call for a legislative response regardless. This is not unlike current developments whereby digital markets are being gradually reigned in, in a (perhaps belated) process known to sociologists as 'cultural lag,'[16] where a more stable non-material culture appears maladjusted to a fast-moving material culture. While recent adjustments by the EU in adapting extant regulatory frameworks such as the General Data Protection Regulation (GDPR)[17] superseding Directive 95/46/

13 See Meier & García (2022), pp. 199–207, listing the examples of good governance, anti-doping and the prevention of match-fixing as candidates for possible future UK-EU tensions in case of clashing policy priorities.

14 For a representative selection of scholarhip, see Brannagan, Scelles, Valenti, Inoue, Grix & Perkin (2022); Dunbar (2021); Houben, Blockx & Nuyts (2022); Macedo, Ferreira Dias & Reis Mourão (2022); Meier, García, Konjer & Jetzke (2022); Welsh (2022).

15 For a distinction between 'speculation' and 'entrepreneurship,' see Keynes (1936); Hecker (2021).

16 Ogburn (1922); Woodward (1934).

17 Regulation (EU) 2016/679 of the European Parliament and of the Council of 27 April 2016 on the protection of natural persons with regard to the processing of personal data and on the free movement of such data, and repealing Directive 95/46/EC (General Data Protection Regulation). OJ L 119, 4.5.2016, p. 1–88.

EC,[18] or even creating entirely new ones such as the Digital Services Act[19] and the Digital Markets Act,[20] exhibit a pattern familiar from the regulatory areas of pollution control, the same might apply to the sport sector.

Similarly, self-interested litigants may also be rendering a (possibly involuntary) service to markets and societies by pushing for a recalibration of the law, where long-established concepts may no longer be apt to catch a complex reality. Where law and politics rely on concepts which may have become legal fictions over time, litigants may acting unwittingly as *de facto* policy entrepreneurs. Where a sector has been allowed to develop unusually lucrative commercial practices while maintaining a largely archaic legal framework, from times when the commercial activities of the sector were much less developed than they are now, perceived assaults by investors on agreed public policy objectives such as access to sport for the general population, or to sports entertainment as (tele) spectators, should perhaps lead to a critical assessment of current governance structures and practices in sport, rather than to a ring-fencing of the same regardless of whether or not they actually meet the same agreed public policy objectives. The current constellation is in fact implausibly attractive, which makes it easy to understand why SGBs can choose between so many business partners. As noted by the authors of a standard German sports law practice handbook (both of them business-friendly and sport-friendly in equal measure), it is essentially a non-profit framework allowing for the intensive commercial exploitation of high-value franchises without the usual strings attached.[21]

In *International Skating Union*, the Commission[22] did not find evidence of a credible solidarity mechanism with funds reaching the actual grassroots; the

18 Directive 95/46/EC of the European Parliament and of the Council of 24 October 1995 on the protection of individuals with regard to the processing of personal data and on the free movement of such data. OJ L 281, 23.11.1995, p. 31–50.

19 Proposal for a Regulation of the European Parliament and of the Council on a Single Market For Digital Services (Digital Services Act) and amending Directive 2000/31/EC. 15.12.2020. COM/2020/825 final.

20 Proposal for a Regulation of the European Parliament and of the Council on contestable and fair markets in the digital sector (Digital Markets Act). 15.12.2020. COM/2020/842 final.

21 According to Pfister & Friztweiler (2020), p. 15, athletes and federations tend to have opposed objective interests regarding revenue distribution, while athletes are at a structural disadvantage. Federations are led by presidents and executives who are neither proprietors nor shareholders, while the IOC even co-opts it members. No shareholder meetings have to be faced, while the usual capital/labour tension is absent, as are (frequently) trade unions and (systematically) works councils. Federations are organised with legal forms foreseen for charities and foundations which, in spite of their commercial operations, relieve them of the obligation to distribute profits to (non-existing) shareholders, allowing to keep revenues within sports.

22 Commission Decision C(2017) 8240 final, 8.122017. Case AT. 40208 – International Skating Union's Eligibility rules, https://ec.europa.eu/competition/antitrust/cases/dec_docs/40208/40208_1579_5.pdf, p. 62, at 246: 'it appears that the ISU does not refer to vertical solidarity (between professional and grassroots sport) but rather to horizontal solidarity (between richer and poorer participants in a given competition).'*Ibid.*, at 247: 'If the purpose is to foster and develop the sport of speed skating, a solidarity contribution to be requested from third party organisers of skating events may under certain circumstances be accepted but such

money distributed by International Skating Union (ISU), (the worldwide federation) to its members (national federations) might be spent anywhere within the national sports pyramid. The General Court, accordingly, while admitting that 'a sports federation with limited revenue may legitimately rely on the right to use the solidarity contribution in order to finance events which, in its view, merit such financing, and to deprive others of it,' stressed that ISU was wrong in making 'the authorisation of events organised by third parties subject to payment of a solidarity contribution which is used to finance only its own events and those of its members.'[23] This is because SGBs maintain a dual role regulating their sports while also benefiting commercially from the activities regulated by themselves: a constellation implying a structural risk of conflicts of interest, especially in connection with the 'one federation' or 'single place' principle (*Ein-Platz-Prinzip*).[24]

It is this unusual duality (at least from the point of view of liberal market economies, inasmuch as the duality is vested in non-profit organisations with a monopoly recognised or at least tolerated by public authorities) which Budzinski and Feddersen, in this book,[25] have pleaded for breaking up, in the interest not only of consumers/fans but also of competitors. While they do admit the possibility of certain 'monopoly bottlenecks' – nodes in the system where a private regulator is needed objectively for competitions to be possible at all – the two economists consider it both desirable and feasible to identify these functions empirically. Following this line of thought, the case could be made for 'granting monopoly governance and exemptions from EU competition law' to an SGB, although it is a 'market-internal regulator' – as opposed to a structurally unbiased outsider – but only if appropriate functions could be identified requiring such leniency. As possible candidates, Budzinski and Feddersen propose 'rule enforcement, licensing and championship design' which, however, must be deconstructed into tasks and sub-tasks to establish necessity and proportionality. Because such tasks should be assessed empirically, they recommend open and transparent tender procedures to determine who should be offered opportunities to participate on the market thus regulated. In other words, the gate-keeping functions of SGBs could be brought more in line with the principles an open market economy if SGBs were obliged (or committed, as may be) to submit themselves to transparent

a contribution should be fair and reasonable, be used to finance grassroots sports activities and not have exclusionary effects.' See also Summary of Commission Decision of 8 December 2017 relating to a proceeding under Article 101 of the Treaty on the Functioning of the European Union and Article 53 of the EEA Agreement (Case AT.40208 – International Skating Union's Eligibility Rules) (notified under document C(2017) 8240). OJ C 148, 27.4.2018, p. 9–12.

23 GC, 16.12.2020. International Skating Union v European Commission. Case T-93/18. ECLI:EU:T:2020:610, at 114.

24 Vieweg (1983); Kornbeck (2020). It is interesting to note that, at the hearings of the CJEU in the cases *ISU* and *ESL*, on 11 and 12 July 2022, frequent reference was made to this originally German concept, with interventions made in English and French even using the original German term, on occasions.

25 *Supra,* Chapter 6.

procedures which could prevent abuse of their indisputably dominant market position. This is an equally original and intriguing proposition, as it suggests that SGBs could – under certain circumstances, with a high level of ambition, strong procedures and outside scrutiny, not just by regulators but also by consumers, competitors and the public (if they were able to consult tender documents online) – possibly act in their dual regulatory and commercial roles without abusing their position. It goes without saying that this would require major reforms and that many sports officials might find it hard to get used to the logic and culture of a system so diametrically opposed to the one they have grown up with.

On the contrary, in the absence of any meaningful structural reforms, the prediction of the present editor – irrespective of how cases will be decided in the short term – is that an increase in administrative complaints as well as litigation should be expected, as alternative event organisers, in parallel or jointly with athletes, will challenge the current arrangements repeatedly. The best way for SGBs to diminish their current discomfort with recent trends would seem to start engaging constructively with them. An example of good practice might be the decision of FINA (swimming), in 2019, as communicated in a highly mediatised way,[26] to stop sanctioning 'their' athletes from participating in alternative events.[27] Another idea might be to claim exemption on the ground of involving consumers (i.e. fans) in the production and development of the services concerned as per Article 101 (3) TFEU: a defence which does not seem to have been attempted so far. In addition to the triptych of, first, unbundling (severing the regulatory functions of SGBs from the commercial ones), second, amendments to statues and regulation and, third, sanction renunciation and light-touch application, identified elsewhere,[28] the proposition of Budzinski and Feddersen deserves earnest consideration. Until further notice, however, the vast majority of SGBs do not seem interested in venturing into such solutions.

In a system determined by the rule of law, any challenge which is not manifestly unfounded and does not represent an obstruction of justice is deemed legitimate. And there is no guarantee that litigants like ISU, ESL and Royal Antwerp will achieve all or part of what they were looking for, just like the CJEU's ruling in *Biffi*[29] must have surprised SGBs. The Court did acknowledge the 'specificity' of sport, including its social integration role; yet for the very same reason, the Court held that SGBs could not discriminate against EU citizens, as this would undermine the very same legitimate objectives already invoked. Such

26 PR 1 – FINA meets with NFs on Athlete participation in international competitions. 15 Jan 2019. http://www.fina.org/news/pr-1-fina-meets-nfs-athlete-participation-international-competitions

27 As foreseen explicitly in BL 12, FINA By Laws 2017–2021. https://www.fina.org/sites/default/files/fina_by_laws_-_16032018_new.pdf. – VC. BL 12.10 : «Failure to comply with BL 12 may lead to possible sanctions in accordance with C 12.6. »

28 Kornbeck (2020).

29 CJEU, 13.06.2019. TopFit e.V. and Daniele Biffi v Deutscher Leichtathletikverband e.V. Request for a preliminary ruling from the Amtsgericht Darmstadt. Case C-22/18. ECLI:EU:C:2019:497.

boomerang effects are not uncommon. As Cukurov has shown, in this book,[30] whether or not SGBs are allowed to discourage clubs from joining the ESL, the Superleague itself risks being a cartel and therefore potentially problematic under EU competition law. According to Cukurov, the very business model of the ESL would imply unjustified restrictions of competition, without improvements to the competitive balance being detectable. Regardless of these considerations, that author does, however, think that the current competition formats need to change to maintain the interest of fans and other consumers, which is why Cukurov pleads for a 'Europeanisation' of football competitions. This would, of course, need to be assessed critically in light of consumer trends, in various generations, regarding sports content versus other types of content.

9.2.2 A sustainable model of governance?

Are recent challenges an anomaly within an otherwise self-contained, balanced and ultimately equitable system of self-regulation (one where interference by outside regulators, however legitimate, is bound to cause disruption to an intricate equilibrium of checks and balances)? Or should they rather be considered the inevitable outcome of a continued enforcement deficit (in the sense that EC/EU antitrust rules always applied in principle, without there being a significant amount of challenges, for a variety of reasons which might be of legal or social causation and which would be open to empirical scrutiny)? The question is not so much one of financial sustainability as one of societal, political and, therefore, also legal sustainability. While the long-term financial sustainability of the current arrangements may be questioned by sports economists and sports management specialists (are we witnessing a bubble and is it going to burst one day?[31]), the focus of this book is on aspects of ownership, control and governance. As Terrien and Chappelet have shown, in this book,[32] the Superleague initiative has considerable disruptive potential, though they also show that the financial stability of the proposed cartel may be questioned. Addressing the ESL legality (under competition law) of the soft law of Fédération Internationale de Football Association (FIFA) and Union of European Football Associations (UEFA), they also note the incompatibility of the proposed format with the so-called European model of sport, while considering the level of litigation around these issues surprisingly modest so far. They stress the support of the EU Council (of Ministers), of the European Parliament and of the Council of Europe for the 'European model' defended by SGBs, while emphasising the role of fans as agents of contestation.

30 *Supra*, Chapter 4.

31 For a non-academic contribution, see Turner, A. (2021) Why the Premier League TV Rights Bubble Really Might Be about to Burst this Time. *City AM*, 18 March, 9:05 AM, https://www.cityam.com/why-the-premier-league-tv-rights-bubble-really-might-be-about-to-burst-this-time/

32 *Supra*, Chapter 7.

The observation made by Terrien and Chappelet regarding the relative absence of litigation is intriguing and should lead to reflections on the culture of the sector, the effects of socialisation within it and a generalised preference for avoiding administrative complaints and court trials. The fact that current arrangements have so rarely been challenged by involving public authorities should not serve as an argument that challenges are unfounded, since potential complainants and potential litigants, despite having standing and good chances of success based on the merits of their case, might nevertheless defer to SGBs for a variety of other, usually more pragmatic, reasons. In this connection, the legal nature of international SGBs organised under Swiss association law may help gaining a deeper understanding of the mechanics behind what seems like an enforcement deficit. For according to Baddeley, in this book,[33] arrangements in place in Switzerland offer SGBs considerable autonomy with only very limited oversight by the public authorities of the hosting country. Arbitration being the preferred mode of dispute resolution, the Swiss Federal Tribunal exhibits regular reticence in reviewing arbitral awards by the Court of Arbitration for Sport (CAS). From Baddeley's explanations, it seems fair to infer that the presence of such an accommodating legal environment at the apex of the global sports pyramid must have repercussions upon the practice of sports governance at all levels between the apex and the base of the pyramid. Against the backdrop of such a reality, it should hardly come as a surprise if athletes and competitors are reticent to challenge decisions affecting them. Similar studies might be conducted in other jurisdictions, yet the status of international SGBs as Swiss associations of crucial because decisions taken on Swiss soil affect sports globally.

In this context, we might also ask whether current sports governance structures provide a voice to all legitimate stakeholders, including athletes and alternative event organisers. Is it normal that most challenges should be brought by disgruntled competitors (usually alternative event organisers, but also potential breakaway leagues) as opposed to athletes and fans, or should we expect to see more 'unusual suspects' in the driver's seat, in the role of complainants in the frame of administrative procedures, or of plaintiffs in trials before courts of law? According to two seasoned German sports lawyers, the closer we get to the top of the pyramid, the less involvement of active sportspeople in governance can be detected.[34] According to the trade unionist Walter Palmer, in this book,[35] SGBs may now have the choice between two rather different strategies, one of which would consist in continued lobbying for immunity from competition law (business as usual, so to speak) while the other would consist in a 'real dialogue' with athletes and other stakeholders to mitigate the anticompetitive effects of their governance model. To Palmer, the 'European model of sport' is nothing more than a campaign for continued insulation and unconditional autonomy,

33 *Supra,* Chapter 5.
34 Pfister & Friztweiler (2020), p. 14.
35 *Supra,* Chapter 8.

where athletes are subjected to the constraints of a monopsonistic market (i.e. a market where only one market operator has the power to sell). Against the current reality of market power concentration, Palmer proposes an alternative based on social dialogue, allowing athletes enhanced bargaining power: a model which would also mitigate anticompetitive effects for other market participants such as alternative event organisers. Agafonova, too, in this book,[36] has a focus on the rights of athletes, and looks specifically to competition authorities for help. Considering that coercive policies of SGBs regularly curb athletes' opportunities to increase their earnings, she underlines the structural, legal, economic and social dimensions of bargaining imbalance. Agafonova assumes that the creation of a level playing field would likely benefit not only athletes but also the market more generally, and sees the *ISU* case as a test case which may bring more legal certainty.

9.2.3 A mature doctrine?

Yet if CJEU rulings on the application of antitrust rules are to increase legal certainty and predictability and help reduce structural inequalities, has EU antitrust law reached a level of maturation such that it is an appropriate instrument to use to achieve such ends, and what has this book shown as regards the development of the law? In the opinion of the present editor, the incremental development of EC/EU antitrust law applied to sport over a 40-year period (1982–2022)[37] makes this field of law emerge as a consistent and helpful battery of norms and tests with which to assess the rules, procedures and practices of SGBs. Moreover, apart from the intellectual and conceptual strengths of this sub-discipline, the enforcement potential is considerable, as Van Rompuy has demonstrated in this book.[38] Emphasising its broad scope of application, Van Rompuy attributes to EU antitrust law a 'unique potential to assert control over the transnational private regulation of sports,' with the test established by the Court in *Meca Medina*[39] constituting a toolbox ready for use at any time. While the dual, public-private nature of the enforcement system does imply some risks of under-enforcement, and while the Commission may dismiss complaints with reference to the decentralised character of antitrust enforcement since 2004 (meaning that athletes and competitors may turn to national competition authorities and courts), public enforcement nevertheless retains appreciable advantages in terms of access, simplicity and efficacy. Administrative complaints do present the same financial hurdles (amounting to effective disincentives) as does private enforcement, while the granting of injunctive relief may have considerable impact (and protect structurally

36 *Supra,* Chapter 3.
37 *Supra,* Chapter 1.
38 *Supra,* Chapter 2.
39 CJEU, 18 July 2006. David Meca-Medina and Igor Majcen v Commission of the European Communities. Case C-519/04 P. ECR 2006 I-06991. ECLI:EU:C:2006:492, at 40–46.

weaker parties). Because competition authorities act in the public interest, they may focus upon the harm done to the market, where civil courts would aim more narrowly at the interests of a particular party. The procedures are different, with wide-ranging investigative powers (even if none of the known antitrust cases involving SGBs are known to have involved dawn raids so far, with documents published by SGBs already providing strongly persuasive evidence of anticompetitive objectives if not effects), while competition authorities can rely on a variety of tools and methods. As noted by Van Rompuy, some recent investigations involved a high degree of empirical economic research, including comprehensive market surveys. The inquisitorial procedure provides further advantages, although the outcome must not, in the end, necessarily rely on coercive means. Positive remedial action with a degree of involvement by the SGBs concerned remains a less confrontational, and potentially more transformative option once an infringement conduct has been established. Above the level of the nation state, Van Rompuy considers the EU the single most important enforcement agent in relation to SGBs, apt to generate at least a degree of general deterrence. For all these reasons, and against the backdrop of a consistent enforcement potential, Van Rompuy surmises that public authorities and self-interested plaintiffs may make even more use of EU antitrust law in the future 'as a meaningful accountability mechanism in sports governance.' Beyond the three cases currently pending before the CJEU, he also considers the possibility that national competition authorities (NCAs) may be more active in the future. As some of them have a proven track record of controlling the market power of globally organised tech companies, their 'outsized influence on transnational quasi-regulatory practices' could extend further into the realm of sport.

The transformative potential of EU antitrust law, as regards the future role of monopolistic SGBs, may be considerable. As we have seen earlier,[40] the incremental development of four decades of interpretation (1982–2022) and two decades of enforcement (1994–2022) suggests that there is room for even more development. A range of cases decided by national competition authorities (NCAs) (2008–2015) and the Commission (2017),[41] including some national and European case law, confirms this impression. At this writing (Summer 2022), the consolidation of EU sports antitrust law would seem to have reached maturity, a fact reflected in legal[42] and even social science scholarship,[43] including a range of German PhD theses in law.[44] Not only had cases been decided by the Commission 20–30 years earlier,[45] but indeed a new wave of administrative cases were decided, all of which

40 *Supra,* Chapter 1.

41 *Supra,* Chapter 1.

42 Van Rompuy (2015); Verdonk (2017); Kornbeck (2020); Cukurov (2021).

43 Brannagan, Scelles, Valenti, Inoue, Grix & Perkin (2022); Brocard, Anglade, Bastien & Mondou (2019).

44 Among these the most recent ones: Cukurov (2021); Fischer (2018); Opfermann (2021); Putzier (2022). Seyb (2020).

45 *Supra,* Chapter 1.

concerned SGBs' rules requiring athletes or third parties to apply for prior authorisation, from an SGB or its affiliates, before participating in competitions or events not organised or not authorised by the same SGB or its affiliates. Together they allow identifying three types of solutions[46] to the problems created, under antitrust law, by the 'double role'[47] of SGBs as private regulators and entrepreneurs, a constellation which seems structurally predicated towards conflicts of interest.

- The first solution, unbundling, involves splitting the activities (and ideally also the legal entities) of SGBs as regulators and entrepreneurs respectively. This 'nuclear solution' is only really represented by a single case, that of the Commission's 2001 FIA (automobile sports) decision.[48]
- The second solution, which covers a quite wide range of cases decided by NCAs or the Commission, consists in the revocation of SGB's statutory rules and commitments made by SGBs vis-à-vis NCAs or the Commission. This category includes the strikingly similar decisions of the Italian NCA in the *FISE* (equine sports) (2008) and *Corse Garcano* (motor sports) (2009) cases; of the Swedish NCA in the *SBF* (motor sports) (2011) and the *SKKF* (bodybuilding) (2014) cases; of the Irish NCA in the *SJI* (equine sports) (2012) case; of the Belgian NCA in the *FEI* (equine sports) (2015) case; and, of course, of the Commission in the *ISU* (speedskating) (2017) case. While the Swedish NCA's *SBF* decision and the Belgian NCA's *FEI* decision were both appealed to national courts, who confirmed and even strengthened the verdict made by NCAs, a case ruled under a slightly different constellation was that from Germany, of the Munich Regional Court (LG München I) 2016 (Basketball) leading to an injunction for an SGB to cease and desist from applying pressure on competitors and/or clubs interested in their business propositions.[49] The German Wrestling League (*Deutsche Ringer Liga*) (DRL) represents a rare case of a successful breakaway league which, after years of litigation, is now able to operate outside the sporting pyramid controlled by the SGB (*Deutscher Ringer Bund*) (DRB).[50]
- The third solution is that of a light-touch application and sanctions renunciation decided freely by SGBs themselves, as practised by FINA (swimming) in 2019, when announcing that disciplinary action would no longer be taken by athletes participating in non-FINA competitions or events without prior authorisation from FINA or its affiliates.[51]

46 Kornbeck (2020).
47 Cukurov (2021), p. 149.
48 Notice published pursuant to Article 19(3) of Council Regulation No 17 concerning Cases COMP/35.163 – Notification of FIA Regulations, COMP/36.638 – Notification by FIA/FOA of agreements relating to the FIA Formula One World Championship, COMP/36.776 – GTR/FIA & other. OJ C 169, 13.6.2001, p. 5–11.
49 LG München I, 2.6.2016, 1HK 0 8126/16; cf. Kornbeck (2020).
50 OLG Nürnberg vom 26.1.2021, Az. 3 U 894/19.
51 *Supra*, fn 26–27.

Finally, in 2022–2023, CJEU rulings were expected in three cases which all had the potential to become landmark decisions. As this book went to press, the outcomes of these cases were still not known, although it is hoped that the views put forward by the editor and contributors will not be invalidated too often by positions taken, either by the AG or by the Court.

9.3 Three test cases (2022)

9.3.1 Athletes competing outside the established pyramid

In *International Skating Union*,[52] the Court, upon appeal from the General Court,[53] had to decide whether an antitrust decision by the Commission European Commission[54] had assessed the selection rules of the ISU correctly. As the litigious regulation (ISU's Rule 102) was based on a strict principle of territorial exclusivity and accompanied by draconian sanctions in case of non-compliance, two speed skaters had taken action against what they perceived as an excessive expression of monopsony power. By preventing them from participating in events not organised or authorised by ISU or its affiliates, they found that Rule 102 deprived them of access to lucrative additional income from alternative event organisers. What the two complainants targeted was the 'one federation' principle[55] currently implicit in the pyramidal organisation of most (though not all) sports in Europe and the World. If the Court were to find against ISU, holding such exclusivity clauses to be (partly or entirely) incompatible with EU antitrust law, SGBs feared an erosion of their model of income generation through pressure from alternative organisers backed by institutional investors raising money on international capital markets. The Commission investigation and the trial before the General Court had, however, revealed that SGBs were wielding their monopolistic powers largely without limitations and accountability and in what seemed to imply a structural predicament for conflicts of interest since, by regulating sports while participating actively in the commercial exploitation of rights and activities derived from the same sports, SGBs were at risk of profiting from their own decisions. Even if legitimate objectives could be invoked, it was not obvious that the measures taken to protect them would be deemed necessary, inherent and proportionate in line with the test developed by the Court in its *Meca Medina*[56] jurisprudence.

52 International Skating Union v Commission. Case C-124/21 P (pending).

53 General Court, 16 December 2020. International Skating Union v European Commission. Case T-93/18. ECLI:EU:T:2020:610.

54 Commission Decision C(2017) 8240 final, 8.122017. Case AT. 40208 (fn 22).

55 Vieweg (1983); Kornbeck (2020).

56 CJEU, 18 July 2006. *Meca-Medina* (fn 39), at 40–46.

9.3.2 Competitions organised outside the established pyramid

In *European Superleague Company*,[57] the Court had to answer prejudicial questions submitted by the Commercial Court N° 17 of Madrid in a case opposing the European Superleague Company (ESL) to UEFA and FIFA. Founded in April 2021 by a small group of professional football clubs, the ESL aimed to organise autonomous, high-level football competitions outside the official calendars of the football pyramid governed by UEFA and its affiliates, effectively establishing itself as a so-called breakaway league.[58] While to North American sports fans this might seem relatively mundane – an independent league, albeit purportedly including the typically European elements of promotion and relegation[59] – the proposal brought many European fans on the barricades and prompted some clubs to leave the ESL soon after. While some scholars have seen the ESL as a largely failed business launch,[60] with the amount of scholarship being published within a mere 8–12 months after the ESL launch being quite intriguing in itself,[61] the reaction of SGBs was more than problematic from the perspective of antitrust law as well as public policy more generally. For even if legitimate objectives could be invoked, UEFA and its national affiliates ignored the injunctions of a preliminary ruling by the national court most blatantly. In submitting preliminary questions to the CJEU, the Commercial Court banned UEFA and its affiliates – national football associations (FAs) – from taking any punitive or dissuasive actions against the ESL founding clubs and their commercial partners (11.05.2021).[62] In direct contradiction with the court order, in an expression of what can only be interpreted as open contempt for a public court of law, UEFA and the FAs had taken a range of measures, including formal decisions, all published in a highly visible and mediatised way, threatening ESL participants with

57 European Super League Company, S. L. v Union of European Football Associations (UEFA) and Fédération Internationale de Football Association (FIFA). Date lodged: 27 May 2021. Referring court: Juzgado de lo Mercantil n.° 17 de Madrid (Commercial Court No 17, Madrid, Spain). Case C-333/21 (pending). See working document: https://curia.europa.eu/juris/showPdf.jsf?text=&docid=244284&pageIndex=0&doclang=EN&mode=lst&dir=&occ=first&part=1&cid=5967904.

58 For an exposition of this concept, see Pijetlovic (2015).

59 On the pyramidal structure and the promotion/relegation principle being the two constitutive features of the European, as opposed to the North American model, see Blackshaw (2017), pp. 5–8.

60 See e.g. Meier, García, Konjer & Jetzke(2022).

61 Brannagan, Scelles, Valenti, Inoue, Grix & Perkin (2022); Dunbar (2021); Houben, Blockx & Nuyts (2022); Macedo, Ferreira Dias & Reis Mourão (2022); Meier, García, Konjer & Jetzke (2022); Welsh (2022).

62 Juzgado de lo Mercantil N° 17 de Madrid. Pieza de Medidas Cautelares 150/2021 – 0001 (Medidas Cautelares Previas LEC 727). A22 Sports Managements SL y European Super League Company SL ./. Liga Nacional de Fútbol Profesional, Real Federación Española de Fútbol y UEFA, 11.05.2021, http://as00.epimg.net/descargables/2021/04/20/184303c283180aada81369542eb7fb64.pdf.

all manner of sanctions. Only a second judgment (20.09.2021),[63] providing for criminal sanctions against UEFA in case of continued obstruction, caused UEFA and the FAs to discontinue this behaviour. Whether or not one might sympathise with the cause of the SGBs, their intimidating behaviour could only force the hand of public authorities.

The Commercial Court in Madrid referred six questions to the CJEU, all of which concerned the compatibility of provisions in the FIFA Statutes and the FIFA Regulation Governing International Matches, including the disciplinary sanctions taken by UEFA and its constituent members (national football associations) to discourage the formation of an independent football league. As the initiators of the proposed European Superleague had challenged the regulatory private authority of FIFA and UEFA, the national court focused on the requirement for prior approval enshrined (Articles 22, 71–73 FIFA Statutes, 49 and 51 UEFA Statutes, 'and any similar article contained in the statutes of the member associations and national leagues'). Noting that FIFA and UEFA had 'conferred on themselves the exclusive power to organise or give permission for international club competitions in Europe,' the national court acknowledged therein a requirement 'for a third-party entity to set up a new pan-European club competition like the Super League.' The Court added that this requirement would apply even 'where no regulated procedure, based on objective, transparent and non-discriminatory criteria, exists, and taking into account the possible conflict of interests affecting FIFA and UEFA.' Following this reasoning, the first question put to the CJEU was whether the litigious rule represented an abuse of dominant position under Article 102 TFEU, while the second concerned the presence of an anti-competitive agreement within the meaning of Article 101 TFEU. The third question focused on 'conduct by FIFA, UEFA, their member associations and/or national leagues which consists of the threat to adopt sanctions against clubs participating in the Super League and/or their players.' Considering 'the deterrent effect that those sanctions may create,' especially if 'they were not based on objective, transparent and objective criteria,' the court asked if this would imply an infringement of Articles 101 and/or 102 TFEU. The object of the fourth question was a wording found in Articles 67–68 FIFA Statutes, identifying UEFA and its national member associations as the 'original owners of all of the rights emanating from competitions' 'coming under their respective jurisdiction.' The court saw therein an attempt at 'depriving participating clubs and any organiser of an alternative competition of the original ownership of those rights and arrogating to themselves sole responsibility for the marketing of those rights,' asking if this provision would infringe upon Articles 101 and/or 102 TFEU. The fifth question again took the arrogation of competence by FIFA and UEFA, as identified in the two first questions, as its point of departure, asking if this presence of such exclusive power meant that a decision by FIFA or UEFA

63 *Ibid.*, 20.09.2021, on file with author.

'to prohibit or prevent the development of the Super League on the basis of the abovementioned provisions of their statutes' would be incompatible with Article 101 TFEU. Speculating about the implied restrictions on competition and the implied limitation of potential competition and consumer choice, the court wondered if such a restriction could be 'covered by an objective justification' leading to the exclusion of abuse of dominant position under Article 102 TFEU. The sixth question, finally, asked the prior approval requirement of FIFA and UEFA, as enshrined in Articles 22, 71–73 FIFA Statutes, Articles 49, 51 UEFA Statutes and in various rules and regulations of the affiliates (national FAs) violated the free movement guarantees of the Treaty (Articles 45, 49, 56, 63 TFEU).[64]

9.3.3 Fielding players trained in other geographical areas of the pyramid

In *Royal Antwerp FC*,[65] finally, the French-speaking Court of First Instance of Brussels was putting prejudicial questions to the Court in a matter regarding an Israeli-born, Belgian-naturalised football player and his former employing club, as opposed to the Belgian FA.[66] The heart of the matter was the compatibility of national rules, enacted by the FA to comply with UEFA's so-called Home-Grown Player (HGP) rule, with EU antitrust law. The player and his club have alleged a breach of Article 14 ECHR as well as Articles 45, 101 and 267 TFEU by the Belgian FA through its national implementing rules. The Belgian FA (URBSFA/KBVB/BFFV[67]) had implemented the UEFA provisions through Articles P335.11, P.1422, B4.106 and B6.109 of its national regulations, which Mr Lior Refaelov and his club S.A. Royal Antwerp FC (RAFC) had challenged in national courts. As a citizen of Israel and Belgium, Mr Refaelov started his professional career with Maccabi Haifa (Israel) in 2004, but signed a contract with Club Brugge in 2011. After acquiring Belgian citizenship, he joined RAFC in 2018 until switching to Royal Sporting Club Anderlecht on 30 June 2021. The challenge was brought against an arbitral award of the Belgian court of arbitration for sport, CBAS, of 10 July 2020. The award was the result of an appeal by

64 Case C-333/21. Summary of the request for a preliminary ruling pursuant to Article 98(1) of the Rules of Procedure of the Court of Justice. Working document compiled by the Court, including a preliminary translation. https://curia.europa.eu/juris/showPdf.jsf?text=&docid=244284&pageIndex=0&doclang=EN&mode=lst&dir=&occ=first&part=1&cid=6173546

65 SA Royal Antwerp Football Club v Union royale belge des sociétés de football association ASBL. Date lodged: 11 November 2021. Referring Court: Tribunal de première instance francophone de Bruxelles (Belgium). Case C-680/21 (pending). Working document: https://curia.europa.eu/juris/showPdf.jsf?text=&docid=251818&pageIndex=0&doclang=EN&mode=lst&dir=&occ=first&part=1&cid=5969529

66 Tribunal de première instance francophone de Bruxelles, Section civile, 4ème chambre des affaires civiles. 2020/5156/1. Lior Refaelov und SA Royal Antwerp FC contre URBSFA. 15.10.2021 (on file with author).

67 *Union royale belge des sociétés de football association,* (URBSFA); *Koninklijke Belgische Voetbalbond* (KBVB); *Königlicher Belgischer Fußballverband* (KBFV).

the player and his club following an appeal to the Belgian national competition authority (NCA), ABC, alleging breach of Articles 45 and 101(2) TFEU. They had also applied for an injunction ordering URBSFA to abstain from applying the UEFA HRP rules, although CBAS, for lack of standing, had dismissed the pleas as well as the complainants' references to the CJEU's *Simutenkov* jurisprudence[68] and to Article 14 ECHR.

The HGP rules were adopted by the UEFA Executive Committee on 2 February 2005. After ratification by all 52 UEFA member federations, meeting at the UEFA Congress in Tallinn on 21 April 2005, they were implemented via clauses inserted into various national statutes and regulations. They do not seem to have been inserted into any official UEFA texts, although it is understood that their obligation to do so is derived, based on the logic of the sporting 'pyramid,' from the intermediary chain of obligations ranging from UEFA through national federations (and regional ones, where they exist) towards clubs and their individual members. The HGP rules limit the scope for clubs to field players not trained within the geographical area of their national federation, while no distinction is made on the basis of the nationality/citizenship of the players concerned. On 29 March 2007, the European Parliament greeted the HGP rules explicitly,[69] thereby expressing its 'clear support for the UEFA measures to encourage the education of young athletes' and putting its 'belief' on record that 'such incentive measures are proportionate and calls on professional clubs to strictly implement this rule.'[70] Despite its unwavering support in principle, Parliament – wisely, one would say in retrospect – could not affirm that these rules, while being 'extremely important for youth development, would, if it were reviewed by the Court of Justice, prove to be consistent with Article 12 of the EC Treaty.'[71] Neither would the Commission issue any such reassurances when publishing an external study carried out by the universities of Liverpool and Edge Hill.[72] In its Press Release,[73] it rather emphasised the need for UEFA to ensure a discrimination-free implementation of the relevant provisions, while reserving its right to investigate at a later stage if needed.

68 CJEU, 12.04.2005, Igor Simutenkov v Ministerio de Educación y Cultura and Real Federación Española de Fútbol. Case C-265/03, ECR 2005 I-02579, ECLI:EU:C:2005:213).

69 P6_TA(2007)0100. Future of Professional Football in Europe. European Parliament Resolution of 29 March 2007 on the Future of Professional Football in Europe. (2006/2130(INI)). OJ C 27 E, 31.1.2008, p. 232–240.

70 *Ibid.*, at 34.

71 *Ibid.*, recital H.

72 Dalziel, Downward, Parrish, Pearson & Semens (2013).

73 IP/08/807. Brussels, 28 May 2008. UEFA Rule on 'home-grown players': Compatibility with the Principle of Free Movement of Persons. https://ec.europa.eu/commission/presscorner/detail/en/ip_08_807.

9.3.4 Potential for change

The defence regarding UEFA's much vaunted solidarity mechanism was used again, at the *European Superleague* hearing of the CJEU on 11–12 July 2022.[74] Although in its ISU decision,[75] the Commission had been unable to detect clear evidence that money distributed within the sport of speed skating actually trickles down to the grassroots, the same argument was used to great effect as reported by the media. A total of 20 EU Member States as well as the Kingdom of Norway intervened over two half days praising UEFA for providing various grants.[76] Surprisingly, however, not a single lawyer instructed by a national government had been briefed to answer questions about the total amounts received, and how many percent of national football budgets they actually covered. Even when the Court gave governments time to request the missing figures from the capitals, not a single government was able to do so. While the present editor is not a budgetary or economics expert capable of filling the gaps, this potentially embarrassing finding confirmed impressions from the last two decades regarding the opacity of financial circuits involving SGBs especially in and out of Switzerland. It also seems to corroborate documented yet isolated evidence suggesting that sport for all may largely be financed by regional and municipal budgets, and/or by households themselves.[77] It is to be hoped that the Court will take this into account and will not give too much credence to claims which were suspiciously similar yet could not be backed by figures.

If absence of sound procedures (in some cases of any procedures) is the central issue – based on 'objective, transparent, non-discriminatory and verifiable' criteria[78] – then it should be possible to keep the European model of sport and possibly also the 'one federation' or 'one place principle.' Yet some sort of action needs to be taken, as it seems unlikely that the Court would fail to address the fundamental problem involved in allowing private organisations with almost total market share and monopoly power to exercise such power without any safeguards against abuse. Conceptually, nothing seems to prevent squaring the circle by making certain rules and procedures mandatory, except that state

74 While the editor is relying on his own notes, readers may wish to use the CJEU streaming tool: https://curia.europa.eu/jcms/jcms/p1_1477137/en/.

75 Commission Decision C(2017) 8240 final, 8.122017. Case AT. 40208 (fn 22), p. 62, at 246–247.

76 Chee, F.Y. (2022) EU Countries Sing UEFA's Praises in Rebuff to Super League. *Reuters*, July 12, 2022, 4:39 PM GMT+2, https://www.reuters.com/lifestyle/sports/eu-countries-sing-uefas-praises-rebuff-super-league-2022-07-12/

77 A decade ago, one study found that HEPA activities are, more often than not, paid by local councils or by private households themselves; see Eurostratégies, Amnyos, CDES & DSHS (2011), pp. 46, 80.

78 GC, 16.12.2020. *International Skating Union* (fn 23), at 118: 'the eligibility rules did not provide the exercise of the applicant's regulatory function with the necessary safeguards to ensure that third parties had effective access to the relevant market. Given the absence of objective, transparent, non-discriminatory and verifiable authorisation criteria, the applicant's broad discretion to authorise or reject such events was in no way limited.'

actors cannot make such provisions without altering the conception of autonomy as it is currently understood and practised in most EU countries, while it seems unlikely that the change needed would emerge spontaneously from within the same monopoly structures. In 2022, the French parliament passed legislation providing for mandatory clauses in the statutes and regulations of sports organisations,[79] while being organised under association law as private entities. Such legislation would probably be met with total hostility in Germany, where the sports movement has so far managed successfully to achieve that their brand of civil society organisations are considered to fall unconditionally under the scope of the constitutionally guaranteed freedom of association;[80] while the French legal framework is based on an understanding of sports organisations as a special subset for which the approval and oversight of public authorities is required in the public interest (while citizens are still free to create all manner of associations, and also to play sports, yet without being part of the monopolistic sporting pyramid). Under such circumstances, it would seem expedient for the sport movement itself to make appropriate clauses mandatory at all levels of the pyramid, although a European solution might be preferable to 27 national ones. Whether the French system based on comprehensive legal requirements would be open to such a move remains doubtful, however.

9.4 The prospect of sport governance reform

9.4.1 A matter of public policy

Against the backdrop of widespread government support for the current arrangements (as witnessed by the 21 interventions during the CJEU hearing referred to earlier), readers may ask why reform should be contemplated at all. At the same time, fan protests against the Superleague business proposition let this initiative emerge as particularly divisive[81] and capable of generating anger and protest: surely, if both governments and populations are more than ordinarily critical of initiatives such as those posed by the ISU and the ESL, the status quo should be easy to defend? Yet there are good reasons for questioning the legal and political sustainability of arrangements whereby private actors enjoy a monopoly situation and control access to their own markets. Fundamentally, the EU Institutions are bound to defend market economic freedom, this mission having been part of the

79 Loi n° 2022–296 du 2 mars 2022 visant à démocratiser le sport en France. JORF n°0052 du 3 mars 2022, texte 2 sur 186, pp. 1–5, NOR : MENX2105502L, https://www.legifrance.gouv.fr/eli/loi/2022/3/2/2022–296/jo/texte. Thanks are owed to Colin Miège for drawing my attention to this important legislative development; see Fischer, Kornbeck, Miège & Stopper (forthcoming).

80 Art. 9 GG (Grundgesetz) (Basic Law of the Federal Republic of Germany).

81 On the role of JP Morgan, see Turner, M. & Brown, S. (2021) JP Morgan Provides €3.5bn for Controversial Football Super League. *Global Capital, 2021–04–19* (London: Euromoney Institutional Investor PLC), https://ca.sports.yahoo.com/news/jp-morgan-finance-controversial-european-100228875.html.

DNA of the Community/Union since the 1950s,[82] while a relative lack of challenges cannot be taken as a sign that these arrangements must be legal. As mentioned earlier,[83] investors looking for unusual opportunities reveal imbalances in established structures, just like George Soros: his £1bn gains on 'Black Wednesday' 1992 only made him a more determined activist for better regulation of financial markets[84] (while campaigning for liberal democracy more broadly).

Whereas ISU failed to convince the Commission[85] that money generated through its solidarity mechanism actually trickled down systematically to the grassroots level, it would be far preferable for sport policies to become more evidence-based and for decisions made by SGBs to be accountable, subject to democracy and rule of law mechanisms, as far as possible. Public funds and lottery-generated money should follow activities, in accordance with specific public policy goals, rather than being sent blindly to particular legal entities merely on the basis of (what political scientists might call) 'path dependency': following a particular path because it has been followed in the past. Cases like those of *ISU* and *ESL* are different, of course, as the SGBs in question are not defending access to public funds but their power to regulate sponsor-generated income. Yet even without receiving public grants, SGBs do rely on the benevolence of public authorities for upholding arrangements which are central to the maintenance of their current, apparently lucrative, business models.[86]

The mere fact that certain arrangements have been tolerated by judiciaries, parliaments and executives for many decades does not have to imply that they will have to be so in perpetuity. For as the example of the new French law on the 'democratisation of sport' shows,[87] remedies may exist which would respond quite neatly to the inconsistencies found in extant arrangements, even if such change may be met with considerable resistance. If the absence of 'objective, transparent, non-discriminatory and verifiable'[88] criteria and procedures is the single most pressing problem, then solutions like the French one, whether by legislators or by SGBs themselves, would seem a rational and targeted way to address them. In June 2022, UEFA suddenly published a set of authorisation

82 Hallstein (1962); Hallstein (1969); Pernice (2001).

83 *Supra,* sec. 9.2.1

84 Schorow, S. (2008) Soros Says Crisis Underscores Need for Regulation. *MIT News*, October 29, https://news.mit.edu/2008/soros-1029: '"I played by the rules. I was a key member of the market. I was doing what other people in the market were doing, with no negative moral implications," Soros replied. "At the time, as a citizen, I was concerned about making the rules better. And I'm still concerned."'

85 Commission Decision C(2017) 8240 final, 8.122017. Case AT. 40208 (fn 22), p. 62, at 246–247.

86 See the assessment of Pfister & Friztweiler (2020) (fn 21).

87 Loi n° 2022–296 du 2 mars 2022 visant à démocratiser le sport en France (fn 78).

88 GC, 16.12.2020. *International Skating Union* (fn 23) at 118: 'the eligibility rules did not provide the exercise of the applicant's regulatory function with the necessary safeguards to ensure that third parties had effective access to the relevant market. Given the absence of objective, transparent, non-discriminatory and verifiable authorisation criteria, the applicant's broad discretion to authorise or reject such events was in no way limited.'

rules,[89] thereby filling the gap identified by ESL. The month before the CJEU hearings in the *ISU* and *ESL* cases, on 3 June 2022, the Federal Constitutional Court of Germany (*Bundesverfassungsgericht*) (BVerfG) handed down a judgment in a dispute concerning an anti-doping rule violation (ADRV) imputed to the German speed skater Claudia Pechstein. Having been defeated in the Swiss Federal Tribunal, the Federal Court of Justice (*Bundesgerichtshof*, BGH) of Germany, and the European Court of Human Rights (ECtHR), Pechstein had previously won in the regional high court of Munich (*Oberlandesgericht München*) (OLG). In quashing the BGH judgment and by focusing on the arbitration clause applicable in the disciplinary procedure related to the alleged ADRV, the BVerfG found a violation of the athlete's constitutional right of access to justice and sent the matter back to the OLG[90] which had previously sided with Pechstein. While the OLG's renewed decision remains to be seen, the BGH had pronounced itself on the structural imbalance between athletes and SGBs in most surprising terms, claiming that the interests of both sides were identical.[91] The BGH's rejection of the mere idea that two opposed 'camps' might even exist is a prime example of the kind of legal fictions protecting SGBs when acting simultaneously as private regulators and entrepreneurs. It will be particularly interesting to observe whether the OLG will comment on this aspect of the dispute, possibly challenging the conclusion reached by the BGH. It may still be possible to preserve the 'one federation' principle, yet not (in the long run at least) without making some long overdue adjustments to the legal framework defining the exercise of power by SGBs over athletes as well as third parties.

9.4.2 Research gaps

Apart from the lessons learnt which have already been summarised,[92] this book will not offer further conclusions. Nor will predictions be offered as regards the likely outcomes of the three pending cases[93] beyond the assumption that, at least, the CJEU can be expected to confirm its own case law as regards the 'obligations

89 UEFA Authorisation Rules Governing International Club Competitions. Edition 2022. https://documents.uefa.com/v/u/_rmtminDpysQUj1VGB01HA

90 BVerfG, Beschluss der 2. Kammer des Ersten Senats vom 3. Juni 2022 –1 BvR 2103/16, ECLI ECLI:DE:BVerfG:2022:rk20220603.1bvr210316.

91 BGH, Az. KZR 6/15, Pechstein ./. International Skating Union (ISU), 7. Juni 2016, Tenor, at d): „Sportverbände und Athleten stehen sich bei der Bekämpfung des Dopings grundsätzlich nicht als von gegensätzlichen Interessen geleitete ‚Lager' gegenüber." – See also Ehle & Guaia (2017), p. 420: 3 'While according to the monopolistic "one federation" principle the ISU, just like other international sports federations, admittedly holds a dominant position as the sport's international governing body, referring athletes to compulsory CAS arbitration does not amount to an abuse of such position. According to the BGH, the athletes and SGBs do not form two different camps with diverging interests; quite the contrary, they have a common interest to keep international sports doping-free.'

92 *Supra*, 9.2.

93 *Supra*, 9.3.

imposed on a sports federation which has a power of authorisation.'[94] This seems a settled baseline, upon which the Court might build additional layers of requirements and tests in line with the *Meca Medina*[95] test. Looking a bit further, the following, more empirical questions – legal and/or economic to varying degrees – would seem to warrant further research in the future:

- Market power concentration: – To what extent do SGBs hold significant, concentrated market power warranting special attention from competition authorities and the judiciary?
- Conflicts of interest: – To what extent are sport-specific structures conducive to conflicts of interest, in particular by conflating regulatory and commercial activities? How realistic and helpful would an unbundling of these conflicting functions be?[96]
- Nature (qualitatively and quantitatively) of financial solidarity within the established European sports pyramid: – How far can it be assessed empirically whether money distributed by international SGBs to their members (national federations) actually reach the grassroots level?
- Specificity' of sport versus orthodox application of competition law (antitrust): – To what extent have the 'special characteristics' of sport (Article 165 TFEU) been taken into account, and what has the outcome been? Is there still room for 'specificity' and is the concept useful or not?
- Brussels effect': – If the outcome of the three upcoming CJEU judgments is going to be transformative for SGBs in the EU, how far will these effects also extend beyond the borders of the Union? Will SGBs such as the IOC and UEFA take new orientations for sport governance into account, or will they show themselves impervious in their Swiss domiciles? Will there be signs of a 'Brussels effect,' as we know it from data protection and the regulation of chemicals,[97] or will the globally integrated *lex sportiva,* and the economic, cultural and political clout of SGBs, show themselves more influent?

If the three cases currently awaiting adjudication by the CJEU are all going to lead to landmark rulings, they can be expected to trigger a fair amount of scholarship over the coming months and years. They might also alter the conditions under which SGBs will be able to exercise their authority as regulators with a simultaneous involvement in commercial activities directly affected by their own regulatory decisions. If the present volume helps shedding light on some aspects which may have been less well understood so far, its editor would find

94 GC, 16.12.2020. *International Skating Union* (fn 23), at 70.

95 CJEU, 18 July 2006. *Meca-Medina* (fn 39), at 40–46.

96 Unbundling was one of the three solutions proposed by Kornbeck (2020). It was also covered by some of the written questions asked by the CJEU to the litigants in the *European Superleague Company* case and debated repeatedly during the hearing on 11–12 July 2022.

97 Bradford (2020).

this a gratifying result, including as further evidence of the pertinence of EU antitrust law in relation to the renewal of the principles, structures and practice of sports governance. As the 'difficulty in defining a single model of governance in European sport has raised questions regarding the adequacy of the standardised pyramidal structure to answer sports organisations' governance issues,'[98] not only test cases but also scholarship seem needed.

Disclaimer

The author is a civil servant in the European Commission, yet opinions expressed are strictly personal and do not render any official positions of the European Commission, nor of the European Union.

Bibliography

Blackshaw, I.S. (2017) *International Sports Law: An Introductory Guide*. The Hague: T.M.C. Asser Press & Heidelberg: Springer.

Bradford, A. (2020) *The Brussels Effect: How the European Union Runs the World*. Oxford et al: Oxford University Press.

Brannagan, P. M., Scelles, N., Valenti, M., Inoue, Y., Grix, J. & Perkin, S. J. (2022) The 2021 European Super League Attempt: Motivation, Outcome, and the Future of Football. *International Journal of Sport Policy and Politics*, 14:1, 169–176, DOI: 10.1080/19406940.2021.2013926

Brocard, J. F., Anglade, M., Bastien, J. & Mondou, J. (2019) *Impacts, externalités et bénéfices du modèle d'organisation du sport en Europe à l'aune de sa professionnalisation*. Limoges: Centre de droit et d'économie du sport. Rapport final, décembre 2019, 268 pp. On file with author but not released at this writing (Summer 2022). Various power point presentations available online, e.g. https://slideplayer.fr/slide/17744153/

Cukurov, D. (2021) *Kartellrechtliche Zulässigkeit von Superligen im Fußball. Der europäische Ligasport vor dem Umbruch*. Baden-Baden: Nomos & Munich: C.H. Beck.

Dalziel, M., Downward, P., Parrish, R., Pearson, G. & Semens, A. (2013) *Study on the Assessment of UEFA's 'Home Grown Player Rule.'* Negotiated procedure EAC/07/2012. Liverpool University & Edge Hill University. https://ec.europa.eu/assets/eac/sport/library/studies/final-rpt-april2013-homegrownplayer.pdf

Dunbar, N. (2021) A European Football Super League: The Legal and Practical Issues. *James Cook University Law Review*, 27, 111–129.

Ehle & Guaia, I. (2017) Bundesgerichtshof, Az. KZR 6/15, Pechstein v. International Skating Union (ISU), 7 June 2016. In Duval, A. & Rigozzi, A. (eds) *Yearbook of International Sports Arbitration 2016*. T.M.C. Asser Press, The Hague, 415–427.

Eurostratégies, Amnyos, CDES [Centre de Droit et d'Economie du Sport] & Deutsche Sporthochschule Köln (2011) *Study on the Funding of Grassroots Sports in the EU. With a Focus on the Internal Market Aspects Concerning Legislative Frameworks and Systems of Financing*. Final Report. Vol. I. Brussels: Eurostratégies. https://www.kenniscentrumsportenbewegen.nl/kennisbank/publicaties/?study-on-the-funding-of-grassroots-sports-in-the-eu&kb_id=10018

98 Sennett, Le Gall, Kelly, Cottrill, Goffredo & Spyridopoulos (2022), p. 25.

Fischer, P. (2018) *Die Rolle des Ein-Platz-Prinzips in der Autonomie der Sportfachverbände*. BerlIn: Peter Lang.

Fischer, P., Kornbeck, J., Miège C. & Stopper, M. (forthcoming) Sports Organisations as Civil Society Organisations and Private Regulators: France and Germany Compared. In Seul, O. (ed.) *Civil Society and the Rule of Law*. Brussels: Peter Lang.

García, B. & Weatherill, S. (2012) Engaging with the EU in order to Minimize Its Impact: Sport and the Negotiation of the Treaty of Lisbon. *Journal of European Public Policy*, 19:2, 238–256.

Gießelmann-Goetze, G. (1987) Das Ein-Platz-Prinzip. In Will, M. R. (ed.) *Sport und Recht in Europa*. Saarbrücken: Europa-Institut (Vorträge, Reden und Berichte aus dem Europa-Institut; 116), 15–26.

Hallstein, W. (1962) Rede zur Ehrenpromotion in Padua: Die EWG – eine Rechtsgemeinschaft. In Oppermann, Th. (ed.) (1979) *Walter HallsteIn Europäische Reden*. Stuttgart: Deutsche Verlags-Anstalt; cit. Pernice (2001), 2.

Hallstein, W. (1969) *Der unvollendete Bundesstaat*. Düsseldorf & Vienna: Econ.

Hecker, C. (2021) How Should Responsible Investors Behave? Keynes's Distinction between Entrepreneurship and Speculation Revisited. *Journal of Business Ethics*, 171, 459–473.

Houben, R., Blockx, J. & Nuyts, S. (2022) UEFA and the Super League: Who Is Calling Who a Cartel? *International Sports Law Journal*, Published online 21 February 2022, DOI: 10.1007/s40318-021-00201-2

Keynes, J. M. (1936) *The General Theory of Employment, Interest and Money*. London: Macmillan.

Koebel, M. (2016) Le profil social et politique des adjoint-e-s aux sports des villes françaises. *Sciences Sociales et Sport*, 9:1, 153–184.

Kornbeck, J. (2020) What can SGBs do to Comply with Antitrust Rules while Maintaining the 'one federation' Principle? *International Sports Law Journal*, 20:3–4, 203–226.

Kornbeck, J. (ed.) (2022) *Sport and Brexit: Regulatory Challenges and Legacies*. Abingdon: Routledge.

Macedo, A., Ferreira Dias, M. & Reis Mourão, P. (2022) A Bibliometric Study of the European Super League of Football – A New Plan or an Old Threat? *Soccer & Society*, online 13 February, DOI: 10.1080/14660970.2022.2038574

Meier, H. E. & García, B. (2022) Brexit and Global Sport Power Europe. In Kornbeck, J. (ed.) *Sport and Brexit: Regulatory Challenges and Legacies*. Abingdon: Routledge, pp. 196–201.

Meier, H. E., García, B., Konjer, M. & Jetzke, M. (2022) The Short Life of the European Super League: A Case Study on Institutional Tensions in Sport Industries. *Managing Sport and Leisure*, online 1 April, DOI: 10.1080/23750472.2022.2058071

Ogburn, W. (1922) *Social Change with Respect to Nature and Original Cult*. New York: Viking.

Opfermann, G. (2021) *Schiedsvereinbarungen zum CAS. Eine Untersuchung aus der Perspektive des Kartellrechts*. Tübingen: Mohr Siebeck

Pernice, I. (2001) *Der Beitrag Walter Hallstein zur Zukunft Europas. Begründung und Konsolidierung der Europäischen Gemeinschaft als Rechtsgemeinschaft*. BerlIn Humboldt Universität (WHI Paper 9/01). http://whi-berlin.eu/documents/whipaper0901.pdf965

Pfister, B. & Friztweiler, J. (2020) Einführung. In Pfister, B., Fritzweiler, J., Summerer, Th. & Alvermann, J. (eds) *Praxishandbuch Sportrecht. 4. Auflage*. Munich: Beck.

Philippon, T. (2019) *The Great Reversal. How America Gave Up on Free Markets*. Cambridge, MA: Belknap Press.

Pijetlovic, K. (2015) *EU Sports Law and Breakaway Leagues in Football*. The Hague & Heidelberg: T.M.C. Asser Press & Springer.

Putzier, K. (2022) *Kartellrechtliche Anforderungen an private Rechtssysteme im Sport*. BerlIn: Duncker & Humblot.

Rodger, B. & Stephan, A. (2022): *Brexit and Competition Law*. Abingdon: Routledge (Legal Perspectives on Brexit Series).

Sennett, J., Le Gall, A., Kelly, G., Cottrill, R., Goffredo, S. & Spyridopoulos, K. (2022) *Study on the European Sport Model*. A Report to the European Commission. Brussels: Ecorys & KEA European Affairs. https://sport.ec.europa.eu/news/new-study-on-the-european-sport-model

Seyb, A. (2020) *Autonomie der Sportverbände. Eine Untersuchung zu wettbewerbsrechtlichen Grenzen der Sportverbandsautonomie insbesondere im Verhältnis gegenüber Dritten*. Tübingen: Mohr Siebeck.

Shapiro, C. (2018) Antitrust in a Time of Populism. *International Journal of Industrial Organization*, 61, 714–748.

Tétart, Ph. (ed.) (2007) *Histoire du sport en France, de la liberation à nos jours*. Paris: Vuibert & Musée national du sport.

Van Rompuy, B. (2015) The Role of EU Competition Law in Tackling Abuse of Regulatory Power by Sports Associations. *Maastricht Journal of European and Comparative Law*, 22:2, 179–208.

Van Rompuy, B. & van Maren, O. (2016) EU Control of State Aid to Professional Sport: Why Now? In Duval, A. & Van Rompuy, B. (eds) *The Legacy of Bosman. Revisiting the relationship between EU law and sport*. The Haguer: T.M.C. Asser Press & Heidelberg: Springer, 153–185.

Verdonk, T. (2017) Rivalry among Sports Associations: The Compatibility of Sports Associations' Exclusivity Clauses with EU Competition law. *European Competition Law Review*, 38:2, 80–88.

Vieweg, K. (1983) Zur Einführung: Sport und Recht. *Juristische Ausbildung (JuS)*, 825–830.

Welsh, J. (2022) The European Super League Debacle: Why Regulation of Corporate Football Is Essential. *Soccer & Society*, online 25 March, DOI: 10.1080/14660970.2022.2054805

Woodward, J. (1934) Critical Notes on the Cultural Lag Concept. *Social Forces*, 12:3, 388–398.

INDEX